AF540131

# FAIRS AND FESTIVALS OF INDIAN TRIBES

# FAIRS AND FESTIVALS OF INDIAN TRIBES

**Dr. Robin David Tribhuwan**

*MA., MSc., P.G.D.I.M., Ph.D., Post Doctoral Fellow*

**Discovery Publishing House**
**New Delhi-110002**

**First Published-2003**

Reprinted: 2013

ISBN 81-7141-640-3



***Published by:***

**DISCOVERY PUBLISHING HOUSE**

4831/24, Ansari Road, Prahlad Street,
Darya Ganj, New Delhi-110002 (India)
Phone: 3279245 • Fax: 91-11-3253475
E-mail:dphtemp@indiatimes.com

Printed at: Dynamic printers, Delhi

# PREFACE

It has been a great experience working with tribals and understanding various fascinating aspects of their culture. After editing the volume captioned, "Tribal Dances of India", I turned my attention to yet another unexplored domain of tribal life namely, "Fairs and Festivals of Indian Tribes". Although, passing references of some festivals made by Anthropologists in monographs on Tribes, in the past, I felt this subject needs to be given real justice. Hence, I thought of editing this book.

An attempt, herein has been made to provide in-depth understanding of the Fairs and Festivals of major tribes in India. I am grateful to all the authors who have contributed papers for this book.

I am sure the subject of Fairs and Festival of Indian Tribes, will pave a way for development of new theoretical insights in Social Sciences. Information provided in the book will also motivate administrators of tribal and culture departments to evolve strategies to preserve these traditions in tribal communities.

This book will be useful to students and research scholars of Anthropology, Sociology, Museology, Tribal Development Studies, Social Work, history, and to general readers as well.

**Dr. Robin David Tribhuwan**
*M.A., M.Sc., P.G.D.I.M., Ph.D.*
*Post Doctoral Fellow*

# CONTENTS

## PART TWO
## TRIBAL FAIRS IN INDIA

# CONTRIBUTORS


1. **Dr. Robin D. Tribhuwan,** Anthropologist and Development Expert, Flat No. 9, Krishna Kunj, Vikas Nagar, Wanowrie, Pune–411040 (India)

2. **Dr. Pratibha Kumari,** Research Associate, (Cultural) Anthropological Survey of India, Harihar Singh Road, Morabadi, Ranchi–834008, (Bihar)

3. **Dr. B.R. Sharma,** Hindol, Kusumpati, Shimla–171009

4. **Dr. Naba Kumar Duary,** Research Associate (Cultural), Anthropological Survey of India, Harihar Singh Road, Morabadi, Ranchi–834008

5. **Ms. Monika Spolia,** # 19–1435, Sylvania Cres. Kelowna, B.C. VI X5J4, Canada

6. **Kunj Bihari Nayak,** Department of Sociology, Shivaji University, Kolhapur, Maharashtra

7. **Dr. L.N. Soni,** Anthropological Survey of India, 2 Ripon Street, Calcutta–700016

8. **Indra Mallo,** I.A.S., Asst. Collector, Ahmed Nagar, Maharashtra

9. **Ms. Sumita Mukherjee,** Lecturer, Dept. of Geography, University of Pune, Pune–411007

10. **Preeti R. Tribhuwan,** Anthropologist, Flat No. 9, Krishna Kunj, Vikas Nagar, Wanowrie, Pune–411040 (India)

11. **Ms. Anuja Arun Majumdar,** 11/12 Sangam Apts., Piramital Road, Dandia Bazar, Baroda, Gujarat

12. **Dr. Narendra Bokhare,** (Ph.D. Anthropology), Reader, Academic Services Division, Yashwant Rao Chavan, Maharashtra Open University, Dnyana—Gangotri, Near Gangapur Dam, Nasik–422222

13. **Talimenla,** House No-26, Pink Building, Liwgrijan Dimapur, Nagaland

14. **Alok Kumar Kunugo,** Research Scholar, Deccan College, Pune–411006

15. **Dr. Laurence Savelli,** 109, ave victor, Hugo, 92140 clamart, France

# PART ONE
# GLIMPSES OF TRIBAL FESTIVALS

# 1

# An Introduction to Tribal Fairs and Festivals: Theoretical Considerations

*Dr. Robin D. Tribhuwan*
*Mrs. Preeti R. Tribhuwan*

## I. INTRODUCTION TO THE CONCEPT OF INDIAN FAIRS AND FESTIVALS

Celebrations of Fairs and Festivals in India form a wondrous and joyful series of events, marking the rights of passage between birth, death and renewal. These moments are determined not; by pre-set dates of linear calender, but by changing luminosity of the sun as it enters new seasons, and in cycles spun out by the waxing and waning of the moon.

Each full moon has its own meaning and is placed in the context of its own rituals sacred or social: The month of May, to commemorate the birth of Gautam Budha, July to honour guru or teacher, November in remembrances of the birth of Gurunanak- the founder of Sikh faith, October, to sip saffron milk in the mellow light of autumn harvest moon.

Along with the concept of consecrated time, there is also the concept of sacred space, that goes beyond the immediate environs of temple, gurudwara, and mosque. The banks of a river, the meeting place of waters, a holy bank, forest, mountains, the sea shore, the tomb of a beloved Pir or saint… . all are places of celebration and communion. Here rituals of prayer, sacrifice, oath and blessings are followed with fasting, feast, song or dance.

In a land of vast distance, and a variety of languages and traditions, the spirit of colour of these religious, seasonal or secular festivals underline the unity that draws together seemingly diverse groups. Fairs and festivals are not new to India, their celebrations goes back to vedic times.

### (a) Vedic Festivals and Fairs

During the regime of Aryans there are references of festivals which were celebrated to honour gods, trees mountains, the forth coming monsoon, the end of winter or the of spring. The celebrations included not only fasting and prayers, but events of social and cultural significance. Even references of airs are given in Hindu literature during vedic period. With the entry of Aryans in India they must have surely brought in new forms of festivals & fairs.

### (b) Fairs and Festivals During and After Moghul Rule

After the invasion and rule of Aryans, followed thc rule of some powerful empires, then came the invasion and rule of moghuls or the Muslim rules. The Muslims ruled over India for several Centuries. During this period their musical traditions, dance forms, folklore, dramas, literatures, fairs and festivals became popular. These above mentioned aspects of Muslim culture became part and parcel of those who accepted Muslim religion and those who were forcefully converted to Islamic religion. Fairs and festivals at the tomb of a religious Muslim leader, warrior or a pir were introduced then.

The impact of Muslim influence, hence retained popular festivals and fairs which are existing among the Indian Muslims. Muslim influence also had its impact on few tribes. One example is of the "Siddis" of Karnataka, few of who are Muslim converts, while some have taken to Christianity.

### (c) Influence of British Culture

Britishers ruled India for 150 years. While they were here, there were conversions from Hinduism to Christianity. Thus, festivals such as X'mas, Easter, Good Friday, New year etc. were introduced. These festivals are celebrated by Christians, Goans, Anglo-Indians and Syrian Christians in India.

### (d) Influence of Other Religions

Not to forget the impact of Buddhism, Jainism and other religious cults. The influence of all these religious cults have given birth to multi-ethnic fairs and festivals of India.

There are more festivals in India than the number of days in a year, not unlikely in a country where small, local village rituals of worship and propitiation are celebrated with as much as fervour as are highly holy days across the nation, occasions that can draw floods of people, numbering half a million or more.

To cite few examples, there are festivals and fairs in India which draw millions of people and some of them are:

*(i)* The Kumba melas of Nasik, Ujjain and Lucknow, in Uttar Pradesh.

*(ii)* The Dasera festival of Mysore, in Karnataka.

*(iii)* The Darga of Ajmer, in Rajasthan.

*(iv)* Pushkar and Vaneshwar Fairs of Rajasthan

*(v)* X'mas Celebrations in Goa, these and several other examples can be cited.

Thus, fairs and festivals are moments of remembrance and commemoration of the birth days and great deeds of gods, goddesses, heros, heroins, gurus, prophets and saints. There are times when people gather together linked by ties of shared socio-cultural beliefs and practices.

Simultaneously fairs and festivals are accompanied with performances music, dramas, dances and more rugged physical activities such as:

- Displays of velour and virility.
- through chariot and boat races.
- Wrestling.
- Fights in which rams, buffaloes, bulls, horses, elephants and even rhino's take part.
- Feasting, drinking and merriment.
- Yajnas (Sacrificial fires), where milk, clarified butter and Somarasa (the nectar of alcohol) are offered to gods before being shaved between the worshippers.
- Special foods are cooked and served, prepared from freshly harvested crops.
- Elaborate garlands and ropes are woven as offering to gods.

- Such an assembly (especially fairs) provides an opportunity for traders to sell and buy all manner of goods, from live stock to silks, species hand crafted objects, clothes and other items of ritual or everyday use.
- Outside home there is brotherhood of community worship.

Every fair and festival celebrated has its uniqueness, which is expressed by people by preparing specific sweets, appropriate to the season and crops. There is the joy of congregational 'darshan' or view of the deity, the sharing of amrit, prasad. or especially blessed food, the immersion of idols led in long processions, the chanting of holy verses and part taking of the basket. These and several activities are associated with fairs and festivals. Given this background, let us look into the definition of festival and fair.

## (e) Definition of a Festival

Festival is an occasions that reinforce the presence of god in the life of the individual and the family and bind them to the community. They are also moments for young people to absorb and be part of age-old, yet still vibrant and living traditions.

Festivals are also about fun and enjoyment, more so when they coincide with agricultural events such as harvest, a time to let go of the cares of daily life.

"According to webster's dictionary the term festival means a day or time of religious or other celebration, marked by feasting, ceremonies, or their observances".

## (f) Definition of a Fair

The term 'Mela' or 'Fair' is quite of connected with festival. The word comes from the Sanskrit root, "mil"- meaning meeting and mixing. In a fair the mixing and meeting occurs on truly grand scale, it is a meeting place for people from different villages, towns and regions.

Mela or fair brings together a large variety of social groups, including devotees, priests, medical practitioners, artisans, musicians, traders, dancers, hawkers of fiery snack foods, vendors of toys, clothes, and household merchandise, sellers of camels, horses, or cattle and families who throng from near and far.

The largest fairs or melas take place over a number of days, and often look gigantic encampments, a multitude of small tents stretched out as far as the eye can see. A dusk falls, the lights of lanterns and cook firs sparkle in gathering darkness, creating an air of romance and magic.

While at some fairs, the ambience of romance is very real, for this is where the young gather to arrange their bethrothals. For example at the Tarnetai in Madhya Pradesh the young men and women wear their best clothes, sing dance and make merry.

The Webster dictionary presents several meanings to the term "fair", but one of them which is relevant to the book is that," fair is competitive exhibition of farm products, live stock etc. often combined with entertainment and held annually. It is a periodic gathering of buyers and sellers in an appointed place. Fairs are expositions in which different exhibitors participate, often with a purpose of buying and selling or of familiarizing the public with the products.

From the above definition, it is evident that the English meaning of the term 'fair' is different from the anthropological and or Socio-logical interpretation of the concept of fairs.

### (g) Difference between Fairs and Festivals

An overview of literature on festivals and fairs reveals that there is a vast difference between a fair and festival. Given below are few points that distinguishes these two concepts.

**Table—1**
**Difference between Fair and Festival**

| *S. No* | *Fair* | | *Festival* |
|---|---|---|---|
| (1) | Fair is celebrated on grand scale by more than one religious, sect, tribe, or a caste community. | (1) | Festival is celebrated by one religious or sub-group, group, a tribe or a community with exceptions to few festivals. |
| (2) | Fair consists of a place which has people from various walks of life such as artisans, musicians, traders, vendors, toy sellers, cattle traders, devotees, medicine men, middle men, drama artists, snake charmers, acrobats etc. | (2) | Festival celebrations are usually accompanied by only one or two ethnic groups. |

*(Contd....)*

| | |
|---|---|
| (3) Fairs are celebrated at a traditional/ Sacred fixed place. | (3) Festivals are not necessarily celebrated at a fixed place. |
| (4) Rituals performed in fairs are common to various ethnic or tribal groups. | (4) Rituals performed during festivals are common to one social group, a religious sect or a community. |
| (5) Food, sweets, fruits, nuts etc in fairs are variety and there is no specificity. | (5) Food, sweets, fruits, nuts etc prepared of during festivals are specific. |
| (6) Number of participants in fair are in millions. | (6) Festive participants are less in number as compared to fairs. |

## II. TRIBAL FESTIVALS AND FAIRS

India is the only country in the world, which has highest number of tribes and tribal population. According to Anthropological survey of India, there are 573 scheduled tribes in the country. Out of these 573 groups 75 groups have been categorized as Primitive Tribal groups by the Ministry of home affairs. As per 1991 Census of India the total tribal population is 68.7 millions amounting to 8.01% to the total population of the country.

Our experience of working with tribals gives us an impression that tribals in India are of two types namely:

*(i)* Tribes inhabiting in remote and inaccessible areas

*(ii)* Those inhabiting on the plains.

The ones who have been living in inaccessible areas such as in valleys and forests on mountains and hills, have not been influenced by the non-tribal groups. Where as those tribal communities living on the plains have been influenced by non-ribal groups. Their long term contact with the Hindus, especially, has resulted into borrowing many hindu cultural traits. Some tribals have been influence by Christianity and Islam as well. Infact there are Christian and Muslim tribals in the country.

It is because of this ecological distinction or separation the influences exerted and the degree of acculturations in both the types of tribal communities by the non-tribal groups differs to a great extent.

### (a) Tribal Festivals

In her paper captioned, 'Asur Festivals" (2002), Pratibha Kumari has stated that tribal society of any region tries to secure favour and active help of supernatural powers by propiation, sacrifices of animals etc, on several occasions or at each new stage in the annual cycle of its simple economic life. Tribal festivals offer occasions for safety and welfare to the people.

On festive occasions they feel free and relaxed from several tensions of their hard life. They participate in the festivals with a sense of solidarity. They participate hastily in feasting, drinking and dancing to celebrate the festivals along with propiations of both benevolent and malevolent spirits to get good harvest, plenty of rainfall and to be protected from disease and natural calamities. A type of gratitude is expressed to the supernatural forces and cosmic beings for helping them in the time of adversity.

Besides providing entertainment, festivals also help in regulating the socio-economic activities of the tribals smoothly. Festivals of tribal people are one of the sacred performances which give them their ritual calender. They engage themselves in feasting and drinks. They seek safety and prosperity to their community as a whole at each new stage in the annual cycle of their simple life. Given this background, let us analyze the types of tribal festivals in India.

## (b) Types of Tribal Festivals

After having studied tribal dances of India and editing the book in the year 1999. We come across the concept of tribal festivals and fairs. Dances of tribals are associated with different festivals. For example the "Kambdi" dance of the warlis is associated with sowing festival called "avni", tarpa dance s associated with harvest and Gauri dance is associated with "Holi" festival. Based on primary data and review of literature on tribal festivals, we have evolved following classification of tribal festivals.

## (c) Classification of Tribal Festivals

*(1) Festivals Associated with Agricultural cycle.*

*(i)* Festivals associated with preparation of agricultural land

*(ii)* Sowing festivals.

*(iii)* Festivals to rejoice over growth of new leafy vegetables.

*(iv)* Weeding festivals.

(v) Harvest Festivals.

(vi) Threshing and storage Festivals.

(2) *Festivals Associated with Seasonal Changes.*

(3) *Hunting Festivals.*

(4) *Festivals of Tribal Gods and Goddesses.*

(5) *Ancestral Festivals.*

(6) *Preventive, promotive , and Curative Health Festivals.*

(7) *Festivals associated with cattle welfare and Health.*

(8) *Festivals of Renewal.*

(9) *Festivals Associated with Cosmic movements and changes.*

(10) *Festivals of Medical Practitioners.*

(11) *War Festivals.*

Let us now look at every type of tribal festival as classified above.

## 1. Festivals Associated with Agricultural Cycle

Tribals are small scale cultivators and cultivable land is their major economic asset. They value their agricultural land a lot Grains produced from the land are used up by the family. In their film captioned "Rice Rituals of the Warlis" Tribhuwan Robin (Scientific Advisor) and signe Ruitgers (2000) have shown how the warli life cycle is interwoven with their agricultural cycle, by showing the cultural significance of rice and its use in various cultural contexts. Food grains are therefore the main nutritional assets and their survival depends on these. Hence, production of food grains is associated with joy and happiness and therefore festive celebration is linked with every stage of agricultural process and production.

### (a) Festivals Associated with Preparation of Agricultural Land

*Holi:* The festival of fire and colours, marks the beginning of summer. To the tribals this time means, they are supposed to prepare their land. Following Holi most tribals, especially cultivators start manuring their land and fertilizing it.

### (b) Sowing Festivals

'Avni' is a popular festival celebrated the tribals of western Maharashtra. Well, this is the time, some where in June-July, when they transplant rice samplings from are corner of the field and sow them in rows. The warlis celebrate this festival by performing the "Kambad" dance.

In their paper on the "dance forms of warlis", Tribhuwan Robin and Finkenaure Maike (1999:339) have documented the symbolism of Kambdi dance. According to Warli myth this dance was performed by Naran (the god of rain) along with other gods to please "Kansari"- (the goddess of food grains). This dance was performed when Kansari brought about famine and hid herself naked under a rock. The essence of symbolism is that a naked seed (Kansari) with out water (Naran- the god of rain) is futile. Hence this dance which is performed only by the males have lot of movents that resemble with the act of sexual intercourse. Hence the appropriate time to perform the dance is during sowing and transplanting symbolically recreating history to appear 'Kansari'.

### (c) Festival to Rejoice over New Leafy Vegetables

This festival is celebrated at family land by the tribals of western Maharashtra. They eat vegetable called "Mataji bhaji" (Amaranthus) leaves to celebrate the joy over production of vegetables in their kitchen gardens, and fields.

### (d) Weeding Festivals

Some tribes, especially in east and north east have festivals of weeding. Weeds that grow in rice fields are taken off. There are several dance forms that depict the action of weeding.

### (e) Harvest Festivals

Most tribes in India, including non-tribal communities celebrate Dasera and Diwali to express their joy over harvest. Some of the harvest dances of various tribes are given below in Table 1.2. *(See the table on page 12).*

**Table—1.2**
**Harvest Dances of Tribals**

| *S. No* | *Tribe* | | *Harvest Dance* |
|---|---|---|---|
| (1) | Santhal | (1) | Sohrae Dance |
| (2) | Warli | (2) | Tarpa Dance |
| (3) | Kokna | (3) | Pawri Dance |
| (4) | Bhil | (4) | Dhol Dance |
| (5) | Thakar | (5) | Dhol Dance |
| (6) | Bhumjis of West Bengal | (6) | Kathi Dance |
| (7) | Garasia of Rajasthan | (7) | Walar Dance |
| (8) | Sauria Paharia | (8) | Snake Dance |
| (9) | Dhurwa, Bhatra Halba and Muria of Madhya Pradesh | (9) | Dandari Dance |
| (10) | Siddis of Karnataka | (10) | Dhamal Dance |
| (11) | Pawaras of Maharashtra | (11) | Bonda Dance |
| (12) | Oraon | (12) | Tunta Dance |
| (13) | Madia/Kolam | (13) | Rela Dance |
| (14) | Korku | (14) | Khamm Dance |
| (15) | Kabui | (15) | Chappa Dance. |

## (f) Threshing and Storage Festivals

Food grains are source of survival to the tribals and hence they give utmost priority and importance. The warlis perform two types of festivals namely.

(i) *Kansari Festival*: This festival is celebrated at the family level and at the level of clan by the warlis. Kansari-the goddess of food grains is worshipped , in order to appease her to be productive and happy with humanity. This festival is performed either every year or once in five years. Celebration depends on the family or clan concerned.

*(ii)* *Muthi Festival:* Warli women make paste from the rice and make fist prints marks on the door, post, doors on agricultural implements. The storage festival is symbolic of prosperity.

## 3. Festivals Associated with Seasonal Changes

Tribals have their own traditional calender, which is based on cosmic changes. There are several festivals which are celebrated due to changes in seasons. Some of the examples of this type are the Ganthan luithan spring festival of the Rongmei Nagas. Holi festival of the Bhils, Rathwa, Garasia, Kathodi, and Pawara.

## 4. Hunting Festivals

Most hunting festivals of tribals in India occur after the harvest i.e. between October to May well, this is the time when they are relatively free as compared to agricultural season. Pasuikao-a festival of hunting is celebrated by the Maram Nagas of North East India.

## 4. Festivals of Tribal Gods and Goddesses

All most all tribes in India celebrate festivals of their gods and goddesses. For example the tribes of western Maharashtra celebrate the festival of Waghya (tiger god) by offering him a goat's sacrifice every year before sowing their seeds. Festivals of Mata (goddess) is yet another example among Gonds and Madias.

## 6. Ancestral Festivals

Tribal believe that their dead ones often visit them in dreams and on festive occasions, especially during ancestral festivals. They believe that the ancestors are very much there in heaven or universe. They perform dances to invite them to be with people. The Thakars and Katkaris of Maharashtra celebrate a festival called "Pitra Amosha", on the new moon night in July-August, they perform the "Dhamdi Dance", whole night and believe that by the dawn their ancestral spirit came into the village. Next day however no one in the village eats lunch unless and until a crow or any other bird takes away food is kept on a leaf on the eastern side of their roof. They believe that these spirits dine with them.

Similarly the Maram Nagas celebrate "Rakka" festival in the memory of their dead fore fathers. The Rongmei Nagas celebrate chakak in March to remember their ancestral spirits.

## 7. Preventive, Promotive and Curative Health Festivals

Most tribals in India and worldover observe festivals of health prevention, promotion and cure. Kolams celebrate the festival of "Gaon bandhani" in which the village priests marks the village boundary and the entire village worships it. They also appease mata (female deity), usually situated on the boundary to protect them from small pox, chicken pox epidemics and other natural calamities. Similarly there are festivals associated with health promotion and cure.

## 8. Festivals Associated with Cattle Health and Welfare

Pola is the most popular festival, of cattle especially bulls and cows, celebrated by tribals of Maharasthtra. On this day they make special food for the bulls and cows, decorate them, rest them and celebrate this festival Atom-Matai is a festival of cattle celebrated by the Maram Nagas they give rice beer to the cattle on this day.

## 9. Festivals of Renewal

Tribals also celebrate festivals of new vegetables. For example Ganthan Luithan-the festival of Rongmei Nagas. Mat-the festival of Thakars, warlis, Koknas, kathkaris, Mahadev Kolis etc of Maharashtra.

## 10. Festival Associated with Cosmic Movements and Changes

Sun is considered to be on of the supreme powers in the universe by most tribals, hence any eclipse of both sun and moon disturb the tribals. Ribes therefore have festivals on new moon nights and full moon nights.

## 11. Festivals of Medical Practitioners

Medical practitioners form an important institution of tribal culture. They do not charge any money for the medical service rendered by them. Hence, they are respected by people. These practitioners have elaborate rituals and festivals associated with collection and preparation of medicine and more importantly with apprenticeship. Thakar shamans train new shamans during 'Navratri" (nine days) festival.

## 12. War Festivals

War festivals are mostly prevalent among the north-eastern tribes. That is where the head hunting cult prevailed once upon a time. For example, the Ling Ngai is the war festival of the Rongmei Nagas.

From the account of tribal festivals presented above, it is evident that one can come out with several sub-categories of festival types. Given this back ground let us turn our attention to tribal fairs now.

## III. TRIBAL FAIRS

Like the Hindus, Muslims, Christians, Parsees, Jains and Buddhists, tribals too celebrate fairs. Tribal fairs are however are not celebrated in grand style. We have classified tribal fairs into two categories namely

*(a)* Fairs consisting of tribal populations and,

*(b)* Fairs consisting of Tribal as well as non-tribal populations.

The first category of fairs have more than one tribe or community participating in the fair. While the later is a mixture of tribal and non-tribal populations.

### Salient Features of Tribal Fairs

1. Tribal fairs are mostly celebrated on mountains, hills, in forests and valleys, with few exceptions, to the rule.

2. Number of participations in tribal fairs are very less as compared to non-tribal fairs.

3. Tribal fairs are managed by tribal religious and political, leaders, and other important personnel, in the community.

4. They are characterized by barter system.

5. In such fairs common dialect is spoken by different tribes participating in the same. For example "Bhilori" is common dialect spoken in Toranmal, Devmogra and Asthamba Fairs of Dhule district in Maharashtra.

6. Traders, artisans, musicians, etc are purely traditional.

7. Economic transactions in tribal fairs is of a lower order, as compared to non-tribal fairs.

8. Temple priest is often a tribal and his post is restricted either to his family or clan.

9. The degree of interference of politicians in tribal fairs is very less as compared to non-tribal fairs.

10. Tribals are involved in drinking, playing music communal dancing, participating or observing traditional games or rituals than buying or purchasing.

## IV. CHANGES IN TRIBAL FAIRS AND FESTIVALS

Over the years, there have been changes in the tribal fairs and festivals as a result of following factors:

*(a)* Constant invasions in India right from the period of Aryans, to the Moghuls and finally up to the Britisher rule.

*(b)* Invaders such as Moghuls and Britishers brought with them Islam and Christianity and hence conversions. christian and Muslim tribals gave up their customs and traditions to a great extent.

*(c)* The process of Hinduization, especially dominated tribals in cities and those living close to town.

*(d)* Impact of education, modernization industrialization and development has been yet another factor of change.

*(e)* Politicians are using the platfrom of fairs to gain political popularity.

## V. CONCLUDING REMARKS

Tribals fairs and festivals are intrinsic aspects of tribal culture. With rapid changes taking place amongst tribals there is a need for tribal Development Ministries, Ministries of culture and Tourism, Museums, anthropologists and other social scientists must make efforts to preserve these traditions by filming or video documenting them, before they are lost.

## REFERENCES

1. Pratibha Kumari, 2001 Festivals of Sauria Paharia, in Tribhuwan Robin (ed) Fairs and Festivals of Indian Tribes, D.P.H, New Delhi.
2. Tribhuwan Robin and Tribhuwan Preeti-1999, Tribal Dances of India, D.P.H, New Delhi.

❑❑❑

# 2

# Fairs and Festivals of the Kinnaras of Western Himalaya

*Dr. B. R. Sharma*

The Himalayas offer a very rich, rewarding and tremendous field for observation, Cultural studies and research on various aspects of life. Since time immemorial, this great mountain has served as a refuge and museum to races and religious faiths and has attracted even the earliest man on earth. Even during the earliest periods of Civilization and Cultural evolution, the spiritual seekers, graziers, nature-lovers, vanquished and victorious including those who fund their mention in ancient scriptures and mythological legends were attracted to find solace and spiritual bliss in the lap of this spectacular creation of the almighty.

Among the mythological races of the remote past we find traces of Yakshas, Gandharvas, Kinnaras, Nags, Asuras, Pishachas, Kiratas, Suras, Trigartas etc. in the various parts of this mighty mountain. It is, in fact, the abode of ancient and mythological races, sages, gods and snow. Not only the ancient tribes, such as, Vidyadharas, Kinnaras, Kimpurushas etc. are mentioned to have occupied the region from time to time but the location of mythical places like Indrapur (the capital of the rain god Indra), Swarg (heaven) Pitrilok (abode of ancestral spirits), Yampuri (the seat of Yama, the lord of death) and Shivloka (the place of Lord Shiva, the greatest of Trinity of Indian mythology) and breadth of this mountain. As already mentioned, we find ample material by way of rituals, living habits, myths, legends, folklore and traditional practices of various communities settled in the region right upto now to support our views on linkage of the pre-historic communities and people with the settlers of the present times. Among numerous communities of ancient times, the Kinnara or Kinnaura who associate themselves with legendary and mythological race of Kinnara and Kimpurusha, is the most thrilling one. These people are found in the present Kinnaur district of Himachal Pradesh.

Kinnaur is the north eastern frontier district of the state and a border district of India. It is about 80 kilometers in length and 65 kilometers in breadth with a population of 70,931 people according to 1991 Census report. On the east, the district is separated from Tibet by the Zanskar mountain ranges. The Dhaula-dhar range separates the region from Rampur Bushehr and Kullu areas. The inhabitants of the district are known as Kinnaras, Kanawaras, Kinnaurese, who associate themselves with khasha or khoshia community of Rajput race. The other communities inhabiting the region are Chamang, Domang, Chanal, Ores and Badhi (Carpenter) etc. River Satluj divides the entire district in almost two equal parts flowing from an elevation of about 3050 metres at its Western boundary. The entire area is marked by high mountains and the villages are situated on the slopes between the snow clad peaks on the upper side and the river passages down below. The total area of the district is 6520 sq. kilometres with nearly 11.5% of the total area of the state and with an average density of nine persons per square kilometer, as compared to 77 for the state as a whole. The entire local population, with peculiarities, such as, language, history and living styles, is classified as Scheduled tribes and Scheduled Castes constituting 74.9% and 10.6% respectively. The upper or the land owning class is khoshia or khash without any further division and the rest are regarded as the Chamang group. Among the latter, the Ores and Domang may intermarry while the Chamang are regarded as low in social status.

The Kinnaur habitats are small and are usually divided into hamlets separated by geographical situations and considerations based on jatis or communities. Villages are generally located around a nucleus which is either a temple, Buddhist monastery, a fort or some old and towering building, usually combined with a trade Centre or market having some small shops housed in residential buildings. The habitants depend mostly on agriculture, horticulture and animal husbandry. The Khoshias or the Khash people, besides being land owners rear goats and sheep for wool, meat and for carrying goods while on business, trade or movement of the herds from one place to the other. The Chamangs serve the Khosias as farm labourers and are also leather workers, weavers and designers whereas the Domangs are blacksmiths and silversmiths and the Ores serve as carpenters. The traditional considerations of social hierarchy and status as well as parental professions have considerably changed now and as a result of openings of earning livelihood and spread of education as well as keenness of the government to allow more and more opportunities of service and welfare to the Tribal and Scheduled Caste people, the life styles are changing fast.

The trade with Tibet has come to an end, and the people have started taking more interest in agriculture, horticulture and animal husbandry. Several types of vegetables and fruit varieties are raised for the local market while apples, dry fruits, such as, Neoza, (Chilgoza), almond, peanuts etc. are distributed for sale to other parts of India. Pars, potatoes and other local products are in great demand even outside the region. Wheat, barley and Millet are the main crops in the area whereas maize and rice are also grown in the lower levels. The rainfall is scanty and the region beyond Kalpa receives only snow during winters. In fact, the most part of the district falls in rain shadow area as the monsoons, obstructed by high mountain ranges on the way, become ineffective while reaching the region. Water is stored either in stone lined pools and tanks or is brought from the neighboring rivulets flowing from the high peaks down below. With the onset of water supply schemes to the habitats, the residents are relieved of water scarcity and troubles of storing water in the houses. Although the social taboos and social hierarchical feelings are diminishing slowly, yet complete emancipation of the Chamang still seems far off as they continue to depend upon the upper class people with an exception of a few. The natural streams flowing near the habitats are guided by the channels into the fields. The use of water for irrigation is decided at a joint meeting of the villagers, where the date and period of one's urn is fixed according to requirements and availability. Bullocks and a hybrid called 'dzo' are used in ploughing the fields.

Previously, traders from Kinnaur had free access to the markets of Western Tibet. Imports into India were salt, boras and wool, while exports included cotton clothing. Foodgrains carried to Tibet were bartered for wool, pashmina, butter, rock salt, Tibetan ponies and yak tails. A trade relationship developed between individual traders on either side of the border. Kinnaur traders used to advance cash or deposit some articles with their respective moshe before returning, on contract, that next year they would take back some specific articles in exchange for their previous investments. Thus, Kinnaur traders used to keep animals like sheep, goats, yak etc. with their Tibetan counterparts, and used to get back milk products and off springs annually, according to the terms laid down in the formal contract.

Under the rule of the Rajas, the whole of Kinnaur was divided into Khunds or divisions. Each Khund has a presiding deity, whose influence has continued to be present day. Every village, had its own special deity inhabiting a temple. A system of mutual visits known as bioling, is a means by which social intimacy is maintained between the villages constituting a Khund. The idols (Mukhang) of the deities are carried in palanquins (Rathang) on the men's shoulders to visit one another. The villagers have to play host to the deity and the people who carried he idol. Every two or three years, a common meeting is arranged between deities. Another tour which the deities undertake every six or seven years over the entire khund, is known as boning. Lastly, the tour which the deity of the khund undertakes to more distant places even outside, is known as parganait.

The temple-gods thus knit together the people of Kinnaur into a kind of ritual relationship. At festivals like Diwali (Deeval) or Baisakhi (Bishu), offerings are made to the village deities for better yield of crops and better health of livestock. Animal sacrifices are made to the demons to check natural calamities like drought, land-slides etc.

Village gods are very popular and common in the region and without the knowledge of the deity noting can happen in the village. The deity is brought out in a wooden palanquin from he temple and is made to dance on festive occasions. The Palanquin is called Rathang (Cariot) in the local parlance. The spirit is not visible but the oracle (Grokch) wile in trance, represents the deity and replies the querries of the devotees. The weight of the palanquin, some times gets heavier and lighter wit the wishes of the spirit, as per belief of the followers.

The mythological Kinnara people were celestial musicians and dancers. According to Brahmand (3.22.56), Matsya (4.53) and vayu purana (47.57;69.31), they had faces of a horse and were called Ashwamukhas (Ashwa=horse, mukh–face). Vau Purana mentions about their Ganas (habitats) in the Himalayas. It is, perhaps due to the fact that they are horse breeders and belong to a region where tis animal is quite useful for carrying household objects from one place to another, as the Kinnara, even in the present times, prefer to shift to places of lower elevation to escape severe winter.

The tribe has typical myths of creation. According to their belief, the Great Spirit' is called 'ISHURAS' or "Ishur Mahadev'. This creator-god possesses mystic powers and an active male personality. The spirit automatically came out from an egg created from a bubble in a pool of water. The body had no limbs and at that time there was a state of darkness every where. With the blowing of wind from the Eastern side, various parts of his body started emerging. The Sun and Moon were formed from the sweat-drops of his body. Vishnu Narayan and Lord Brahma were created by him and they came out from his wrist. There was no sky or Underworld. The sky was lifted by the creator with the blow of his head and Underworld got developed due to the pressure of his foot. He created KALU LUHAR (Kalu, the blacksmith) in order to get his help for creating the Universe.

The creator-god, with the help of Kalu Luhar, tried to make human beings. The earth was made out of black clay as white and soft ones could no longer bear the burden. Man made of gold and later from silver was sent across the mountain, but he couldn't respond to the call. The experiment failed. Then a man of copper and brass was tried but he, too, could not succeed in hearing to the call given to him. At last, a man of clay and ash was created and to their surprise, he responded. The creator-god, on seeing this got outraged, as according to him, the body of the creature was sort-lived and was to be cremated. The animal world was created later.

The creator-god was a bachelor but his companions including Vishnu Narayan wanted him to get united in family ties. A suitable ride was not easy to be found. A massive search was initiated. All the godlings were sent on a mission to find out a suitable partner to the great-spirit. But some of them would forward their own claim side tracking the main issue. Ultimately, Vishnu Narayan advised Ishuras to go out in search of bride himself. They reached the house of the snow god, YUKUNTRAS. The creator god was in the guise of an ascetic and sat outside in the courtyard. The son of Yukuntras was contacted by lord Vishnu Narayan. He, on knowing that Ishuras wanted to marry his sister, asked the black crow to bring heavy snowfall. The crow instantaneously brought about twelve feet of snow but the ascetic remained unaffected. Yukuntras locked her daughters Gore and Gange inside seven halls. All the rooms got unlocked with mystic powers of the sage and Gore came out smiling. She intended the ascetic to demand her hand in marriage from her father. Ultimately, Yukuntras had to agree but with some conditions.

The marriage day was fixed 8th day of Magh month (January). The father of Gore wanted to avoid Vishnu Narayan and shepherd as he thought them to be shrewd. He wanted them not to be included in the marriage party. At last the auspicious day came. The marriage party reached the palace of the Snow-King. At last the auspicious day came. The marriage party was served with 20 Pathias (20 kilograms) or rice, a big goat and one Patha (about one kg.) of salt to be consumed by him alone. One seeing the quantity, all were amazed but couldn't think of a successful plan to cope with the condition. Vishnu Narayan, on seeing the situation, emerged from a drum and suggested that the quantity meant for a single member be consumed collectively to pave the way for total consumption. The blunt hammer (Ghan) was sharpened while dancing and rubbing it turn by turn by the dancers. The whole lot was, thus shared turn by turn. Gore was wedded to Ishuras but Gange also accompanied her to her in-laws house. Later, she also got married with the creator–got. According to Indian mythological literature, Gauri or Parvati, the daughter of Himvan is the consort of Lord Shiva. According to Shiv Puran, Mahadev went to Parvati to test her determination and devotion. He was in the guise of a Brahman, but in the present context, he was an ascetic and Gore suggested to ask her father for her hand in marriage. Gauri and Ganga are two important characters of Indian mythological literature but their unification with the creator-spirit symbolises the uniqueness of Kinnara mythology. The question remains that Ishuras obeing the creator-spirit, is the originator of everything on earth but Yukuntras, the snow-king existed even before him. This question finds no solution. It however becomes sufficiently clear that the primitive mind of the people of the Tribe can't think of the world without snow. However, Lord Ishuras and her two consorts Gore and Gange are exhibited on the palanquins of village gods in the form of metal images in the region and their metal images are given prominent positions.

The Kinnauras have another myth of deities too which is distinctly related to the myth of creation. According to a ballad, the father of eighteen principal deities of the region, BANASUR met the goddess-HIDIMBA at a place near Sungra Village. On enquiry he told that his name was banasur Dev and he belonged to Chantang (Tsaprang) in Guge province. Hidimba told him that she was coming from Kullu-Lahul area. Later, they got married and stayed in a cave named 'Gorboring Ag'. They gave birth to eighteen sons and daughters who are worshipped as deities of various areas in the district. The temple of Hidimba goddess is in Kafor Village and the spirit of Banasur is believed to stay the upper storey of Sungra Maheshur temple in Sungra. Chandika, the eldest sister of the deities, divided the area among her sisters and brothers. She gave Sarahan-Sungra area to her eldest brother Sungra Maheshur, Bhaba area to her next brother Bhaba area to her next brother Bhaba Maheshur, Rajgramang to her third brother Chagaon Maheshur , Nichar area to her sister Usha or Ukha, and Chaitralekha who is also mentioned as their sister, was alloted Tranda Village. One of their brothers settled at Mebar Village and goddess Chandika got Koshtampi or Kothi Village as her share. She managed to conceal Ropa Valley in her plait and later found her worshippers in that area also. The legend goes that Chandika asked her sister Usha to send her husband 'HONU' to accompany her to Tibet for the purchase of salt. Honu agreed to do so and went to Kothi Village where he was asked by the goddess to wait inside a watermill till her arrival. The goddess killed him while his beard got stuck in the watermill. The goddess didn't know that the demon had some mysterious powers due to which her body got re-assembled. The resuscitation of Honu put Chandika to great difficulty and she called each one of her brother for help. But annoyed with the division, none of them responded. In the end, she called Markaling, the god of Khawangi Village to come to her rescue. Markaling was related to her as her nephew. He came and found that he did not have the powers to free his aunt from the clutches of the demon. On his request, Chagaon Maheshur came for her rescue and suggested that she should first of all kill the fly hovering over the dead-body of Honu. She at once killed the fly which was the spirit or soul of demon.

The legend gives enough evidence to a primitive belief that the spirit, on leaving the body, hoves like a fly and can be killed again. Honu, the husband of goddess Usha, a Pauranic Character is mentioned as Anirudha in Srimad Bhagwat (10.63) and Vishnu Puran (Ch. 32, P. 470).

Banasur, according to records belonged to the lineage of Kashyap, Hrinyakashipa, Prahlad, Virochan and Bali. Bali's son Banasur was a great devotee of Lord Shiva and his daughter Usha got married to Anirudha, the grand son of Lord Kirshna. Chitralekha has not been mentioned as a real sister of Usha, the daugther of Banasur in the Epic, but according to a popular belief she was given a share in the property and folklore of the region mentions her as the daughter of Banasur and Hidimba. In Shiv Puran (Ch. 55-56) she is mentioned as the daughter of Kumbhand, a minister of king Banasur. All the Asura kings referred to above were Shaivites where as Lord Krishna, the incarnation of Lord Vishnu, was a Vaishnavite.

Hidimba was a powerful goddess of the Himalayan region. She, at one time, had a vast number of followers. Dimapur, in Asam is associated with her name. The temples of this goddess are found at various places in Himachal Pradesh. According to the great Epic, she married Bhima, one of the Pandava brothers during their sojourn in the Himalayas. Hidimb was her brother and on seeing the Pandavas, he sent her to kill them. But on seeing Bhim, she fell in love with him and Kunti allowed her to stay with him on the condition that she would leave him after the birth of their first child and they would never stay together during the night. It is, perhaps, due to the belief that demons get very powerful during the night and she might harm Bhim, even when she was wedded to him. Hidimb was killed in encounter and she, later left Pandava brothers after the birth of Ghatotkach.

Hidimba is worshipped in the name of 'Hirbani' during the festival of Bhunda- a rope sliding ceremony at Nirmand in Kullu region. The festival takes place, on the advice of the village god, after twelve or more years. It is witnessed by thousands of people. A man from Beda community performs the rituals. The worship of Hirbani on the occasion, makes her the presiding deity of the festival and reminds of the days when human sacrifice might have been in vogue in the Himalayan regions. Rope sliding is now a ritual only and the Beda has no risk of life. This ceremony, according to the legends, had been performed at Nichar in Kinnaur region where goddess Usha, the daughter of Hidimba is the Presiding deity.

The spirit of Banasur is still believed to be visiting the places of his sons and daughters from time to time. In Chagaon village, the inhabitants, at the time of untimely storms, inclement weather and chilly winds, consult the deity whether the spirit of is father had come to the village. If the Grokch (Oracle) replies in affirmative, it is the duty of the population to give a warm send off to the spirit on an appointed day and the villagers, in their best attires and musicians, come out in a procession to bid farewell to the spirit. The palanquins of the village gods (Maheshur and Vishnu Narayan) are also on this occasion decorated and brought out of the temple to be taken in a procession. The spirit is seen off, according to her wishes, at a place outside the village. The same is worshipped as a snake made of flour and put in a basket with a lamp. The followers keep the basket closed and nobody opens it afterwards. They make it a point not to see backward while coming to their village. The ceremony is called 'Shu bonu samyamu' (Shu = deity, Bonu = to father, Samyamu = departure). In Bhaba Village, the spirit is received on its arrival. In Kafor village, where Hidimba, the wife of Banasur is the principal goddess, the spirit is given saltish dish (doo) and, seen off. In Sungra village, a festival is held in honour of the arrival of the spirit is arranged. It is called the festival of reception of the father of the gods' (Mahadevu Bau Karmu). After this festival, it is believed that the spirit would take rest for about three years and would not go out.

Besides their staunch faith in major deities belonging to the family of Banasur and Hidimba, the Kinnauras have Nag and Nagini (serpent gods and goddesses), Narayan or Vishnu Narayan, Buddhist gods, viz. Dabla, Yulsa, Milayung etc. as their village deities. Kimshu (household god), crop gods, evil spirits like chan, khon, Khungch etc. and mountain goddesses, Saonige or 'Saoni are also believed and worshipped. The Saoni spirits are invited to households during the Faguli festival and served with fine meals. The Saoni or the mountain goddesses feel attracted to the villages during various festivals and it is believed that they attend every ceremony during which musical instruments are played. The inhabitants don't allow the spirits to stay back in the habitats and as a remedial step, obscene and vulgar sentences and songs are uttered by the participants. People believe that on hearing the obscene language, the spirits feel ashamed and opt to leave the habitats. According to some scholars, the tradition of vulgarity is a substitute to the idea of Nudity found among various primitive tribes of India and abroad. It is with this idea that obscene songs and loud vulgar voices are allowed during various festivals to drive away such spirits. The Kimshus (household gods) control the affairs of a family and Khatingshu (courtyard deity) controls the surroundings or premises of the house.

The Kinnara deities have great regard for hierarchy. During the princely regime, the Rayasat (state) god was considered to be the supermost spirit or Principal deity of the state who was followed by khund, Ghori, Deshang (village), Padeshang (hamlet), Kimshu (household) and Khatingshu (courtyard deity) gods and goddesses. Bhimakali was the state goddess of Rampur Bushehr State and Maheshur deities headed various Khunds (parganas). Maheshur deities are called 'Monshir" in local parlance, and it is believed that they might be the gods of 'Mon' tribe in ancient times. Out of total six khunds of Kinnaur region, five were dominated by the deities of Monshir clan. In Hangrang valley, the traces of village god system, according to Hindu Pantheon are not traceable but Buddhist gods are worshipped. The tribe has a typical system of Parganait according to which the village gods of different villages pay a visit to other villages and stay as guests of the villagers and their deities. The rotation is decided by the respective gods and conveyed to the followers through their oracles (Grokch). All the deities of the region are believed to pay a visit to Indrapuri during winter. Indrapuri is not located on earth and, most probably, is a mythical place. The godlings, under the guidance of Basehru god, assemble invisibly at Sarahan and leave for Indrapur. In some of the villages, the functions of departure of the deities are arranged and in some others, the deity is received after the visit.

According to legends, the deities try to get major share of prosperity for their fellow beings at Indrapur. But sometimes, floods untimely deaths, famines and other calamities haunt and are predicted. In Chagaon village, the festival of departure of the deity is called 'Ragul'. During this festival, the villagers take out the palanquine of the village god to the courtyard (Santhang) of the temple and try to lift and throw it up upward with a jerk presuming that the spirit is leaving the palanquin and going upwards.

During the absence of the village gods from the villages, no functions are held and feelings of isolation and loneliness prevails. In some of the villages, people make pictures of ghosts and demons on entrance points feeling that such acts would help keeping ghosts away from the habitats. Agricultural work is totally forbidden during this period and even loud voices are prohibited. There is a common feeling that the benevolent spirits being away to Indrapuri, there would be none to help in case of any crisis in the village and, as such, everything is kept in dormant stage. The oracle predicts the return of a particular deity and on the appointed day. On that day the people assemble in the Santhang or in the house of some person on whom the god wished to come down first of all. The oracle or the desired person receives him while going into trance. They greet the deity and the oracle relates the ordeal of the spirit to bring more and more prosperity to the people. In some villages, the oracle (Grokch) makes the statement but in some others there is a tradition of unfolding a particular cloth used to wrap the images of gods. On some villages, it is believed that the cloth wrapped around the images during this period carries the indication for the fate of the devotees during the ensuing year. In case objects like coal, grains, hair, clay etc. are found with the cloth on being unfolded, the predictions are deciphered likewise. Coal depicts more deaths and grams promise better crops.

The polyandrous Kinnaras have typical customs of birth, marriage and death. The mother gives birth to a child in the lowest room of the house. This room is meant for animals and is called 'Khud'. The child is brought out alongwith his or her mother after three or four days. In upper areas, Lama (Buddhist priest) performs the rituals of purification but in other places, the family gets sanctified after entertaining the villagers on feast. There is a custom in some amount of money is offered. In Ropa Village, the father of a male child is symbolically beaten by the villagers in the ceremony arranged in the promises of the temple on 'Ukhyang' festival day with the bone-sticks of the offered goat. There are five types of practices to acquire a wife in the area. These are:

1. Zanekang or Zanetang — Marriage through settlement.
2. Nyotang Meerang — Only two persons go as representative of the bridegroom and bride accompanies hem to the house of in-laws.
3. Damchalshish — Love marriage
4. Darosh Dab Dab — Marriage by Force

5. Hari — This is typeof abduction by consent. The married lady, if not satisified in her in-laws house, sometimes leaves her husband/s and the new husband, after making good the expenditure incurred by the first husband, re-marries the lady.

The village god plays an important role in the selection of a suitable match. In some cases, the father of the boy having more than one matrimonial alliance offers to his son, goes to the temple and consults the village god with flowers in his hands. The god, in that case suggests the girl for whom a particular type of flower is meant and the case is settled. The middleman or 'Maj Omi' plays an important role in performing the marriage. The Kinnaras believe that the soul, after leaving the body goes to mountain tops. Raldang, a legendary place situated in deep snows on the mountain of Kinnaur Kailash, is the heaven of Kinnauras. All the departed souls reach Raldang (Ralang=spirits, Dang=place) through a place known as 'Kumshutring' (a rock of confusion). All the spirits stay at Raldang till the next command of the Ishuras. Mourning in the family is for about one year i.e. till the next 'Fulaich' festival. Fulaich is the festival of flowers. On this day, flowers are offered to the deities, family members and the mourners. On the day of death, the relatives and villagers as well as friends assemble in the house of the departed soul. This night is called 'Dum Rating' (the night of assemblage). The dead is made to take bath in a big Tub called 'Lam Kunyal' and his legs are not kept straight as it is feared that in that case, the dead could dance and go away.

While being taken to Cremation ground, two persons holding white piece of cloth called, 'Om Kaphra' (the cloth showing the way), lead the way as it is believed that in case the way is not shown to the dead, the spirit may come back to the village or night remain their and disturb the atmosphere. On Chhnantiyamo day, wine is offered to the participants and relations. In upper Kinnaur, the Lama, performs death rites and chants mantras for the salvation of departed soul. Through 'Foa' (saying sacred words and pulling the hair of the head), he paves the way to his unknown journey. Professional singers known as Gitkares sing the mourning songs on Phulaich festival. In Chagaon, the 'Gitkaras' narrate the story of the departed soul and its journey to 'Raldang'. They have to sing a traditional song while standing and moving throughout the night. If any of them falls down or stumbles, it is feared that the departed spirits would no allow him to see the next Phulaich festival as they would be annoyed. The singers narrate that the family members have brought gifts for him and that was an old tradition so there is nothing would not allow him to see the next Phulaich festival as they would be annoyed. The singers narrate that the family members have brought gifts for him and that was an old tradition so there is nothing unusual in it. The family members then come out with their gifts which are offered to the Gitkares to be handed over to the dead. They accept wine, honey, tobacco and other eatables etc., and the members shed tears in the memory of their departed souls. The god of death (jhonrajas.)

In Ropa village there is an interesting practice that whenever the water channel (kuhl) of the village requires cleaning, each one of the family has to distribute especial food (Poltoo) to the workers in the name of their ancestors. The purificatory ceremony arranged in the villages practicing Buddhist faith is called 'Chhotpa' and it is performed by a Buddhist monk (lama). The monk, after reading from the religious scriptures, writes the name of the departed man on a piece of paper and puts the paper to flames after tearing it off. This ceremony, in Spillow and Kanam villages is called 'Shugu Lama' (Shugu=papter, lama=do). A religious book is read in this occasion and afterwards uptill 49$^{th}$ day after the occurrence of death. The book is called Bordo Thodol.

The folklore of Kinnaras is very rich. Belonging to the high mountain region, they carry with them even the most primitive and prehistoric legends. Their elders relate long folk tales during long winters and all the members of family, while sitting beside the hearth, listen to them during nights. Their Proverbs and idioms tell about their folk wisdom. The folksongs and ballads of these people are the source of their great historic past and day today happenings in the region. It is interesting to note that even small happenings, such as, untimely death of a person, elopement of beloved, punishment to evil doers or any other incident of social attraction including the visit of a dignitary to the region is recorded in the folk songs which continue to be sung by the local folk dancers. Folk theatre and folk dances form which has various shades and local nomenclatures. The monks perform their dances in the monasteries and 'Chham' is the most popular dance drama. The deities have full control over every dance, musical instruments and all sorts of ceremonies in the region.

The fairs and festivals of the region are indeed marvellous. Chaitrol, Bishu, Jyesthang, Ashlechang, Shonechang, Deeval, Jagro, Phaguli, Sazo, Ponasing, Jatrang, Homang and Shivratri etc. are some of the festivals on whom, the impact of Hinduism can be seen. According to Buddhistic traditions, the festivals of Losar, Ramadis, Lamoch, Shirkin, Zine, Kumzod, Chhyangkulma, Ramnas, Gampa Zalkha, Kangyur Zalma and Paza are celebrated.

The third category of festivals and rituals include such ceremonies which don't fall under the first to categories mentioned above. These contain comparatively more primitive or prehistoric rituals and include:

1. *Phulaich, Ukhyang or Phulayach* i.e. the festival of flowers. The festival is held during the months of September and October when the flowers on the mountain peaks bloom. The young boys and girls selected by respective village gods go to the peaks called 'Rang' or 'Kandha' in local parlance and collect flowers to be offered to the village god at the time of festival of flowers (Phulaich). Before plucking flowers, the collectors have to abide by the instructions of the concerned deity and observe absolute piety. They can't make noise and do anything not liked by the village god. The Festival speaks of nature and spirit worship among the Kinnaras and thier love for flowers. *Airatang* festival is arranged only in few villages during summer whereas 'Namgan' is arranged in upper Kinnaur areas where Buddhism is a popular religion. In some villages, Chhota Phulaich or small Phulaich is also celebrated. Om Mahang Songaan i.e. 15th day of Magh (Feb-march), the Kinnars, arrange a great festival. According to their belief the whole universe was created during the month of Magh and it is this month that their gods go to attend a meeting of the celestial spirits at Indrapur. On this day, there is a tradition in some villages, that the village gods give farewell to Indrapuri, whereas in some others, these spirits are received back. *Khepa* festival is prevalent only in upper Kinnaur region and is related to Buddhism.

2. *Dakreni or Dakshinayan* is arranged during the months of July and August. This is a very typical festival. Dakreni, in some villages, is celebrated in the compound of the shrine of village gods but in some other villages, the inhabitants, go to high mountain peaks where monoliths (Kotang, Shakari or Shekhar) in the name of those who went to their heavenly abode during the past, are already constructed. These monoliths are decorated with coloured flags and large poles on Dakreni. Dishes are offered in the name of ancestors at the foot of the monolith and new flags and poles are offered to it to celebrate the occasion. Dakreni at Pangi and Shaung villages is of great attraction. On this occasion, obscene songs are also sung to drive away the wild spirits known as Saoni yogini and Dakini etc. who are believed to haunt the mountain peaks. In order to appease them for good crops in the uplands, they are invited to the villages on the occasion of Phaguli festival arranged during winter season. Deeval is not exactly the festival of lamps

(Deepavali) in Kinnaur. It is arranged to drive away evil spirits from the habitats. In some villages, Chhota Deeval (small Deeval) is also arranged. Khepa and Suskar are arranged only in upper Kinnaur region.

The participants in these rituals are mainly the village folk but relatives of the inhabitants also do make it a point to attend such functions. None can think of a function without the arrangement of local wine, folk songs and dances. These ceremonies have great significance for these people as in some cases, marriage settlements or ancestor worship rituals are performed on these occasions and local food is also served to the invitees. The whole community, thus finds opportunities to come closure with relatives, friends, well wishers and even adversaries. These functions contribute in maintaining age old traditions, use of garments and Jewellery and enthuse new life in otherwise dormant and routine rural hill life. Fairs in the region are only a few. Independence day and Republic day, s well as, visit of dignitaries are the festival occasions these days. The tribals take keen interest in such activities. They discuss about developments and drawbacks, if any. They are happy go lucky and jovial people and take life quite sportingly. They have maintained the local dialect 'Kanauryanushad' with about 10 shades very well and like to speak in their own language, though Hindi and even English is followed by majority of the population. The Buddhist monks (lamas or Rimpoche) are given due respect and people are known for thier hospitality and integrity.

The Kinnaras, with their own graceful mythology and historical back ground, are a very significant mountain tribe which serves as a bridge between mythology, history, primitive and modern ways and thought process of Indian culture. The tribe can serve as a key to the unresolved and unsolved problems of Indian mythology including the concepts of 'Suras' and 'Asuras', Dasyus, Kiratas, impact of Himalayan Buddhism and related to social and religious life during the hoary past.

# 3

# Asur Festivals

*Dr. Prathibha Kumari*

Tribal society of any region tries to secure favour and active help of supernatural powers by propitiation, sacrifices of animals etc. on several occasions or at each new stage in the annual cycle of its simple economic life. The festivals offer occasions for safety and welfare of the people. On festive occasions they feel relaxed, and free from the several tensions of their hard life. With a sense of Social solidarity, they participate heartily in feasting, drinking and dancing to celebrate the festivals along with the propitiation of both benevolent the festivals along with the propitiation of both benevolent and malevolent spirits to get good harvest, plenty of rainfall and to be protected from disease and natural calamities on individual as well as on community level. A type of gratitude is expressed to the supernatural powers for helping them in at the time of adversity. Besides providing entertainment, festivals also helps in regulating the socio-economic activities smoothly. Majority of the festivals are associated with the occupations both past and present. Asur festivals are associated with agricultural activities except the worship of 'Sansi Kutasi' (Pincey and hammer) which is solely attributed to the iron smelting works which has become a thing of past.

## THE COMMUNITY

The Asur are one of the nine primitive tribes of Bihar. They live in the Netarhat Plateau within the Chhotanagpur plateau. Traditionally Asur are iron smelting tribe. They claim to be the descendants of the ancient people of that name were associated with the art of working in metals and were maker of metal relies discovered from Asur sites in Chhotanagpur (Leuva, 1963). Risley (1891) has described them as a small non Aryan tribe who lived almost entirely by iron smelting. To Risley (1891) Asur appeared to be the true representative of the Australian aborigines. They speak 'Asuri' dialect which comes under Austro-Asiatic Mundari group of languages. They also speak 'Sadri' and Hindi with other tribal and nontribal people. Sadri is a lingua franca of Chhotanagpur. Asur are mainly distributed in the districts of Gumla, Lohardagga and Palamau. Their locality is known as 'Pat' area which literally means level hill tops. Their population in the state according to 1981 Census is 7783 and their estimated population according to 1991 Census is 8862.

The Asur tribe living on the 'Pat' area consists of three divisions namely the Bir Asur, the Birjia and the Agaria. In Bihar Birjia has been classified as a district Scheduled Tribe while Agaria is a Scheduled Tribe in Madhya Pradesh.

Asur society is divided into sixteen clans which takes their names from some animals, plants or materials. Totemistic clan exogamy is the characteristic feature of the Asur social organisation. Post puberty marriage is the rule, girls may be below eighteen years of age. Marriage age of boys varies from 18 to 22 years. Asur have adopted the six ways among the eight ways of acquiring mate. Asur have a term to denote the married life for which no essential on marriage ceremony has taken place. It is called 'Idi-me' in Asuri dialect, which means to lead the girl from her parents house to the boy's house for the purpose of cohabitation. This practice of Idi-me is found only among Asur tribe which distinguishes the tribe from other tribes of Bihar in particular and of India in general. It is an unique institution of Asur because 'Idi-me' cannot be included in all the eight types of marriages prevalent in the tribal India.

Impact of Hinduism is observed to a great extent in their religious life. Very few of the Asur have embraced Christianity though, they still retain some preconversion practices. Resistance to change in the Asur is very strong and Christian missionaries have found it difficult to prose tytise a large number of them rapidly.

Asur pantheon consists of a number of deities and spirits. 'Pat Deota' is a village deity who protects the village from sickness and other natural calamities. They have sacred grove the principal trees of which are Sal (*shorea robusta*) trees. The spirit living on the sal trees is recognised as 'Sarna Buri' she receives sacrifices attended with the most elaborate ritual at the annual Sarhul festival. Asur have much faith in their ancestral spirits which are considered benevolent. These spirits are invoked and offerings are made to them by their living relatives at every feast and on every suitable occasion. This ancestor worship in a simple ceremony of offering a drink and sacrifice of a fowl to the dead ancestors. 'Darha' and 'Masan Mua' have been categorized as evil spirits.

Iron smelting was the principal means of their livelihood for several centuries, along shifting (Beonra) cultivation. They used to grow crops like maze, til (*sesamus indicum*), surguza *Guizotia abyssinica*) etc. on the field prepared by slashing and burning, spread over a period of three years by rotation. (Leuva, 1963). But after the implementation of National forest Policy (1952) the practice of iron smelting and shifting cultivation came to an end. They have adopted settled cultivation as their primary source of livelihood. They raise maize crop which is their staple diet. They also cultivate cereals like Arhar (*cajanus indicus*), Urad (*phaseolus radiatus*), millets like Marua (Eleusine coracana), gondli (*Panicum milliare*) and also Seasonal vegetables. Besides they also collect edible forest produces. Since last two decades Asur have taken to potato cultivation for economic gain.

Though Asur have land for cultivation, yield of food crop in not enough even for family consumption throughout the year as there is no wet cultivation. They depend on rains because there is no irrigational facilities. Soil of the landholding is laterite void of humus-extend. It cannot maintain its fertility without regular manuring. Fertile soil on the top is washed away by heavy rains during monsoon. In 1960 Government leased may surface mines of Bauxite to the private owners whose exploration work is going on in the entire 'Pat' area. Many Asur youth work as unskilled labourers. Poor economic conclusion in 'Pat' area has resulted in seeking employment elsewhere to get some cash. Some of them have emigrated to Assam, West Bengal, Punjab etc. and taken up wage labour works. A number of adult Asur boys and girls migrate seasonally to other towns and cities to work as a labourer in the brick kilns. Few Asur are Government employees e.g. Peons in district hospitals, cooks and teachers in residential schools etc.

## FESTIVALS

Festival calender of Asur includes Sarhul, Hariari or Ashad Bata, Noakhani or Kharwaj, Sohrai or Kartik Bakhra, Phagu/Sendra etc.

### Sarhul

The annual cycle of festival starts with Sarhul which is celebrated with gaiety and merry making jointly with other neighbouring tribes. Sarhul is celebrated during

March or April when Sal trees are in full blossom. Baiga is the chief priest. Though the post of the Baiga is strictly not hereditary, in practice the office passes from the father to the son in order of patrilineal line of succession. Some economic benefits are attributed to Baiga such as a plot of free land and a number of Mahua trees. Asur also worship the Earth as a goddess. Flowering of Sal tree is regarded as sign that the Mother Earth is in her menstruation. On this festival the marriage of the Earth goddess with the Sun god is celebrated. The 'Baiga' (priest) along with her wife observe fast on the day preceding the holding of the Sarhul. They may take rice beer only. At night Baiga offers a chicken in the inner chamber of the house or 'Orah Bhittar' which is the abode of ancestral spirits as Asur believe. After offering the sacrifice of chicken to ancestral spirits, Baiga and his wife take food at night but they do not take anything after day break till the festival is over. In the early morning of festival day. The Baiga and village chief 'Mahto' followed by a number of village men assemble in the sacred grove or Sarna place. A small patch of the ground under the principal 'Sal' tree is cleared. The ground is sprinkled with water and small circle drawn on it with rice floor. Baiga and others sit in a group facing the east. The Baiga has by his side a sacrificial winnowing fan and knife used in previous year. The Baiga makes two small heaps of Arua rice by the side of circle. He holds in his hands two chicken which had been washed by his assistant before handing them over for sacrifice. Then the Baiga begins to chant prayers addressed to Lords of spirits both benevolent and malevolent and is joined by the Mahto and a few others. Then he makes the chickens to eat some rice grains from the two heaps. He cuts the necks of the chickens one by one with the sacrificial knife without severing them from their bodies. He drops the blood over the white line of the circle. Those of the Asur who had taken a to offer such a sacrifice to the deities and spirits presented their chickens and pots of rice beer to the Baiga. This beer is later on drunk by those present. At some distance from the Sarna place a few of Asur males prepare the sacrificial dinner of rice and the meat of sacrificed chicken. After the end of the ritual, Baiga is then carried back to the village on the shoulders of a strong man. Near the village women meet them and wash their feet. With the beating of drums and singing, dancing all prodeed to the Baiga's house. Then the usual form of marriage is performed between the Baiga and his wife, symbolising the supposed union between the Sun and Earth. After this ceremony they had nothing to do, except to eat, drink and make merry. Asur men and women assemble at the dancing place, Akhara of their village and there they sing Sarhul songs and dance for the whole night till the morning.

The Asur are forbidden to start sowing operation in is fields before the sacred marriage of the Sun and the Earth on Sarhul festival.

## Oeoroh Bakhra (Sowing Ceremony)

The 'Oeoroh Bakhra' or sowing ceremony is connected with the plough cultivation. For 'Beonra' or shifting cultivation also they used to observe a similar ceremony called the 'Baidea'. This ceremony is held on the onset of the monsoon, in the month of Jaistha May-June). The head of the family collects a small quantity of all kinds of seeds grown in a bamboo basket called 'Nachua'. He sacrifices a hen in he main living room but not in the 'Orah Bhittar' or the inner chamber, keeping the basket with seeds near allowing a little of oozing blood of the sacrificed hen to fall on to the seeds. The hen is sacrificed in the name of ancestral spirits and spirits of the clan. The seeds of the basket are then mixed with the seeds stocked separately for sowing.

## Hariari or Ashad Bata

Like Sarhul, the Hariari is also an agricultural festival. It is celebrated in the month of July-August, when the fields remain covered with the green seedlings. Transplantation of the green seedling of millets does not take place unless this festival is celebrated. The village elders select a day for this festival. In the morning of the festival day the head of the family sacrifices a chicken in the inner chamber of the house uttering prayer for good crops and the welfare of family. He propitiates the ancestral spirits. The head of the sacrificed fowl is dressed and cooked in the Orah Bhittar as well as some rice. The cooked food in small quantity is offered to the spirits and the remaining food is eaten by the head of the family. The remaining part of the scarified fowl is cooked and eaten by the family members.

## Kharwaj

This festival is celebrated when the crops are harvested for the first time in the months of Bhadra (August-September) and Ashwin (September-October) for different types of lands. The newly harvested grains are not consumed before the celebration of this festival. The occasion is celebrated with liberal consumption of food and rice beer. On the day of the festival, the head of the family sacrifices a chicken in the name of ancestral spirits. Some newly harvested grains is cooked by his wife. Cooked grains alongwith cooked chicken and rice beer are offered to he ancestral spirits in the inner chamber or 'Orah Bhittar' of the house. Another harvesting festival known as 'Pahar Kharwaj' is observed in the month of November-December (paus) for 'Beoura' or sifting cultivation which is practised upto very little extent these days.

The rituals are performed by Baiga in open field near his house. Baiga's wife assists him by collecting one chicken from each house having Beonra cultivation. The men, women children gather at that place. Baiga sacrifices fowls one by one in the name of the spirits of rocks and forests. The head of the sacrificed birds are cooked separately and a portion of the cooked and shared by everybody present. Before ordinary 'Kharwaj' is observed people often cay the harvested crops to home but not a single grain from Bconra crop is taken home until 'Pahar Kharwaj' is observed.

**Sohrai or Kartik Bakhra**

This festival is associated with the domestication of cattle and is celebrated on the New Moon day in the month of Kartik. In the evening of the festival, earthen lamps or diyas are lighted in the cattle sheds, manure pits and kitchen gardens. The lamps are kept burning the whole night if possible. Mea in the form of boiled grains are prepared in each house for the cattle. Next day the cattle are bathed at stream or river and then taken into the cattle shed where rice beer is sprinkled on heir hoofs by some female members. The horns and hoofs of the cattle are anointed with vermilion diluted in oil. Some put colour them. The cattle are given hearty feed of grains boiled overnight. In a few families a fowl is sacrificed at the cattle shed to its presiding deity called 'Goraia Deota'. Some families who own buffaloes a black pig is sacrificed to the 'Goraia.' Ordinarily the pig is purchased by the subscription from the villagers who may own buffaloes. Sacrificed fowl or pig is cooked in the cattleshed and eaten there by the members of the family.

**Phagu Sendra**

The festival takes place every year in the month of Phagun or March. The festival is celebrated between the first appearance of the moon at night in the month of Phagun until the night of the full moon.

On the festival day Asur families engaged in iron smelting or blacksmiths in their crude forges perform 'Sansi' Kutasi' worship is done by the Asur who are involved in blacksmiths. All the implements required for iron smelting and blacksmiths are collected in a verandah of the house. A cock and a hen both of red colour are sacrificed during the worship. The offering is said to be accepted if the bird partake some of the rice from the small keep. Which is kept there. The cock is caught by the neck with a pair of pincers (sansi) and its head is crushed with a hammer (Kutasi) by keeping it a stone anvil. The hen is also scarified in the same manner while making a fatal blow on chicken's head he cutters incantation for higher yields of iron from the Kuthi (furnace) and for saving the person working with the furnace from any accident. The presiding spirit of the iron smelting furnaces the *'Kutsand Bhat'* is worshipped on this festival. Here is an instance of magic which is resorted to by the Asur for securing good iron in his productive activities.

The head of the hen sacrificed earlier is cooked and aportion of it is offered to ancestral and clan spirits. The flesh of fowl are separately cooked and shared by all those present. Lastly, the women of the locality come to the iron smelter with a small cup of mustard oil and rub the oil on his body, feet and hands. He is also offered a pot of rice beer to drink. Ever women fans him with winnowing basket moving it up and down enacting the operation of the bellows (Chapua) and with tis ends he Fagu Sendra festival. Evening and nights are spent in dancing and merry making.

The peculiar feature of this festival is that musical instruments which are so essential for all social ad festive occasions are not played on this occasion when the youths and girls are engaged in dancing. It is the last festival the festival calender. I the performance of rituals during festivals men dominate, women only assist them. Offerings and sacrifices of fowler other animals to the deities or spirits are solely done by men folk. Women accompany their community men in dancing and singing. Ancestral spirits are propitiated with great devotion on every festival, who are always considered benevolent.

Propitiation of the deity of sacred grove, earth goddess, and Sal tree expresses their reverent attitude for nature and their ecology. They directly or indirectly worship nature in different forms during their festivals. Festivals bring joy and merriment, a positive change in their hard life for time being. Festivals also promote community feeling and social solidarity.

## REFERENCES

1. Census of India 1981 Special Tables for Scheduled Tribes, series–4, Bihar Part IX (III), Govt. of India, New Delhi.

2. Dalton, E.T. 1872 Descriptive Ethnology of Bengal, govt Printing, Calcutta.

3. Jha, Makhan, 1994 Glimpses of Tribal life Hari Prasad & Tribal Series of India, Series

4. Kamla Agrawal. T- 159, Inter India Publication New Delhi.

5. Kapthuama, B.B.1995 "Bihar Tribal Sub Plan' an Overview" in Bulletin of Bihar Tribal Welfare Research Institute, Ranchi vol. XXXIV.

6. Leuva, K. K. 1963 The Asur: Bhartiya Adimjati Sevak Sangh, New Delhi.

7. Risley, H. H. 1991 Tribes and Castes of Bengal, Vol. II, Calcutta.

8. Singh, K. S (Ed) 1994 The Scheduled Tribes, people of India, National Series III Oxford University Press.

# 4

# Festivals of Sauria Paharia

*Dr. Pratibha Kumari*

Festivals of tribal people are one of the sacred performances which give them their ritual calender. Festivals make them jubilant and enthusiastic. People engage themselves in drinks, dance and feast. Festivals usually last for more than one day and are celebrated annually. Deities are worshipped suitable rituals and offerings are made on all the festive days. Tribal people seek safety and prosperity to their community as a whole at each new stage in the annual cycle of their simple economic pursuits and feasting, rejoining and social reunion that make their successful termination. A greater interaction with nature on one hand and spirit on other, can be observed in the mode the celebration of tribal festivals.

Sauria Paharia are one of the nine primitive tribes of Bihar State and also one of the tree sections of Paharia inhabiting Santhal Pargana Plateau. The other two sections are known as Mal Paharia and Kumarbhag. The Kumarbhag is not recognised by the Government as being a tribe. Sauria Pahariya and Mal Paharia have different social economic religious and political systems. They have no matrimonial relationship with each other. The Mal Paharia consider the Saurias, as unclean because they eat beef and the caracases of dead cow. The Saurias are also known as 'Maler' in 'Malto' language which is their dialect, which means the persons living on hills. 'Malto' language comes under Dravidian linguistic group.

Risley (1891) described Sauria Paharia as Dravidian, but Sarkar (1936) classified them as pre-Dravidian. Vidyarthi (1964) proved beyond doubt the affinity of Sauria with Oraon. The concentration of Sauria is heaviest in the Sahebganj and Godda districts of Santhal Pargana Plateau. They live on hill tops and hill slopes. These days few Sauria hamlets are found on the plane also and they are engaged in plane agriculture. But majority of them prefer hills as the hill surroundings around their habitat contain various useful fruit bearing trees, timber, bamboo and silk cotton trees and sabai grass with which they prepare rope and associated materials. Their population was 39,269 according to 1981 Census and their estimated population according to 1991 Census is 44,716.

They practice shifting or slash and burn cultivation which is known as 'Kurwa' in their language on hill slopes and grow millets like maize, Bajra (*Pennesetum typhoideum*) pulses like Arhar (*Cajanus indicus*), vegetables like barbatti or bean, a type of gourd known as Khaxa (*Trena Palitoria*) seasonally. The availability of the forest produce, and shifting or Kurwa cultivation has led them to stick to their hilly habitat; though they have to face an acute shortage of potable water. The Sauria women carry potable water 200-300 ft. down from their habitat.

Fishing in summer is also common among them. Besides, cultivation, many Saurias work as wage labourers in stone quarries, and at crusher and construction sites. Few of them are Government servants.

## RELIGION

Among the sacred beliefs the faith in spirits is most common with the Saurias and thus animism. Every child, adult and old very commoner and specialist has some sort of conception in his mind about the spirit and super-natural world which he calls by the common term 'Gossaiyan' which is used to denote a group of spirits that are believed to guide their destiny. Ancestral worship is an important aspect of their religion. They are very cautious in performing the rites and observe all ceremonies carefully. The newly dead person is believed to have joined the earlier dad ancestors. The ancestral spirits are worshipped annually and occasionally during sowing and harvesting of crops also.

Among 'Maler' Jiwe Urkkya' is their ancestral spirit, the spirit of the dead relatives. Urkky means "has left}. Thus Jiwe Urkkya means the soul of the dead. This spirit invariably becomes a source of fear till the first feast normally given on the fifth day of the funeral. Later the Maler conceive ancestral spirit as essentially benevolent spirits. The death anniversary or 'Bhoje' ceremony is marked with the solemn sacrifices (*Karra Pujar,*) buffalo's worship is most preferred). Communal feast and every thing desired by the spirit of the dead is given through the *Demano* (village shaman to appease it. They consider the words of *Demano* (Shaman) coming straight from the mouth of a dead ancestor. The offerings to the dead are made generally after the harvesting season or are combined with *Bandana* festival. They further conceive that the ancestral spirit goes back to the sun God, the Bero Gossaiya when it is well satisfied with the offerings. Thus, the worship of the ancestor is of prime importance to the Sauria. The awe and fear of the displeasure of the dead ancestors hang heavily in the hearts of the Sauria Paharias. At every turn and twist of a Sauria life economic pursuits and social observances, ancestors are remembered and are offered due sacrifice or propitiation.

Gossaiyan are considered as benevolent spirits. They conceive of a Gossaiyan associated with almost every phenomenon in the nature and society. The Gossaiyan in terms of gender Male and Female, but are not sure about which Gossaiyan is which, there is no consensus on this aspect at all. Gossaiyan termed male by one may be called female by another. The Gossaiyan among Saurias are Singpate, Kanaiye, Chal, Rakhshi, Tunde, Mula, Atgo, Charka, Addo, Yam, Bender, Beru, Bilpu, Bindke etc. Here it must be remembered that these names of Gossaiyan are not always consistent and very often, one may come across only a few of these in one particular village and ten quite another in other villages. Indeed it seems, the name and spots vary in different villages depending on the area and topography of the village. This is also an indication that the Gossaiyan are conceived in adaptation to nature.

The Addo Gossaiyan (home god) is represented by a door and is worshipped at the time of new crop or a new house construction. The Gomo Gossaiyan (pillar of the house) brings health and happiness in the family. The Atto Gossaiyan is their hearth deity. The Sohar Gossaiyan lives in the cattle-shed and protect them (Vidyarthi, 1963:153-54).

Besides, Saurias also believe in evil spirit which they called *Alchi* or Bhute and Chargani or Witchcraft. These are considered to be malevolent who bring only death and destruction miseries and calamities. They believe in six types of ghosts living in different places in forests with different grievances and different disposition. Services of diviner are sought to counter the evil effects of the Bhute. They recognise witchcraft practised by certain evil women of their villages. Some evidences show that suspected women witches have been mercilessly beaten and driven out of their villages.

But strictly speaking the first two i.e. Gossaiyan and Jiwe Urkkya because of whom religiously the Saurias are obsessed. There are a number of sacred centres for the propitiation of different Gossaiyans or spirits. The most important them is *Manjhi Than* where the village deity, resides, this is the most important Gossaiyan of Saurias. It is supposed to be a male Gossaiyan. It is represented by five black stone under a small tree. Sacrifices are made by the Manjhiya twice in a year, the solve specialist for this than, once during Bandana festival and then just before sowing operation in the Kurwa field.

Another important sacred centre is Gossaiyan Adda which literally means the house of Gossaiyan, Female gossaiyan is supposed to reside there who is worshipped by 'Gurait' who offer a black fowl to it. Bender Nadu is another sacred spot represented by four stones, where female Gossaiyan is worshipped during annual festival and pig is sacrificed.

Kaneya Nadu also a sacred centre where a male Gossaiyan reside, is a bit far from the main village. Gorait sacrifices goat or pig at this centre during Saliani or annual Puja.

Chal nadu, situated on hill top is another important sacred centre where that Gossaiyan is worshipped. A cluster of white and black stones seven in number represent the Gossaiyan. Pig fowl are sacrificed there during the Bandana festival and other times when some family has to worship to appease it. Chal Nadu' is sought for when any calamity befalls on a village.

'Masani' or graveyard is also sacred centre where many offerings are made in the name of ancestors on the day of death, one the fifth day from death and during 'Bandana' festival. The head of the family or the nearest relative of the dead does all the offering and sacrifices of fowl. In addition to the above sacred centres, there are many spots in the hut of Saurias it self which become sacred centre sometimes. These are Bali (door), Gummo (pillar), Attu (hearth), Adda (hut) etc.

In every house, abode of the ancestor is near the hearth. First fruit or first crop of the fields are offered to the ancestor by the head of the family.

Outside the village settlement but within the village boundary, many trees, ponds and springs are supposed to be the abode of certain evil spirits. Among the Malers there are there sacerdotal functionaries at the village level viz the *Kando-Majhi, Kotwar* and *Chalwe*. The Kando Majhi controls and directs the ritualistic life of the people. The selection of Kando Majhi is based on the supernatural force which guides the desting of Sauria from him. He is supposed to be chosen by God. For his selection, villagers gather in the middle of the village in front of the house of the secular headman. Incense is burnt there and the kotwar invokes the help of the deities for the selection of the Kando Majhi. If everything goes well, it is believed that the Gossaiyan has accepted him. He is then formally declared Kando-Majhi or the head priest of the village.

As assistant to the head is the Kotwar. He performs the actual worship including offering of sacrifices to the deity. A Kotwar has life tenure and is selected in the same manner as his chief. At the time of his selection the Kando-Majhi invokes the aid of the Gossain. Chalwe is the assistant of the Kotwar. He is also selected in the same manner as the other two sacred specialists.

## RITUALS ASSOCIATED WITH CULTIVATION OF CROPS IN KURWA

The main ritual or sacred performances of the Saurias is to offer some sacrifices alongwith a few other things to the spirits they worship. In other words the performances constitute killing a fowl, pig, cow or a buffalo and pouring the blood over the sacred centre, at the same time uttering the name of Gossaiyan. In some cases, specially to the ancestral spirits, some food in the forms of puffed maize, rice, pulse of ghaghra (a type of bean) and a glass of wine is also offered. The blood of the sacrificed animal is most important in every sacred performances. The belief behind this is that all the spirits are invariably non-vegetarians, who can be appeased only when they are 'offered animal of thier choice. It is because of thier choice that they are to be offered red or black fowl or goat.

The relationship of the Sauria with his super-natural world is more of a trade than any inherent urge. It is as if "I do not understand your powers which are very great indeed. Please take what I have to offer and let me live in peace. I do not want to displease you and given the choice, I shall have nothing to do with you". So, in case of Sauria the term 'Worship' properly so understood does not apply. It is more a sort of 'give and take' or exchange.

There are some sacred performances at family level as well as at village level before sowing and after harvesting of crops. Just before sowing operation in Khallu or Kurwa cultivation, sacrifices of red or black fowl is made at the Manjhiya than and Chal Gossain, the 'Chief deity' is propitiated for getting better yield in Kurwa. Sacrifices of fowl is done by the head of the family. The sacred performances on the family level are numerous and important. The welfare of the family depends as they believe in propitiating the Gossaiyan which control the Kurwa produce and also on the ancestors who are primarily interested in their respective families and which are their prime target. The sacrificial objects on family level are small, the fowl, pigeons and rarely pigs and goats. Other items are wine (pochoi) prepared out of maize and millet, different varieties of food preparation of maize pulse like ghaghra etc.

During the latter part of Bhado (August-September), on getting Bhadai maize (Tekalo) from the field the Saurias propitiate first Chal Gossain at Manjhiye Than or chal Nad; and then in their houses. At the village level, all Sauria families contribute to get a he-goat and one or two children. Four maize corns are suspended to the 'Chal Nad' (attached to the Sal (Shores robusta tree) and goats and chickens are sacrificed by the 'kotwar' after burning *dhumna* (incense) and daubing the goat and chickens on their head with vermillion. At the end of this ritual, Saurias perform the ritual on family level in their houses. Every head of the family in each house this cook maize and alongwith the maize preparation sacrifices one or two chickens in the name of thier dead ancestors in front of their hearth. Only after this ritualistic observance, they eat the food grain got from the fields.

"Ghaghra Puja" is performed during the latter part of 'kartik' (October-November) after getting the crop from the field, before they eat the same. Ghaghra is dried seed of a variety of bean. The ritual is performed by each household to their dead ancestors.

In the months of December and January, when 'bajra' (nanto) millet is ready for harvesting, another ritualistic observance is made by the Saurias before they eat the millet. On behalf of the entire village, one he-goat is scarified at the 'Manjhiye than' by he 'Kotwar'. After this collective ritual, each Sauria family performs the ritual in every house. In front of the hearth a chicken is sacrificed and the preparation of bazra millet is also offered in the name of their ancestors.

Most of the sacred performances at the village level are made during the annual festival known as 'Bandana' and just before sowing operation in Kurwa (Kadchake). The sacrificial animal required for village level performances are large in size and also more in umber. Naturally, the expenses are high, which are met with by raising subscription from the villagers.

## BANDANA: THE ANNUAL FESTIVAL

Banana is a four day festival held during February-March after the harvesting. Since drinking and dancing are also a very important part of this festival, friends and relatives from other villages are invited. The Manjhiye himself acts as priest and kills the sacrificial animal (buffalo or cow) every alternate year. In some villages, he-goat, pig and chicken are sacrificed if they cannot bear the expenses of buffalo or cow. In those villages buffalo is sacrificed on every sixth year to the 'Chal Gossain', the presiding village deity.

A wooden pole, suitably carved and festooned is fixed just in front of manjhiye than and the buffalo is tied to it. By night fall the worship of the other sacred centres beings. The Garait assisted by a few others goes to each sacred centre in turn and sacrifices the fowl uttering at the same time certain words in which he pleades the Gossaiyan to be happy with the offering and not let the disease and calamities befall on the village. The sacrificed animal is brought back, but just outside the village settlement, the meat is fried and eaten by all who are present. At the same time the last rite of the death which occurred after last Bandana festival are also completed. The family, in which the deaths occurred go to 'Masani' or burial ground and worship the ancestors.

The sacrifices of animals mostly chicken before the different Gossaiyan takes most of the night because the different centres are quite distant from the village settlement which has to be visited in turn and each scarified animal is to be cooked and eaten first before proceeding to the next. The buffalo which had been tied to the pole in evening under goes much torment during the night. He is never allowed to stand at rest. People keep poking him with bamboo stick to make it angry and irritated all through the night. The idea behind doing so is to make it so irritated that it may attack and wound a few people. Then it could be said that the buffalo which was scarified was so much dangerous. In fact, the ferocity of buffalo sacrificed is remembered. Perhaps, this is a way to justify the killing of animals, though only buffalo is treated in this way. Other animals are spared. In the morning of second day feasts are arranged by the families mourning the dead. Rice and pork is offered with millet bear or 'Pochoi'. In the afternoon, the buffalo which has spent a sleepless night is sacrified. First of all, its four legs are chopped off so that it may fall on the ground. Then the Manjhiye the main sacred specialist beheads the animal by axe (masu). The head is hung in the small hut specially constructed for this occasion and the body is thrown down hill. Its meat is not eaten.

The rest of the period is spent in drinking and dancing which is a hearty scene to watch. All the Saurias, young and old male and female clad in new coloured clothes, and drunk dance and sing for hours together through the night. Next morning village bears a deserted and desolate look, as everyone being exhausted falls asleep at the dawn, in comparison with the previous night's noise and activities.

It is clear that worship and sacrifice go hand in hand in the life of the Sauria Paharia. Their belief in the presence of spirits both malevolent and benevolent necessitates their right and reasonable propitiation to ward off the dangers befalling the individuals and the village as a whole. They consider thier ancestors as their important benefactors. So they are worshipped with great devotion on each festive occasions. No ritual is complete with out offering to the ancestral spirits as these are considered the guardian spirits.

Thus the Saurias have adopted their belief in spirits in the background of the ecological settings and social needs which can be easily found out in their festival and their mode of celebration. A type of close interaction with nature on one hand and spirit on another is deeply maintained by the Sauria.

## REFERENCES

Census of India 1981 Special Tables for Scheduled Tribes, Series-4 Bihar Part IX (III), Govt. of India, New Delhi.

Dalton, E. T 1872, Descriptive Ethnology of Bengal, Govt, Printing, Calcutta.

Kapthuana, B. B. 1995 "Bihar Tribal Sub Plan" An Overview" in Bulletin of Bihar Tribal Welfare Research Institute, Ranchi Vol. XXXIV.

Risley, H. H 1891, Tribes and Castes of Bengal Vol. II, Calcutta.

Singh, P. K. 1984, The Maler: A Restudy of Nature-Man Spirit Complex. Ph.D Thesis submitted to the Deptt. of Anthropology, Ranchi University, Ranchi.

Vidyarthi, L. P. and B. K. Rai 1976, The Tribal Cultures of India, Concept Publishing Company, New Delhi.

Vidyarthi, L. P. 1963, The Maler: A Study in Nature Man Spirit Complex of a Hill Tribe, Bookland Pvt. Ltd., Calcutta.

□□□

# 5

# Disuasendra in Santhal Society

*Dr. Nabakumar Duary*

## INTRODUCTION

The Santhal is the third largest tribal community in India having with a population of 4,260,842 (1981 Census). This tribal group is mostly inhabited in Bihar, West Bengal, Orissa, Tripura and Assam (the Santhals of Assam are not a Scheduled Tribe). The traditional gathering, hunting economy of the Santhals have been changed to settled agriculture but it is remarkable fact that presently many socio cultural traditions exist among their society. As for example they traditionally practice cutting of the umbilical cord of the new-born baby by an arrow head. The male child first heas the term sendra (hunting) in his mothers lap. Whenever the child experience choking at the time of sucking milk or drinking milk or water, the mother of the child use to say politely for his relief that "you mothers of the hunting party take this baby for hunting" (Murmu, 1983:129). Regarding the disua sendra (it is also known as Ajodhia sendra) there is a very common folk tale in Santhal society that "Kora gidra hueakate jahae Ajodhia sendra bae cholaoakena, unido engat kukhirega", means if a male Santhal has failed to attend the Ayodhya hill hunting since birth, he is still supposed to be in his mother's womb. This proverb is sufficient to understand the importance of disua or mel sendra (disua or mel means public or mass) is their traditional socio-cultural life and values of the Santhal society. Therefore, all capable male members of this community try to participate in this hunting festival every year or take minimum chance in their life time. Drinking, dancing and singing, manifestation of the same of raska (i.e., fun) are characteristics of santhal festival (Bhattacharya, 1995:257). It is also fact that all participants participate in this festival mainly to fulfill their traditional socio-cultural values. But some of them used together there only for observing hunting festival at that place and to visit some important mythical places/ things viz. Sitachatani (place), Sitakund spring, streams, big termile hills in the jungle, and also to get together with their relatives and to participate in that recreation during the disua sendra at Ayodhya hill.

## THE SETTING

The Ayodhya hill is an important and famous sacred place of the neighbouring tribals in general and Santhals in particular for their traditional disua sendra festival. This hill is situated in south West part of the Puruliya District in western frontier of West Bengal. This hill and its surrounding area is an attractive picture within the Matha forest range. It's landscape shows undulating topography with the presence of hills and hillocks of different altitude and no many streams, and springs in a L shaped area. This region is a continuing part of the Chotanagpur plateau of Bihar. The total area of Ayodhya hill is 98.20 sq. km. and its average altitude is 1200 ft. There are thirty villages situated on the table lands of the Ayodhya hill and predominated by the Santhals. According to the Government report there highest percentage (i.e. 63%) of land is covered by the forest being looked after by the state forest Department. It is fact that the thick forest have been gradually reducing along with the population of wild animals and birds proportionally. But the most famous traditional disua sendra festival of the Santhals is not abolished, it is held on Ayodhya hill with same Disuasendra.

The Santhals Strictly celebrate six different hunting festivals Pun hunting, Jarpa hunting, Bithi hunting, Baha hunting Disu hunting, Gira hunting festival on different occasions throughout the year, these are associated with nature, forest including their traditional socio-religious beliefs. Only the male members can participate in these huntings. The disua sendra is one the most, important and biggest public hunting among the Santhals. The present study is mainly concentrate in disua sendra. It is held at Ayodhya hill in a particular day on Buddha Purnima or Baishakhi Purnima (bengali month). Every Santhal waits keenly for lunar day and try to participate in this hunting, Even other tribals and non-tribals also assemble there. This hunting council La-bir-baisi consists of the hunting pargana, dihiri and some important persons from the gaonta. The head of the hunting council known as sendra pargana.

An aged and experienced Santhal informant stated that earlier the disua sendra was very much risky for the life of its participants, because there was possibilities of encounter with the big wild animals. Therefore, the married participants had carried the iron bangles of their wives and who morally allowed to remarry then; if he could not came back from Ayodhya hill to his residence. Even today it is also observed that during the hunting period wife of the participants does not comb her hair, does not wash their cloth and family members of participants put a full lota (small brass pot) of water at the abode of ancestors place in their respective houses and she strictly observes its water level in time to time till his return back. If she feel that the water level drops down, and the surface of the water covered by dust, tis signifies bad symptoms for the participants.

Before proceeding in disuasendra the Santhals make mental as well as material preparation. They worship the ancestors in their houses for blessing and to keep them safely from all sorts of dangers in this hunting festival. In every village has a hunting deity (name is secret) and worship by village priest during festival time. The participation in this hunting is symbolised as bravery, successful hunters earn the social prestige, respect by the others and it has also many traditional socio-cultural significance of the Santhal society. Therefore, thousands of Santhals come to Ayodhya hill from the different districts of West Bengal and its neighbouring States Bihar and Orissa with full of zeal to participate in this hunting. On the particular day or one day before of this hunting Santhal participants gather at the foot of Ayodhya hill carrying with their traditional hunting implements viz. aak (bow), sar (arrow), Kapi/ tabbla (battle axe), budia (axe), barlaam (spear); some musical instruments like tamak (cattle drum), dhak, charchari, regra, sakwa (made up of bison horn), banam, tiriya and rice, tobacco and mahua/haria liquor.

Santhal who follow the traditional religion have their Gods represented the nature (Singh, 1984:1045). It is also mentionable that before the journey to Ayodhya hill they worship the hunting God at there (i.e. a fixed place of the foot hill) for good hunting and to protect themselves from wild animals (the name of this deity is kept secret). The Santhal people of the dihiri (hunting priest) village contribute the money to purchase of fowls, vermillion, earthern pots. This worship is held at forenoon on the lunar day. Then they prepare food and also take it. Afternoon all participants start to climb on the Ayodhya hill for operate the hunting. The hunters proceed for hunting operation with their own group members in a particular area of the jungle which has already decided and in a particular area of the jungle which has already decided and declared by the hunting pargana. During the hunting operation they beat the drums which echoes all around. As the result birds and animals come in motion use to escape here and there, on dry leaves, on trees and in sky. This become appropriate time for hunting. In this situation hunters wait for appropriate scope, searching for their games. Before proceeding they are divided into two groups. The forward group members hold big weapons i.e. battle axe, axe, spear and enter into the jungle following a line to encoutner the wild animals as well as to protect the others hunter group. Some times they blow sakwa for communication and convey different informations (like danger or precaution from the wild animals) to other participants. At that time they do not fear. The more forward in a very systematic way with full of vigour and hunt the game like zill (deer), Jhink (procupine), sukri (headgenog), kulai (hare), bana (bear), sim/askal (fowl) etc. till the evening. After completion of the hunting operation all hunting members gradually go with their hunt at gipitij tandi (i.e. prefixed place for night halt). Then every hunting group separately prepares rice, meat and enjoyed the delicious meal. Then some of them sing their traditional hunting songs, perform war dances such as danger, singrai etc. in the moon light and a few people also participate in thier traditional jocking, folktale about their genesis and discussing sex education within the jocking relations. During this mood they prefer to take mohua and haria (local liquor). Most of the hunting songs express their love affection and disattachment in love among the lovers on other members of the family. In this regard one of the common song given below:

Gatin do Ayodhiya sendratey

Chalao akan

Sendra rey sikar ocoyen

Gatinko jalao ekan

Hilge dhuwa kotanok kan

Gatin do menae geyare

The meaning of this song is oh dear you have proceeded for hunting. But in turn you were hunted by the wild animals. The blue smoke of your burning funeral pyre is spreading in the sky. I believe, you are alive. We will meet again. At dawn they again assemble in a particular holy place on the hill known as Sitachatani. Here is a spring named Sitakund, where they took bath early in the morning. Their belief that at the time of disua sendra this spring will be failed with water naturally. The Santhals interestingly noted that there are also found a thin parasitic plant nearby the falls sitakund. It is etymologically known from them these parasitic plants are evidence of the Sitadevi's hair, when she came to this place at the time (one of the hindu epic) of Ramayana. There is also held a hunting council meeting in that morning for mitigate the dispute in hunting games. When the wounded game manage to escape but die beyond their territories then, disputes arise. More than one members of the hunting parties claim the same game and try to prove its right. Because it is a largest public hunting and all hunters are coming from different areas. If this dispute is not solved on spot then it is taken to hunting council la-bir-baisi. There is no illegal interference by the others council like as gaonta on a court of law etc. The members of the la-bir-baisi go to spot verification systematically i.e. They observe line of breeding, distance of shooting, sign of Khand (cut marks on the tree for evidence) and make enquiry about the evidences of inserted arrow in the animal body i.e. type of arrow (according to shape, size and material used). Then hunting council members identified the actual killer and they recognise is possessiveness. In this context the santhal society have a proverb "Sengel ate do, dorbar bako durpa; lotadak ate geko durup a". It significantly means that every hunter have their hunting weapon, but they are not allowed to use these in the disputed assemble. If both parties do not agree with the above decision then it is forwarded by the la-bir-baisi to hunting priest dihri to solve the dispute through traditional customary laws i.e. hunting ritual kalka operation. But it is now diminishing due to modern impact. Moreover, during the traditional hunting council meeting they also solve any unsolved social disputes at village level like illegal sexual relation on intra clan or inter caste marriage and take bitlaha in the final decision i.e. excommunication in presence of mass participants. The mass people have heir own right to opine in the decision making.

In the afternoon they start getting down from hill and before leaving the place the hunters collect the champa baha (i.e flower of Michelia champaca) from the near by jungle and keep in safe place. The members of the family wait anxiously in he house for their return of the tired participants. When they reach there, the young members washed thier legs with oil and water, then he offers the champa baha to his wife receives it in her anchal (a free part of her cloth). Then she keeps it in a corner of the wall of the house of their ancestors place.

## CONCLUSION

The disuasendra is an integral part of the Santhals life and culture. It has a traditional socio-cultural values in their society. The tradition preserved collectively as an expression of their identity. Moreover, their socio-cultural festivals and ceremonies are a response to the rhythm of nature.

## Note

1. **Haria:** A kind of rice beer. It is prepared from boiled rice and mixed with tables ranu of powered bir/biro. These are prepared from unboiled rice with some herbal concoction juice. It helps in the fermentation.

2. **Mohua Liquor:** It is also an indigenous liquor, prepared from flower of Madhuka indica by a crude retrot method.

3. **Kalka:** A ritual of tribal ceremony to worship the supreme God Dharam for solving the hunting disputes in the Santhal community. It is materialised only in some case where claiming the right over the killed animals by more than one hunting parties. This is the last and ultimate method for deciding the cases of hunting disputes.

## Acknowledgement

The author is immensely indebted to Mr. Dalapati Murmu, Asst.. Anthropologist (Cultural) of Anthropological Survey of India, Field Station, Ranchi for his encouragement and valuable suggestions without which this article would not have acquired this shape.

## REFERENCES

Bhattacharya, Kumkum 1995 "The religion of the Santhals" "Sociology in the Rubric of social Science" Edited by R.K. Bhattacharya and Ashok Ghosh, Anthropological survey of India.

Census of India 1971 District Census Hand Book, Purulia, West Bengal, Govt. of India.

Murmu Dalapati 1983 Kalka: A Ritual trial for Hunting Disputes in Santhal Community, Journal of Indian Anthropological Society, Vol. 18, No. 2, Calcutta.

Singh, K. S. 1994 People of India, National Series, The Scheduled Tribes Vol. III, Oxford University Press, Delhi.

❑❑❑

# 6

# Tribal Fairs and Festivals of Rajasthan

*Ms. Monika Spolia & Dr. Robin D. Tribhuwan*

Rajasthan is one of the most historic and culturally rich state of India. Unfortunately, it is also one of the most underdeveloped state. Despite its rich context for a writer's inspiration, not a lot of scholars have displayed much interest in this part of the country.

However, Rajasthan attracts a lot of tourism because of its uniqueness and perseverance of age old traditions. A lot of traditions are not completely lost, instead they are in the process of adapting to the newer era. The most famous Rajasthani fairs for the tourism purpose are:

1. Pushkar Fair
2. Maru Fair
3. Mewar Fair
4. Bagar Fair

The fairs mainly related to the tribal population of Rajsthan are:

1. Vaneshwar Fair—held in Baswara District
2. Goti Amba Fair—held in Dungerpur District
3. Jarga Ji Fair (Shiv Ratri Fair)—held in Udaipur District near Ranapur

4. Siyawa Gour Fair—(Siyawa is the name of the village) held in Sirohi District. The main participants are from Garasia tribe.

5. Sita Bari Fair—held in Kelwara village, Baran District near Kota. The main participants are from Sehria Tribe.

6. Gautameshvar Fair—held in Arnodh village in Chittorh District, of Pratapgarh Tehsil.

The national integration and attempts of adaptation of the tribal population to the mainstream culture of India is reflected in the festivals celebrated. The following festivals celebrated by the tribal are the mainstream Indian festivals as well except Gavri.

1. Holi

2. Diwali

3. Raksha Bandhan

4. Gavri

## GAUAMESHVAR FAIR

The name Gauameshvar is depicted from Gautam Rishi.[1] Gautameshvar is combination of two words: Gautam and Eeshvar where Gautam is the name of the Rishi and Eeshvar means God in Hindi. Thus, Gautameshvar refers to god of Gautam.

This fair is held in Arnodh village in Chittorh District, Pratapgarh Tehsil.

The core place of this festivity is no less than natural beauty of mother nature. It lies about 1000 feet below ground with a diameter ranging from 500 to 700 feet. It is not in perfect circular position, but has rather non- geometrical shape. Vannangali is another natural spot approximately 30 x 30 feet about 12 stairs down from the top. The rocks around are soaked in water and the excess water falls ten to fifteen feet down in the Kund[2] which is about one and a half feet deep.

Sometimes, there is no natural water in the Kund during festival time, so the tankers are brought in to fill the Kund. There are more than one legends related to the celebration of this festival.

**Legends and Myths**

One of the legend is obviously related with Gautam Rishi. Gautam Rishi was accused of killing his father. As a consequence his body had decolored and deformed. He was wandering from place to place in order to repent for his sin. He passed one night in a hut with an adivasi[3]. During the night, Gautam Rishi heard the conversation between a cow and its calf.

The calf was going to be sold to a Brahmin the next day, but it was refusing to let go of its mother. The cow was crying its best to explain to the calf that it is their life style to serve the human community, in specific the Brahman community. The calf kept on insisting on not leaving the mother in the morning.

It laid its plan like this to the mother: when the Brahmin comes to get it in the morning, it will charge the man with its horns and kill him. The cow was against because killing a Brahmin is one of the biggest sin with unforeseeable circumstances.

The calf not only seemed to be already familiar with the consequences of killing a Brahmin which will be that its whole white body will turn black, but it also knew of its cure. It will have to travel to a particular Kund of water, which is visited by all kinds of Sadhus, Rishis, Yogis etc. and has duly acquired some supernatural powers which can cure the biggest sin even that of killing a Brahmin. No matter how much the cow tried to persuade the calf to give up its idea of killing the Brahmin, but the calf stuck to its words.

Gautam Rishi, who was wise enough to understand the language of the animals, decided to follow the calf after the killing of the Brahmin so that he could also repent his own sin and find solace. Thus, the plan was carried out.

A Brahmin showed up early in the morning on the hut-door of the Adivasi. The plan was carried out as discussed earlier. When he was about to take the calf with him, it charged the Brahmin and stuck its horns in his stomach. The Brahmin died instantly and the white body of calf turned all black. The cow stood there motionless and prayed for its baby. The calf started running away. Gautam Rishi knew where the calf was going and so he followed the calf.

It just so happened that there was only knee deep water in the Kund at the time. As he calf jumped in the Kund, it landed on its back with its feet up. Because the water did not get on its hoofs and nose, these two parts stayed black and the rest of its body returned to its natural white color. To this day the cow's feet and nose are always black.

Gautam Rishi also bathed in that Kund and returned to his original form and color. There and then, he meditated and prayed for Lord Shiva[4]. Then a Shivling[5] erupted from the earth.

Now, people from around 100 kilometers believe in this. Whether someone has killed a cat, committed another sin, or one performs mundan, one bathes in the Kund to repent and/or finalize the ritual/ceremony (as is the case in mundan). Nowadays, there is a small charge for bathing in the Kund and even a receipt is issued. This is done in order to convince the community of one's visit to the Kund for the desired purpose.

Another legend is linked with old history of India about the time of Mehmood Gajnabi. Gajnabi had passed that way to dismantle the temple of Soamnath. He followed the stairs, passing by the Kund to the Shivling and attacked the statute of Shivling. A lot of honey-bees came out of the statue and heavy avalanche of rocks followed from above. A lot of his army men died and another good portion got wounded. This blasphemy really took Gajnabi by surprise.

He, then, prayed that he will reconstruct the temple. And up to now the place is in Mugul Shelly i.e. it reflects middle eastern Islamic architect.

There is a lot of preparation that goes into celebration. The merry-go rounds and other kinds of rides are there. Many people set up little shops in the bazaar.[6] One can find in the market anywhere from clothes; artificial jewelry (i.e. metal, stone or bead jewelry); clay and stone pots and pans; harnesses for the animals; many varieties of toys for children; decoration pieces; clay and stone statutes and sculptures; photographs; and of course the sweet shops and food shops.

People come all the way from Banswara Jila and its surrounding areas, Chittorh and Pratapgarh, Dhariaved Tehsil, and Udaipur Jila to participate in this festival. Mainly the Bhil and Meena tribe participate. It is just too far for Garasia and Sehria tribe. Regardless that it is a tribal festival, a lot of India families also participate with the same spirit and same beliefs. Still it has not caught the fancy of the tourists as yet.

The participants usually come with their clothes and blankets to spend at least two to three days there. They cook Choorma and Bati in the clay pots which are left behind after the use. Some people put ashes of their dead relatives in the water. But mainly they come here for repenting their sins.

Meenas have been looking after the temple for generations. Brahmins have tried to interrupt this routine by making a Radha-Krishna[7] temple there, but still the main donations are handed over to the Meena care-taker family.

In the middle of the roof of Shivji temple here is a hole so that one can look straight down at the shivling without having to go through the gate. There is normal size wall (about 3 feet high) surrounding the hole. People go around that wall by circling their waists. This act is called Gadha-lot i.e. Donkey-circling. This act is performed with the belief of being rid of the donkey life[8] in the eighty four lakh birth cycles in hindu mythology.

It is a two day fair. Nowadays, this festival is organized by the Tehsildar, Additional District Magistrate (A.D.M.), Project officer and Rajasthan Administrative Officers. The development officer looks after the management. There needs to be some extra care in cleanliness and fresh food because there has been an incidence of food poisoning three years ago.

### Gavri

The month of September is the month of dance; it is a month of own merit among the Bhils. Gavri is organized in Bhadra Pada month of Hindu Calendar from Krishna Ekem' to Ashwin Krishna Navmi[2]. Depending upon Hindu calendar, it varies from 37 to 40 days for example, Gavri was organized from September 2nd to October 10th i.e. 39 days in the year of 1993. Bhopa[3] of the host village watches for the appropriate time and seeks permission from the goddess. He also decides with other Bhopas from nearby villages about the villages which are to take part in playing Gavri. The Sarpanctes[4] of these villages are then informed.

The origin of Gavri is not traced precisely perhaps because of the dynamism of oral tradition and its ability to adapt to contemporary situation at hand. However, people state that Gavri was organized previously and today also to please Shankra[5] and Parvati.[6] Pleasing the gods will cure them of all evils like diseases, poverty, famine etc.

The significance of this festival is also attached with the importance of brother-sister relationship. Traditionally, villages unmarried girls are sisters tot he men of that village. These girls are married off to nearby villages. Thus, rotating of Gavri performance is representative of visiting the sisters of a paetiwlar village.

## Observance of Ceremony

Rural social economic life is wrapped around its religiously and spirituality. The participants, especially the performers, have to follow some rules. Daily intake of meat and wine is prohibited. Only green vegetables are to be eaten. Celibacy must be practiced. One must sleep on the grass bed on the floor. Cutting of trees, even for wood, is prohibited.

Sometimes, a test is laid out to see if everyone is observing the rules. Daily intake of meat and wine is prohibited. Usually, a fire is lit and the participants are led by the Bhopa to walk on fire. The belief is that if the person is abiding by the rules, the fire won't hurt him, otherwise, it would. Someone disobeying the rules, righout is punished by the panchayat. It is believed that if someone breaks the rules but escapes the punishment will eventually be punished by the heavenly powers.

## Initiation Ceremony

Gavri is usually played within an imaginary sacred line. The Bhopa of the village draws this line to protect the performance of Gavri from evil. Bhopa senses any outside evil through the grace of goddess and immediately cures it.

He then establishes within imaginary line the sacred "Trishul[7] of Devi" along with the statues of Lord Shiva and Parvati. This sacred trishul is made out of iron and is received from the village which last hosted this festival. Further, it is marked with saffron color near the top (either on middle prong or underneath it) and shinning gota is tied in the middle of it.

Finally, a Jyot[8] is dipped in ghee[9] in an earthern deepak[10] to mark the opening of Gavri festival. Bhopa along with his male family members lights this jyot and keeps it lighted for 39 consecutive days.

## Folk Play

The host village starts the Gavri ballet. Usually, Bhopa assigns the roles and characters to people to play. The performers are brought within the imaginary circle, sprinkled with holy water, and are asked to abide by the rules. Then the main performers, Boodia and Rayo symbolizing Lord Shiva and his wife, Parvati, respectively are brought in front of the Sarpanch who presents them the costumes for the ballet. One person can not take part in two successive Gavri ballets, though he may perform it every other year.

The script for the play of Gavri is based on many stories representing their beliefs and local incidents. Some of the scripts are described below:

(a) **Shiv Parvati:** This paetiwlar script must be played everyday before sunset in every village where Gavri is taking place. Once Shiv Ji and Parvati Ji went to the forest for hunting. Shivji went quite a distance while following a hunt. Meanwhile, Bhils hid Parvati Ji. When Shiv Ji returned looking for Parvati Ji, Bhils demanded that he puts life into one of their dead man shiv Ji enlivened the dead man and Bhils returned Parvati Ji.

(b) **Baba Bhasmasur:** Bhasmasur was a Rakshas (demon) who meditated for Lord Vishnu for thousands of years and received a magical bangle as a boon. According to the boon, anyone will turn into ashes instantly upon touching that bangle. With his mind set, he proceeded to kill Shiv Ji, so that he could marry Parvati Ji. Shiv Ji and Parvati Ji escaped his attack narrowly.

Then Vishnu Ji disguised himself as a beautiful dancer and blocking Parvati Ji asked Bhasmasur to dance with him/her. During the dance, Bhasmasur touched his own bangle and turned into ashes instantly.

(c) **Nahar and Kali Mata:** As the Gavri play goes on, the mother goddess, kali Mata seated on the lion, watches Gavri with other spectaters e.g. other divine deities, gods and goddesses. They shower blessings on everybody performing the play. Kali Mata also assures them no fear of demons.

(d) **Goma Meena:** He was a tribal decoit who used to worship the goddess, "Choti Mata", especially before going on his mission. However, once he committed a theft in a temple and that of the goddess herself. The goddess became so angry that she transformed herself alive at that instant of, theft, killed the man and turned back into her idol.

(e) **Bhanvara-Bhanvari:** They represent Devar and Bhabhi. Devar is the brother of woman's husband and Bhabhi is brother's wife. Bhabi asks her devar to bring some honey. Devar goes to the forest but is attacked by the honey bees. He returns, worships mother goddess and proceeds with her blessings to the forest again. Here he collects honey and gives it to his bhabhi.

(f) **Natni and Jamai:** This script is based upon a local comedy. Natni is a beautiful woman. Jamai refers to son -in-law in hindi. After Natni is married, she takes leave with her husband. She weeps bitterly. Jamai also starts crying uncontrollably. When questioned for his crying, he, in turn, questions Natni's weeping. His mother-in-law explains to him that Natni is crying because she feels sad for leaving behind her parents, siblings and relatives with whom she grew up. He replies in between his sobs that he is also sad for leaving behind his parents-in-law, brothers/sisters-in-law etc.

(g) **Ambor and Kalukar:** Kalukar is brother to Ambar. Once she was taking bath by the sea shore. Suddenly her ring slipped off her finger and a fish swallowed it instantly. It was the dearest ring of Ambar for she would not stop crying. Kalukar took his net and sat by the sea shore until he caught the fish with the ring. He brought the ring back to his sister.

The costumes of players are the common ones. For example, ghaghra Choli[11] with dupatta[12] is worn for the part of females. Dhoti-Kurta[13] with turban is worn for the part of males. The performers further dress themselves up according to the part and thier taste. They put on powder, lipstick, small crowns, shinning ribbons etc.

Usually, females do not perform in the play. They prepare the meals and look after other arrangements. The gavri parties are invited by the rich people in the village for feasting.

On the last day of Gavri, i.e. on Ashwin Krishna Navmi, the Shiv Parvati story is replayed and a havan of 'dhoop' and 'ghee' is performed. Havan is a ceremony that takes place around the sacred fire. Bhopa burns somethings in the fire while repeating mantras. Dhoop is incense and ghee is the purified butter which helps light the fire and keeps it lit. This havan is to purify the environment and keep the evil off.

Finally, statue of elephant is brought that represents conveyance of Parvati Ji. Swamani of food (Choorma and Bati traditional. Rajsthani food) is prepared for the elephant which is distributed amongst the people as prasad.

Before sunset, a large crowd of dancing and hopping villagers follows with the shivji and Parvati Ji Statutes on top of the elephant statue to the nearby river bank or a pond. The statues are immersed in the water which marks the end of the Gavri festival.

**Notes**

1. Krishna Ekem—Krishna refers to the darker side of the moon and Ekem refers to one in hindi; thus, Krishna Ekem is the day after Amavas (dark moon).

2. Ashwin Krishna Navmi—Navmi refers to nine in hindi, thus, Ashwin krishna Navmi refers to ninth day after Amavas (dark Moon).

3. Bhopa—is the priest /Pundit of the village. He is also treated as a link between the layman and god.

4. Sarpanch is the head of the village Panchayat which is administrative unit in the village.

5. Shanker is another name for Lord shiva in Hindu Mythology. Lord shiva is the Lord of destruction and underworld.

6. Parvati is the wife of Lord shiva.

7. Trishul is a metal spear like weapon with three prongs instead of one. It is the weapon of Lord shiva in partiwalr.

8. Jyot-raw cotton rolled

9. Ghee purified butter.

10. Deepak is usually a clay pot in whcih the jyot is placed dipped in ghee and lighted for prayer to goddess/god.

11. Ghaghra—Choli Ghaghra is an ankle length pleated skirt. Choli is a blouse usually waist height.

12. Dupatta—the long scarf going over head and tocked into the waist of the skirt, ghaghra.

13. Dhoti—Kutra-Dhoti is about 21/2 meter long material wrapped around the waist of Indian men. Kurta is a shirt with buttons only half way in the front.

**Footnotes**

1. Shivling—sex organ of shivji.

2 Shiv Ji—is Lord of destruction.

□□□

3. Radha Krishna-Radha is manifestation of Laxmi and Krishna is manifestation of her husband, Vishnu.

4. Pujarees—Priests of temple who look after rituals and ceremonies.

5. Healing Ritual—For instance, if someone has a problem, then pujarees can suggest special offering to them and repeat some mantras for the victim etc.

6. Savari—is the ride, in this instance it is parade.

7. Magh-Purnima—Magh is a month in hindi calendar which falls usually in January-February. Purnima means full moon in hindi.

8. Moksh—Moksh is breaking the life-rebirth cycles. According to Hindu philosophy, a human being goes through eighty four lakh yonis (life cycle) to be born as human. The basic idea is that the first physical birth of a spirit starts from the smallest imaginable insect, something like bacteria, goes through the stages of insects, birds, vertebrae, mammals etc. until it reaches the last potential birth, that of a human being. So praying for Moksh refers to the concept of stopping the birth of the spirit in a physical body and attaining the debated spiritual plane of soul where the spirit is a free spirit and not bound physically in any way. Moksh is similar to liberation or Nirvana of the soul.

1. Rishi is spiritual person

2. Kund a water hole.

3. Adivasi In hindi Adi means start of origin and vasi means inhabitants, this, meaning original inhabitants. Whereas the English interpretation of it is tribals.

4. Lord Shiva is lord of destruction and underworld in hindu Mythology.

5. Shivling—is a statue of lingham that represents lord Shiva, it is worshipped for fertility, prosperity, strength etc.

6. Bazar-Hindi word for Market.

7. Radha-Krishna-manifestation of Laxmi and her husband Lord Vishnu respectively.

8. In Hinduism, the belief in reincarnation is that a person usually goes through more than eighty four lakh lives before being born human again.

❑❑❑

# 7

# Celebration of Life: Festivals in Jhauba

*Dr. Narendra Bokhare*

## JHAUBA: LAND & HISTORY

Jhabua is one of the districts of Madhya Pradesh state in central India. The district of Jhauba comes under Malwa region. The northern border of Jhabua touches to the State of Rajasthan, at west it shares borders with the State of Gujarat, and towards south it touches to the State of Maharashtra. The district of Jhabua is dominated by the tribal population which comprises of Bhil, Bhilala and Patelia tribal communities. Total tribal population of the district is around 16,26,626, which forms 83.48% of the total population.[1]

The area now known as Jhabua district is situated on the Western boundary of Madhya Pradesh at the foot hills of Vindhya mountains. The Jhabua dynasty (Riyasat) was founded by Jhabbu Nayak of Labana clan in 1584 A.D. From the end of 13th century to the beginning of 16th century, the southern region of Malwa was repeatedly attached & looted by a clan of Nayak belonging to Labana community from Rajasthan. These people rose in mutiny against the then Mughal emperors. In 1605, Mughal emperor Jahangir sent a huge army under the leadership of Keshav Das, who belonged to the royal Rajput family of Jodhpur, a princely state in Rajasthan. There was a fierce battle between the Mughal army led by Keshav Das and the Nayak army which fought under the leadership of Jhabbu Nayak, who died in this battle. Keshav Das named the conquered territory as Jhabbaha, after Jhabba Nayak which later came to be known as Jhabua. Emperor Jahangir rewarded Keshav

Das for his bravery by presenting him ten districts in South Malwa. Thus, Keshav Das founded his own riyasat—Jhabua—and ruled over it until 1607. Since then twelve generations of Keshav Das ruled over Jhabua. Thereafter, during the British regime, the State affairs of Jhabua were looked after by the political Department of Malwa Agency of the British Raj. After India achieved independence in 1947, the State of Jhabua was assimilated into the federation of States of Central India on May 28, 1948.[2]

Today there are around 1364 villages in Jhauba district which are inhabited by Bhil, Bhilala and Patelia tribes. Since Jhabua district shares borders with Gujarat State and Nimad region of Madhya Pradesh, the languages spoken by those tribals show Gujarati and Nimadi dilacts. There is no literary evidence about the origin of adivasis of Jhabua. However, it is possible to infer from the folkore and legends that these may have migrated from Badhaka (Gujarat), Dholka (Rajasthan) and Khandesh (Maharashtra). According to a legend, ancestors of Bhils living in Rajasthan and Gujarat had quarrel with Meghraj—the Rain God—and as a result there was constant drought. Therefore they came and settled in Jhabua while searching fertile lands.

Among the adivasis of Jhabua, Bhil, Bhilala and Patelia are three major communities. Besides, Tadvi and Rathiya are sub-groups of Bhils. Each of these communities follows distinct way of life and traditions. The Bhilalas believe that they are descendents of the royal Rajput clans. Most of them are stout, strong and sharp featured. The main occupation of the adivasis of Jhabua is agriculture.

## FAIRS AND FESTIVALS

Although the socio-economic condition of the Jhabua is poor, their cultural life is very rich. Against many social odds such as illiteracy, harrowing poverty and political injustice, they celebrate several rituals, fairs and festivals. These celebrations are associated with their deities of archaic origin, with the Hindus deities as well as wit seasons. Their life may be full of difficulties created by the nature and by the humans as well, but they celebrate various festivals with enthusiasm, gaiety and deep faith throughout the year. The tribes of Jhabua celebrate the following major festivals:

### 1. Akha Teej (आखा तीज):

This festival is celebrated on the third day of the bright half in the month of Chaitra (May). A week before the festival, young boys visit each house carrying wooden plough and ask elders for the directions for ploughing fields. This motivates elders to give up lethargy and start field activities. On the day of Akha Teej, adivasis abstain from liquor and restrict to vegetarian food. Men go to the fields and start works such as ploughing, spreading manure, mending fence around the field and alike. They do not sleep in the night of Akha Teej but collect dry foliage, garbage and burn that in their fields.

Young girls make images of bride and groom out of leaves of Palash tree and celebrate their marriage. In the evening, the images are immersed in the river. This is a message to stop wedding celebrations in the village, as now, even the trees have been married off. Therefore villagers stop singing and dancing until the Navai festival when the crops would be ripe. Thus, the message of the festival helps them to keep away from mere entertainment and concentrate on the field activities. From this day, tribals start using 'new' leaves of palash trees.

## 2. Hovan Mata ki Chalavani (होवन माता की चलावनी):

The fair of Chalavani is celebrated in order to seek protection from the supernatural calamities which might befall on villagers. Generally, three to four weeks after seeds are sown, each household in the village contributes a certain amount of money & deposits it with the chief of village for performing rituals of Chalavani. Villagers fix a Sunday or Tuesday to celebrate Chalavani. Celebrations begin on the previous day of the Chalavani. On that day, the chief of the village (Tadavi), the priest (Badwa) and a few young men who can sing gather at the boundary of the village. Women are not allowed near the place of Chalavani celebrations. On this day, houses in the village are not cleaned and people do not go to the farms for working.

As a preliminary preparation of Chalavani, a wooden replica of bullock cart alongwith bulls is prepared. This replica is known as Khapper. Symbolic wooden figurines of buffaloes are placed in Khappar alongwith red flags. These are treated as representations of various deities. Tadvi (chief) and Badwa (priest) sit facing each other near Kahppar. Badwa closes eyes and begins chanting prayers. His companions start playing a musical instrument called Kimandi. Gradually Badwa enters into trance and gets possessed by the goddess Hovan Mata. In trance, Badwa, in fact the goddess warns the villages to follow the traditions. If the goddess expresses displeasure for certain wrong doing on part of villagers, the Tadavi seeks pardons of the goddess and pacifies the goddess who speaks through the medium of Badwa. This continues almost until early morning. At the end Tadavi offers liquor to Badwa and begins worship of Hovan Mata offering her coconut, dhoop, camphor, water and flowers and a bottle of liquor. The worship lasts until the late morning of the next day, the actual day of Chalavani. Thereafter the main rituals of Chalavani begin.

Badwa first worships the Khappar and a goat is brought for sacrifice. After worship of Khappar, Badwa pours left over water and liquor on goat. If the goat moves his ears, it is believed that the goat is ready to be sacrificed. If the goat does not move his ears, it is considered as bad omen and another goat is brought for sacrifice. After 'consent' of goat, he is beheaded with sword in a single attempt. As soon as the goat is killed, four young men pickup headless body and pour its blood over the Khappar and start running towards village border carrying body of the goat, Khappar and other things, used in sacrificial worship. Villagers gathered outside the village pay their respect by offering water and grains of corn, sesame, moong and udid. Then the goat meat is cooked outside the village border and distributed to people as *Prasad*. It is strongly believed that the khappar takes away the illnesses, diseases and other misfortunes from the village.

### 3. Savan Mata ki Jatra—(सावन माता की जत्रा)

Savan Mata is believed to be the goddess who ensures abundance of field produces by the tribals of Jhauba. When new seedling come out of earth after sowing seeds, Badwa, Tadavis and other villagers worship and pray to Savan Mata that whatever has been sowed should came out in the multifold abundance. From this day until Navai festival, villagers do not plaster or smear their house walls and floor, men do not shave off their beard.

### 4. Diwasa (दिवासा)

The festival of Diwasa is celebrated on the full moon day in the month of Jeshtha (June) in honour of Baba Dev who is the main god of adivasis of Jhabua.

On the day of Diwasa, people go to the sacred grove—a protected part of forest for deities—near their village where Baba Dev is installed alongwith other deities. They offer sweets made of wheat, rice and udid to Baba Dev and drink liquor. On this day, they begin playing flute which continues until the festival of Dipawali.

### 5. Navai (नवाई)

The festival of Navai is celebrated after the crops are ripe and ready for harvest, generally in the month of August. Villagers collectively decide a day to celebrate Navai. On this day new crops are worshipped before people start consuming them. On Navai morning people offer new crops of corn, rice, milk and vegetables to the village deities believed to reside in the sacred groove near the village. After returning home, the new crops are offered to the family deities, clan deity and the totem deity. At the same time, they offer thanks giving prayer to Mendh—The Rain and cloud God — expressing gratitude for his blessing. They also offer worship and prayer to the farm insects and pests requesting them not to eat away the crops.

As an expression of humility and gratitude towards the Nature the new crops are offered to the various deities. On the day of Navai, people clean and renovate the village temple. Then they gather at the house of the village chief (Tadavi) and sing collectively in praise of village god (Gram Devata) alongwith the village priest (Badwa). The singing continues till midnight. Meanwhile Badwa gets possessed by Gram Devata and talks to villages about their general well being, rewards them with blessings and forecasts future for the forthcoming year.

On Navai, each household carries milk, new corn and fresh vegetables for offering to the village god. In addition, each person brings a fistful rice or jawar grains which are used for cooking feast for the whole community. The Badwa is offered liquor which he drinks before getting possessed. The village god, ancestors of many villagers as well as other deities possess Badwa turn by turn and bless their respective worshippers and descendants.

## 6. Malkani—Gruhanee (मालकनी गृहनी)

Malkani is believed to a form of Mahalaxmi. The festival of Malkani is celebrated on the full moon day in the month of Bhadrapad (September). This festival is normally celebrated collectively by tribals of eight to ten villages. A ritual specialist, Panda—who has to be cow-header—performs rituals of Malkani. He makes a big clay figure of elephant near a sacred grove. The decorations on the elephant figure are made using grains of new crops. Men and women from the nearby villages assemble together on the full moon night wearing their finest adornments and offer corn, vegetables and other field produces to the clay elephant. Groups of young men sing and play flutes while young women dance. Several groups of singers and dancers come from different villages. Dancing among the adivashis of Jhabua begins from the day of Malkani which lasts till the month of Chaitra and ends on the day of Akha Teej.

## 7. Navaratri (नवरात्री)

Navaratri festival is celebrated in the month of Ashwin (October). On the first day of this nine-day festival, people sow various seeds in the sacred grove near the shrines. Badwa the priest, looks after the growing seedlings. After nine days, he observes growth of seedlings and forecasts about the intensity of mansoon. He further advises people for preventive care of cattle from diseases and about crops to be sowed in the forthcoming season. All the gods, goddess and souls of ancestors are worshippd during the festival of Navaratri.

### 8. Dashara (दशरा)

The adivasi people of Jhauba district celebrate Dashara to worship mother goddess Ma Chamunda, who is also called as Savana Mata. Ten days before Dashara, the villagers mix wheat grains in black soil in small bamboo baskets kept in the temple of village god (Gam Devata). The baskets are watered for nine days. Throughout these nine days, people offer worship playing small drums with utmost devotion and reverence to goddess Savana Mata. During nights, some persons get possessed by the Mata. The goddess is worshipped with coconut oil, dhop, ghee and flowers. From the second day to the ninth day either a goat or a cock is sacrificed at the temple. On the day of Dashara each household sacrifices goat or cock to Chamunda Mata. In the evening people root out sapling of jawar and put them in nearby river or lake in order to 'cool' the crop from the heat in October. People also worship their weapons on the day of Dashara.

### 9. Dhan Teras (धन तेरस)

The festival of Dhan Teras is celebrated in the month of November in honour of goddess Jasma Mata. Jasma Mata is treated as the goddess of wealth and abundance. Householders gather outside the house, sing in her praises and worship the goddess at the threshold of the house.

### 10. Roop Chaudas (रूप चौदास)

The festival of Roop Chaudas is celebrated in the month of November. It is a day for collective fishing. In the morning of this day all men from the village gather at the river, stream or lake carrying a cloth called dhoti. After gathering, they form into groups and stitch their cloths together. This long cloth is then held across the water current by people in such a way that fishes jump into the cloth-net. The catch is distributed amongst the people.

According to a legend, once upon a time a Bhil went to a river to catch fish in order to feed his ailing and hungry family. However, he could get only one fish.

Thinking that it would not be sufficient for his family, he offered if to Shiva Linga. Bhagawan Bholanath (Shiva) was very much pleased by it act of generosity and granted boon to the Bhil devotee that from that day onward fish will jump in his cloth net, and if he would offer a fish to Bhagwan his house would never be afflicted by illness or hunger. It was the day of Roop Chaudas and since then Bhils and other adivasis of Jhabua have been practicing ritual of collective fishing.

The day of Roop Chandas is also important for preparing indigenous medicines. Some people catch crabs for making medicine for common, cold. This day is also important for ancestral worship. Some people install colourful, decorative memorial stone slabs carved in memory of their ancestors or diseased loved ones.

## 11. Dipawali (दीपावली)

By the time of Dipawali festival in November, most of the crops are ready. Therefore all the adivasis celebrate Dipawali, with joy and enthusiasm. They renovate ad paint their houses with bright colours, and clean the cattle sheds. On the day of Dipawali they worship cattle and field produces and light lamps in the evenings. In the late evening, the village boys and girls dance together, sing humorous songs, play riddles and thus entertain themselves.

## 12. Gai Gohari (गाय गोहरी)—Festival of cows and cow-herders)

On the next day of Dipawali, people wash and decorate their cattle and feed them the best available fodder. They brand the cattle with hot iron believing that it would protect them from diseases.

Gai means cow & Gohara is a cow-herder in Bhili dialect. Gai Gohari is an unique event performed in Jhabua. On the day of Gai-Gohari all the cattle are assembled in a narrow lane in village. In this lane the cow herders, wearing new clothes, lie down on the road. Then other people burn crackers behind cattle so that the frightened cattle would run through the narrow lane jumping over the herders. It is believed that the herders remain safe in this stampede of hundreds of cattle. Indeed, so far there has not yet been any recorded mishap during the Gai-Gohari festival.

## 13. Chhoti Diwali (छोटा दिवाली)

Festival of Chhoti Diwali is celebrated on the fourteenth day in the bright fortnight of Kartik month (November-December). This day is marked for installation of Gatala—

carved stone memorial in the name of family members who have died accidental, unnatural death. Other ancestors are also worshipped on this day. In the night people dance at the place where Gatala is installed.

## 14. Holi, Bhagoriya and Dhulendi (होली, भगोरीया और धुलेंदी):

Holi is the most popular and eagerly awaited festival of the adivasis. Indeed, not only Holi, but the whole month of Phalgun (March), which marks onset of spring season, is joyous and festive month for the adivasis of Jhabua.

Holi is celebrated on the full moon day in Phalgun month. A wooden pole called Holi ka Danda is fixed to the ground by the village chief a month before, that is, on the full moon day in the preceding month of Magh (February). On the evening of Holi, the whole village starts gathering near Holi Ka Danda. Almost everyone is inebriated and engrossed in singing, dancing and playing music. As the midnight approaches, young men & women dance with increased vigour. Badwa worships the Holi pyre and the Tadavi lits is with fire. All the people curcumanbulate seven times around the Holi fire. While returning home, people carry some fire from Holi for burning their hearths with it. Some people attempt to keep this fire kindling throughout the year. The whole night is spent in singing & dancing.

The most attractive event impatiently awaited during Holi celebrations is Bhagoriya Hat. Hat is a weekly market held in adivasi areas. The Bhagoriya is organized a week before the day of Holi. Men and women of all ages clean their clothes, jewelry and other adornments days before Bhagoriya day. Men clean and mend weapons such as swoard, axe and bow-and-arrows. Women embroider their clothes with cowri shells, beads ad glittering tinsels. On the day of Bhagoriya Hat, young men and women start making up themselves from the early morning. Everyone takes great care that his/her finest attire, apparels and adornments would be displayed explicitly. Friends and peers are called together by playing special tunes on flute. The groups of young people march together towards the Hat area in joyous, humorous mood while singing and playing flutes. Everyone carries a mirror, comb and available cosmetics in order to rearrange make up on the way and after reaching the Hat. Once they reach the Hat, young men look for the girls of their liking. If a boy likes a girl he goes near her and applies red colour to her face. Then they both walk away to some distance & talk to each other. If the girl also likes the boy, she offers him pan (beetle nut leaves) and they both run away, symbolically, from their parents. Such a pair mutually approved by each other, is later married off with the consent of their parents and elders. In rare cases boys use force to take away girls.

Dhulendi is celebrated two days after Holi. Villagers contribute money to enjoy community feast. Some young men apply black and white colours on their faces, body and dress-up themselves as clowns and go around the village enacting comic roles. Women sing bawdy, lascivious songs and stop men to collect money from them. The whole day is spent in entertainment and drinking liquor.

## 15. Gadh (गढ):

This festival is celebrated on the twelfth day from Holi. A strong wooden pole of about 50 feet height is erected in the main square of the village This pole is called Gadh. It is treated with oil and soap in order to make it smooth and slippery. Then the young men are challenged to climb on this pole and eat Gur (jaggary, raw sugar) kept on top it. Unmarried girls stand around the pole holding thin cane sticks in their hands. As men attempt to climb over the pole, girls beat them on the bottom with cane sticks. After hard and determined efforts a few young men succeed in climbing the pole and eat gur. The man who climbs first gets the privilege to choose any girl of his liking to make his wife. Many adivasi young men from nearby villages come to participate in this ritual with their dance groups.

## 16. Indal Mela (इंदल मेला):

This fair is celebrated in honour of God Indal—the Rain God. Any person wishing to gain wealth or ward off misfortune or illness can take a vow to celebrate Indal Mela. There is no fixed day for Mela. It is celebrated on a convenient day to the host. A week before the Mela, announcement is made in weekly village market about the day and place of Indal Mela.

Three days before celebration of Mela, the host offers liquor and lits a lamp near a Kadamb tree to invoke and invite Indal God. On the day of Mela seven branches of the Kadamb tree are cut and buried in the field of the host. Thousands of people gather to participate in the mela and all night they sing and dance holding swords & bows to the tunes of drums. In the morning five goats are sacrificed to Indal God. The branches buried in the field are placed in water since this 'cooling' of branches is believed to appease Indal—the Rain God.

## 17. Father Ka Tyohar or Festival of Father (फादर का त्योहार):

Some adivasis have been converted to Christianity. Nevertheless, they still follow their traditional adivasi customs. In addition they incorporated newly adopted faith in their traditional cultural framework. Father —the Christian priest/preacher-is now one of the deities of Christian adivasis. Christian as well as non-Christian adivasis celebrate this festival on the eve of Christmas. Every year on December 24, troupes of adivasi dancers gather near the Church in Jhabua town with their drums and flutes. Entertainment stalls, merry go rounds, sweet-shops are installed near the church. Christian adivasis attend ritual service in the local catholic church, others wander around and amuse themselves in the fair.

## SUMMARY

The main occupation of Bhil and other adivasis from Jhabua is agriculture. Therefore the festivals and rituals related with the growth of crops are celebrated with joy and happiness. These people start sowing seeds by the end of summer and beginning of monsoon. As the crops start growing, people start expressing their joy and gratitude towards the nature and various deities through various festivals related to different stages of agriculture. Akha Teej is celebrated to give message to community to give up lethargy and start working. Hoven mata ki Chalavani is performed to appease supernatural forces and seek protection from their wrath. Savan Mata ki Jatar is, in fact, a thanks-giving ceremony. There is a purpose behind each celebration and each has rich traditions and heritage.

Almost all the festivals are celebrated on the community level. This ensures social cohesion and harmony in the village. During festivals, the whole village gathers together and people dance shoulder to shoulder with each other. In this way they get rid of their mundane problems, tiredness and emotional disturbances by sinking in the rhythm of music and footsteps of dance. The difficulties faced in daily living are dissolved in the festive atmosphere.

These festivals are not celebrated simply for their own sake. In each case, they have a pragmatic aim and are associated with other mundane human activities. In general sense, these festivals have a useful organizing power. They assure confidence to those who perform them, and help them understand the nature and the seasonal changes. They are too deeply interwoven with the basic fabric of human emotions. The festivals give strength to people to forget their poverty and related evils and to find emotional gratification and spiritual satisfaction.

Above all, the festivals provide guidelines to the poor adivasis to look at their, otherwise difficult, life as a celebration.

**Notes**

1. The figures, percentages cited have been obtained from the District Statistical Office in Jhabua town white interviewing District Statistical Officer on July 26, 1995.

2. Jhauba Kāl aūr Aāj (Jhabua: Past & Present). Hindi; Editor Yaswant Ghodawat, 1988, Republic Day special issue.

3. The data on the description of various festivals and cultural events narrated here have been collected during my ethnographic field work in Jhabua town in July—August 1995 which was a part of research project funded by the Canadian International Development Agency. I am thankful to Dr. Michael Ames, Professor, Department of Anthropology and Sociology, University of British Columbia, Vancouver, Canada for inviting me to associate with him for the project. I also thank Radhu Bhilala, Parik, and the staff of the Collectorate in Jhabua and many adivasi informants for providing the relevant cultural information.

❑❑❑

# 8

# Fairs and Festivals of the Bhilala Tribe

***Dr. L.N. Soni***

The Bhil and related tribes are spread over the central uplands of the Indian peninsula, and bulk of them live in the regions covered by the forest-clad areas of the Vindhya, the Satpuda and the Sahyadri in the states of Madhya Pradesh, Maharashtra, Gujarat and Rajasthan. In Madhya Pradesh, the Bhil and related tribes are mainly found in Dhar, Jhabua, west Nimar (Khargone) and Ratlam districts. They have also been enumerated in Dewas, East Nimar (Khandwa), Shajapur and Indore districts. Their population, according to 1981 Census, as 2,500,530 which includes the tribes of the Bhil, Bhilala, Barela and the Patelia. The Bhilala, described as a mixed tribe, sprung from the alliances of the immigrant Rajputs and the Bhils. Separate population figures for the Bhilala tribe are not available as the community is notified with the major group, the Bhil. The Bhilala are closely related to the Bhil, Barela, Patelia and other groups inhabiting the Vindhyas and the Satpudas. The Bhilala claim Rajput descent and are considered to be of higher status than their neighbouring tribal groups in the area. They are more hinduised than their tribal neighbourers, so we find a number of Hindu festivals celebrated by them. This observation is based on my fieldwork in two villages of western Madhya Pradesh viz. Bhilkhera (Khargone district) and Padalya (Dhar district) in 1979 and 1981, respectively.

The Bhilala celebrate a number of festivals and participate in fairs which are held locally. These fairs and festivals make their life lively, bring change in the routine habits and add happiness in their life. These are the occasion when they assemble, enjoy and celebrate the festivals jointly with vigour, joy and mutual cooperation.

## HOLI

The festival of Holi is celebrated jointly by the Bhilala with other groups of people living in the villages on the full moon day of Falgun (Falgun Poornima). The Bhil do not attend the village bonfire (Holi). On the day of Holi, the Balai (drummer) makes around of the village (Bhilkhera) in the evening giving shouts to the people to gather in the Holi ground. The Patel (village Headman) worships the Holi and sets fire. The men who have sons below one year and the men who have got married in the same year, offer a full coconut to the bonfire. Those who have daughters below one year and those who have given their daughters in marriage in the same year, offer half a coconut (*batki*) to the bonfire. These coconuts are taken out by the attending persons and relished with joy. At Padalya, half portion of the coconut is returned back to the profferer.

In the next morning, the mothers (or any other relative) go to the place of the Holi bonfire with the children below one year of age and make a round at the bonfire, so that the child may get some heat and may be healthy. The children are given garlands and sugar-cakes, which are snatched by the persons assembled over there irrespective of their community affiliation. The women who go to the Holi bonfire offer water first to Sheetala Mata at her shrine and then go a round the bonfire pouring water from a pot.

It is found that a *Semal* stick is fastened in the Holi ground about a month ago which is brought from other villages. It is properly guarded by the village chowkidar, so that it is not stolen. It is believed that if the stick is stolen, then the prosperity will not come to the village and they will face a lot of problems. Crops would not be ripening fully. *Semal* stick gets easily burnt in the fire and is assumed to be the symbol of peace. Half-burnt semal stick is taken out in the morning and dipped into the well water (Padalya). The villagers never fasten a stick cut from their own village.

The Bhilala go on collecting the wood, cowdung cakes, dry twigs and straws at the place of the village bonfire. On the day of Holika *Dahan* (burning of the bonfire), the Patel goes to the place of the village bonfire and worships that ritually because he happens to be the ritual head of the village also. He then sets fire to the heap of the collected wood after offering jowar and water enchanting hymns. He again goes to the place of Holi bonfire in the morning and offers coconut, lemon, etc. At some places, sacrifice of a chicken is also made. Thereafter, the village women come there singing songs. They make salutation to the Holika Mata, offer jowar grains and then pour water on the Holika.

Sweet dishes are prepared in the house and relished with gaiety by inviting their sisters and daughters on that day.

On the day next to Holi and on the fifth day, the Bhilala play with colours. Works are mostly suspended during this period and they remain in festive mood.

## GANGOUR

Gangour festival is celebrated from the tenth day of the black fortnight to the fourth day of the bright fortnight of the Hindu month of Chaitra (March-April). It is celebrated for happiness and good-luck to the people. The persons who vow to invoke goddess (Gaur Bai) and Baba (Dhaniyar Raja), bring five baskets, 1.5 kgs. wheat and an earthen lamp in the temple on the tenth day of the black fortnight of the Hindu month of Chaitra. Out of five baskets, four are meant for goddess and one for Dhaniyar Raja. The invocation of Dhaniyar Raja is not compulsory for all. He is also known as Chandul Raja, Ishwar Raja and Brahm Raja. Likewise, Gaur Bai is also known as Ranu Bai, Sait Bai and Rohin Bai.

The womenfolk of the village assemble at one place on the tenth day, at night. They go to the place of Holi bonefire with the accompaniment of the village drummer. Water is sprinkled on two spots and chauks (floral designs of flour) are made. One vessel (*lota*) with water is kept over one floral design and seven pebbles are put on the other. They are worshipped by offering rice and *gulal* (red powder). Then earth from that place and seven pebbles are brought to the temple. Earth is spread around the baskets in the temple and seven pebbles are placed there as the emblem of Lord Ganesh.

*Keshar* is then prepared. It is a mixture of black soil and powdered cow-dung. Keshar is placed in the baskets in three layers and wheat is broadcasted over each layer. A man is appointed to water them four times a day till eighth day, so that seeds may sprout properly and grow healthily.

On the second day, the women gather for dancing and singing. They distribute roasted maize (*tamol*) and groundnut there. At Bhilkhera, it is held in the temple-ground. The *Badawa*, a man with divine power, comes there and treats the suffering people. He is also known as *Jhar*. On the seventh day, the room for the goddess is cleaned and all the spiderwebs of the house are removed. The room is besmeared with cow-dung paste. The women of the house pound flour at night for the morrow's feasting of the invited couples (*Joda Baithhana*) Maize, jowar and wheat are pounded in *ghatti* ( a stone device for making flour or grind-stone). This work is initiated by a couple and then carried on by the womenfolk of the house. Milk-rice and thick *chapatis* are the main food items of the day.

Women assemble in those houses at night where Gaur Bai and Dhaniyar Raja are to be invoked. They sing devotional songs. This continues upto the last day of the festival. People play with cards for recreation and to pass their time. They also gamble. This is a unique feature of the area. Generally, it occurs in other parts of Madhya Pradesh during the festival of lights, Deepawali.

The Bhilala wear new garments on the eighth day of the Gangour festival. They go to the place of the *jawara* and worship the goddess by offering yellow clothes and coconuts. They make ready the wooden chariots in the morning. It is made up of wooden seat and bamboo-sticks. This chariot is adorned with colourful clothes and ornaments. The chariot of Dhaniyar Raja is worn a shirt, a scarf (*dupatta*) and a garland. A colured head of baked earth is fitted on the upper portion of the chariot. The chariot of Gaur Bai is bedecked with dress and ornaments of a female. Dhaniyar Raja is also seen holding a sword and a gun. Four baskets with *jawaras* and one earthen lamp is kept in Gaur Bai's chariot and one basket with one earthen lamp is kept in Dhaniyar Raja's chariot. This work is done by the malefolks. After making ritual worship by the village priest, the chariots are lifted by the women. A woman lifting the Dhaniyar Raja's chariot leads the procession. The procession moves slowly with the accompaniment of the village drummers. The *badawas* also join the procession. Some of the women get possessed by the deity and they move quizically. As soon as the procession reaches the house of any chariot carrier, a long cloth is spread on the road upto the room where the chariot of the deity is to be placed. The room is first cleaned by sprinkling cow-urine and then the chariot is placed on the fixed place. The procession goes to each house where the chariots are to installed and at last, the procession is dispersed.

The women bring fresh water from the well and invite to the couples for meals. The men and women are seated on separate rows. The husband and the wife are asked to utter each others' name. They do like that and pay tribute to the goddess. They visit the goddesses rooms after taking meals. Outsiders are not allowed to enter this room and secrecy is maintained by both the parties.

The chariots are taken out in the courtyard in the evening. Women and girls dance around the chariot for a while, worshiping the goddess and distribute tamol among the assembled persons. The worship is made for four times at night. Someone from the house awakes for the whole night and takes care of the lamp lighted near the goddess and also checks the entry of any animal in the sacred room.

Worship is made thrice on the ninth day. The chariots are taken out and inside for four times in the evening and finally brought to the temple-ground. People come with groundnut and *tamol* which are distributed there. Now, the chariots are lifted by the women and they proceed towards the river at Bhilkhera for immersion of the jawaras. The procession is stopped on the outskirts of the village. The chief badawa makes predictions about the future and warns the villagers about the breakthrough of the epidemics and diseases, if any. He also forecasts about the crop-position in the coming year.

He suggests the ways to meet and avert these calamities. Then the procession moves forward. The lemons are cut in the name of the village deities on the way to river. After reaching there, clothes are spread on the sand and chariots are kept down. Ritual worship of the deity is made and coconut is offered. The Jawara is taken out and immersed in the water. The lower parts of the chariots are dipped in water and washed. The men now lift the chariots and move hastily towards the village, sometimes running and sometimes walking fast. Other people including women also walk fast. Again, they stop at the boundary of the village. The chariots are kept down and then lifted by the women. Now, they proceed towards the village and stop in the temple ground. The dance for a while and then go to their houses. The water brought from the river is sprinkled in the house. The chariot is dismantled.

*Sewai* ( a sweet preparation) is prepared in the houses and relished with joy. Different items of wheat flour are made in the form of ornaments, fried in oil and served to the married persons only. The Balai (drummer) collects grains from each house in the village in the morning and thus, the festival ends.

## RAMNAVAMI

It is celebrated on the ninth day of the black fortnight of the Hindu month of Chaitra. People assemble in the temple and worship the god by doing *arti* (waving a lighted lamp before the idol of Lord Ram).

The Bhilala worship their clan deities on this day and the Patel worship the village deities, especially Moti Mata who is worshipped thrice in a year on the days of Chaitra Shukla Navami, Shrvan Shukla Navami and Shrvan Amavasya.

## HANUMAN JAYANTI

It is celebrated on the day of Chaitra Poornima. Money is collected by raising contributions from the villagers and ritual worship of Hanuman is done before sunrise.

## AKHTEEJ OR AKHATI

It is the main agricultural festival celebrated on the third day of the bright fortnight of the Hindu month of Baisakh. It is the beginning of the new agricultural season. People enjoy this day be feasting and decorating their animals by the use of colours. They do not sleep in day time and remain busy in work for the whole day.

## DIWASA (JIROTI)

It is celebrated on the day of Shravan Amavasya. The graziers start grazing of the village animals from this day. Village deities are worshipped on this day and sweet preparations are made in the houses.

## RAKHI

It is celebrated on the day of Shravan Poornima. A silk thread is tied to a stick and kept on the door of the house. It is worshipped and a coconut is offered. After this, the sisters tie *rakhi* to their brothers. Sisters visit their brothers, houses on this day and celebrate the occasion.

If there are no rains in due time, the Bhilala cook food outside their houses in the Hindu month of shravan (July-August) near a well or any water resource in the morning and worship Indra Deo, the god of rains. Jugdhari (jowar) is worshipped on this day by the village Patel and his wife and then it is brought to the temple. Goats are sacrificed in the evening facing north. The goats are purchased from the common fund by the villagers.

There are a number of festivals like Ganesh Chaturthi, Hartali reej, Rishi Panchami, Halchhat, Dol-gyaras, Janmashtami, etc. which are observed by the tribals in this area. Some of them are traditional Hindu ones while others are purely local and tribal.

## KELYA POONAM

It is celebrated on the day of Kwar (September-October) poornima. The Bhilala worship the domestic animals. The person who possess a good number of cattle and get enough milk, do not sell milk on this day. They prepare curd, ghee and whey out of milk on these days. They distribute whey to others mostly at night and before sunrise.

On the day of Poornima, a black earthen pot is filled with water in the evening and kept at the place of *gotrej* (clan deity). It is put over a heap of wheat grains and is marked at five places with vermilion mixed with ghee. *Khir* or rice is also put at five places. *Hom* offering made to fire is done and a coconut is offered. coconut is distributed among the members of the family.

## DIWALI OR DEEPAWALI

It is celebrated on the day of Kartik (October-November) Amavasya, but the festival starts two days earlier from the day of Dhanteras. On this day, a cow is worshipped, fed jowar and is decorated with peacock feathers. A lamp is lighted in the cattle-shed. Grains and ornaments are worshipped on this day.

The next day is known as Roop Chaudas or Bodaga Chaudas. The Bhilala make *morka, machkundi, nath, ras*, etc. from ropes which are used during different agricultural operations and are related to animals. These are of different colours. They bring an earthen pot (bodaya) from the market and put ash, nail, cowrie-shells, hair, neem-leaves, *karkumba* bush inside that pot. They then sing the following couplet

*"Aisa Paira ko door kar do*

*Gay-Bhais ka bada bhar do"*

Meaning take out the straw and fill up the cattle-shed with cows and buffaloes, and go outside of the house striking that pot and break that into pieces. This is done in the evening. Earthen lamps are lighted at night. On the day of Amavasya, they put some colours on the animals, light lamps at night and invite their close relatives for meals.

On the day of Pariwa (first day of the bright fortnight of the Hindu month of Kartik), the girls visit others' houses and worship the bullocks to get money. They sing songs and dance also. At Bhilkhera, the girls make a circle around with the drummers. Crackers are burnt on these days.

## TIL SANKRANTI

This festival generally falls on 14th January every year. *Laddu* (Sweet ball) of sesame is eaten and also distributed. *Khichara* of jowar (gruel of jowar cooked with ghee and jaggery) is prepared in the houses. Cattle of the village are collected at one place on this day and fed fodder.

Thus, the Bhilala celebrate a number of festivals throughout the year which enliven the social life with joy, happiness and visits of relatives. In some of the festivals, they interact with other groups of people and celebrate them jointly. Bhagoriya Hat and Gal Jatra are two important market festivals which bring life and sense of beauty after the arduous work in the fields during the rains.

Along with festivals, fairs have a very important role in village life, especially in tribal villages. They provide an occasion for personal meet, marketing, sale and exchange of materials, exchange of greetings and thoughts, etc. It also becomes a means of goat attainment.

## BHAGORIYA HAT

Spring season (i.e. in the month of March) begins with Bhagoriya Hat eloper's market) which culminates in Holi. Two market days before the festival of Holi are important. The market day, a fortnight before the commencement of Holi, is called Tehariya Hat i.e. Festival Market and the one just before Holi is called Bhagoriya Hat or the eloper's market. On this day, young boys and girls move out of their houses in their best possible attire. They reach the fair hoping to find a suitable match for themselves. Colourful *lugdas* (woman's wear), red and blue shirts, huge turbans and jewelleries change the otherwise dull look of the market.

The young boys and girls are seen flirting and throwing *gulal* on each other. Young boys roam about purposefully to attract the opposite sex. If a boy likes a girl, he applies *gulal* on her face. If the girl also returns it by applying *gulal*, it signifies her approval. Then a betel leaf is offered to the girl by the boy. If the girl accepts the same, it becomes clear that she is ready to marry him and then they run away from the market to the boy's house or may go to any relative's house. They may pass 2 or 3 days in the jungle also.

It is not always the case that the unmarried boys and girls only select their mates in the Bhagoriya Hats, but sometimes married women also fall in love with some men and run away from the market. In that case, her former husband is entitled to get a compensation from her second husband. In these markets, the Bhil and the Barela show much interest and they particularly get involved. The Bhilala show a little interest and examples of elopement is rare among them. The markets following Holi are appropriately called Ujadya hat (deserted market). The eloper's market functions like an institution for mate selection followed by elopement, which is later on approved by the community.

## GAL JATRA

Gal markets are held in a number of places in the area. These markets are held on the day of Pariwa which is also known as Dhuleti, the day following Holi. On this day, the persons who have taken vows (*mannat*) come to the market and make five rounds in the Gal. Before swinging on the Gal, Bheru Baba is worshipped and sacrifices are made. During swing the person continues throwing of rice on the earth.

Another observance is of Chuli Mata. The woman who has taken *mannat*, walks on fire bare-footed. Chuli Mata is worshipped and offered a coconut.

Besides these, a number of village deities as well as household deities are worshipped by the Bhilalas which act as a bridge between the people and their supernatural world. The fairs and festivals change the routined cycle of work and make afresh and lively. It relieves them from overgrowing tensions and burdons of life and to start a new with enthusiasm and joy.

# 9

# Tribal Festivals in Maharashtra

***Dr. Robin D. Tribhuwan***

## INTRODUCTION

The Tribals live in the forests and naturally isolated regions as culturally distinct groups. These people are known by different names, such as Vanyajati (castes of forest), Vanvasi (inhabitants of forest), Pahari (hill dwellers), Adimjati (original communities), Adivasi (first settlers), Adimjati (Primitive people), Anusuchit Jati (Scheduled Tribes) etc. is the constitutional name covering all of them.

According Bose (1971:2), nearly all tribal people living in India have been in continuous contact with their Hindu neighbours, who live by farming and a large number of specialized manual industries.

This long term acculturation has resulted into tribals borrowing certain customs and traditions of the Hindus. This borrowing is certainly observed among tribes living on the plains. Fairs and festivals are therefore no exception to the rule. Most tribal festivals and fairs have Hindu elements in them.

For example, some of the popular Hindu festivals such as Diwali, Dasera, Pola, Holi etc. are also celebrated by the tribals. What is different, is the degree of glamour associated with festive celebration is far too less amongst tribals than the Hindus.

Despite of this some the traditional festivals of tribals still prevail. For example the Divasa festival of the Dhodia, is exclusively for unmarried girls, the Bada dev festival of the Raj Gonds, the Bhat chasal festival of the Raj Gonds, the Gauri festival of the Malhar Kolis, the Akhaji and Pitra Amosha festivals celebrated by the Bhils and Thakars.

Tribal festivals have certain typical cultural features which are as follows:

1. They celebrate festivals of their village and clan deities. e.g. the Waghdev festival of Bhils.

2. Rituals and ceremonies are given importance.

3. Communal dancing, singing and drinking is associated with festive celebration. Liquor is offered to deities as well.

4. Festival celebration is linked with seasonal changes to the tribals and ultimately on the agricultural occupational pattern.

5. The members of traditional Panchayat are given due respect and recognition during festive celebration.

Given below is an ethnographic account of some of the festivals celebrated by the major tribes of Maharashtra.

**(I) *Festivals Of Mahadev Koli***—Mahadev Koli found in Ahemadnagar, Raigad, Nasik, Pune and Thane Districts. Their festivals are as follows:

**1.** *Holi/Shimga*—Holi is the most important Festival of Mahadev Kolis. All the communities in the hamlet come together to celebrate, the festival collectively and make merry, for couple of days. It is also an important festival of all Scheduled Tribes in the State.

Fire is lit at a common place in the hamlet and worshipped as a Holi. Five coconuts called 'Vatya' and five Bhakris of rice flour called 'Papdya' are tied to the top of the pole. The firewood kept around the pole is theem lighted and fire is worshipped as Holi by a man who enjoys the hereditary right of doing so. Persons assembled around the Holi, they throw pieces of firewood and dung cakes into it and worship it. A few persons of the tribe also take fire rounds around the Holi. Generally each household in the hamlet is expected to tie atleast five papdyas of rice flour to the pole on this occasion. Generally Holi is lit in the evening after Sun-set and is kept burning through out the night. After worshipping the Holi, those who are given to drinking liquor enjoy till late at night. On the next day they mostly indulge intaking liquor and throuwing coloured water on each other.

2. *Pola*—Pola is the festival of bullocks celebrated on the last day of Shravan. On this occasion the bullocks are washed with water and decorated. Their homes are painted. In the evening, all the bullocks are assembled in the open ground of the village and later on taken to the masters house where they are worshipped and given cooked food to eat. No work is taken from them on that day.

3. *Dasera*—It falls on the tenth day of bright half of Ashwin. It is not so much important to the Mahadev Koli.

4. *Diwali*—It falls on the last of day of Ashwin on the first day of Kartik. This festival is observed as a holiday except offering worship to household deities. Their hamlets are decorated. They wear new clothes and enjoy fire work.

(II) ***Festivals of Warlis.*** Warlis are Predominently found in Thane District. Their festivals are as follows:

1. *Nag Panchami*—On the Nagpanchami they worship "Varul" (ant hill) with an offering of milk and eggs. Some draw picture of a serpent on a wall and worship it with an offering of milk.

2. *Pola*—Pola is celebrated by those who own bullocks. Those who do not possess bullocks obsere the day as a holiday.

3. *Pitru Amavasya*—It is observed in memory of all the dead ancestors and put a portion of the food into the kitchen chulah (hearth) for some purpose. They offer cooked food to the crows in the name of their ancestors.

4. *Dasera*—They worship household dieties. In the evening they distribute Apta leaves (Bauhinia racemosa) among elders and friends. They also worship Chedha and offer a coconut.

5. Diwali—They celebrate this on the last day of Kartik. Worship household deities with an offering of chavli, cucumber and such other vegetables. They drink liquor, dance and make merry. Women also dance on this occasion.

6. *Holi*—It is observed by this tribe. A bamboo pole is erected in an open place in the hamlet. Faggets, dung cakes, grass and dried leaves of trees are put around it. Fire papdya, cakes of rice flour and a garland of some pieces of coconuts are tied to the pole. The pole is worshipped and the heap is set

on fire. Any person who wishes to worship Holi then throws a coconut in the fire. Lights and inconce sticks takes out the half baked coconut and its kernel is distributed as prasad to the persons assembled.

A newly married couple are expected to celebrate the first Holi at the house of the girl's father. On this occasion the boy and the girl take coconuts in their hands, move round the Holi and throw coconuts in the fire. The borne fire continues for a couple of days. Fresh mango is offered to the Holi on this occasion. When worship of Holi is over, those interested take liquor, dance and make merry.

**(III)** ***Festivals Of Kokna***—Kokna are found in Nasik, Thane and Dhule Districts. Their main festivals are as follows:

1. *Padva*—Padva is celebrated by the Koknas on the that day. It is celebrated by hoisting a Gudhi (metal pot over a stick) on the house. All the house hold deities are worshipped on this occasion and sweets are made.

2. *Akhaji*—It is observed especial by the Koknas. They sow seeds of rice, nagli, warai, maize and khurasini in a basket filled with earth some days prior to the day of celebration and water it every day so that the seedlings sprout on the festival day. These seedlings are worshipped on this day and later on thrown near the wall or a temple. Family deities are also worship women ding songs and dance. Some Koknas offer food to crows in memoy of their ancestors.

3. *Teriavas*—is celebrated in Ashadhi amavasya. It is principally observed by the Koknas. They offer leaves of Teri plant to their family deities that day. The leaves are cooked as vegetables, offered to their deities and eaten as prasad by family members.

4. *Diwali and Dasera*—Koknas celebrate Dassera by worshipping family deities and exchanging apta (Bauhinia racemosa). They worship village deity-Mhasoba and Vetal on this day. Some Koknas observe a fast for nine days.

Diwali is celebrated for two days. Bullocks are worshipped, liquor is taken and pawri dance is performed.

5. *Holi*—Holi is an important festival of the Koknas.

6. *Pitru Amavasya*—They observe Pitru Amavasya on the last day of Bhadrapad, offer cooked food to crows on that day, in the name of ancestors.

7. *Community Festivals*—Koknas also celebrate certain common festivals with other tribes such as Warli, Thakars and Katkaris. Those are

   ***(a)*** *Khadicha Dev*—On a convenient day in June before sowing of seeds to protect the new crop. They worship Kortoba and some grains of Nagli, rice.

   ***(b)*** *Saticha Dev*—This is celebrated on full moon day of Margashirsha for the production of crops and fields.

**(IV)** ***Festivals Of Thakar/Thakur***—Thakurs are found in Pune, Nasik, Ahemadnagar, Raigad and Thane Districts.

1. *Pitru Amavasya*—The Thakurs celebrate Pitru Amavasya to enjoy the company of their ancestral spirits, who are believed to visit the village on Pitru Amavasya. On this eve, they perform a dance known as Dhambdi. This dance is performed by the elderly folk. On the next day they offer cooked food to the crows.

2. *Dasera Diwali*—The Thakurs also celebrate Dasera and Diwali as the local Hindus do.

**(V)** ***Festivals of Katkari***—Katkaris are found in Thane, Raigad, Pune, Ahmednagar, Ratnagiri and Sindhudurg Districts.

(1) *Holi*—Holi is one of the important festival of Katkaris, they light a separate Holi in their Hamlet. They erect a bamboo pole preferably after sunset, with five papdyas (cakes of rice flour) lied to its top, each tribal household in the Hamlet is expected to tie five papdyas faggots and dung cakes are piled around this pole. The pole is worshipped and the firewood is set-on fire as holi by the tribesmen, who enjoy the hereditary rites of doing so he goes five times round the fire, after that tribesmen assembled their throw fire wood dung cakes and coconuts into the Holi. Some interested persons drink liquor and dance till late night. On the next day they worship the household Gods, dance to the Dhol music house to house and demand gift from the villagers. The money collected is mostly spent on the drinks, and dances staged by them on this occasion are restricted to men only.

(2) *Diwali*—Among the Katkaris, Diwali which falls on the last day of Ashwin and the following two days in mostly on occasion for rejoicing and merry making, drinking liquor, singing songs and dancing. The Katkaris of Thane stage tarpa dances on this occasion both men and women participate in the dances.

**(VI)** ***Festivals of Malhar Koli***—Malhar Kolis are found in Thane District.

**(1)** *Gauri*—Gauri is celebrated on the seventh day of the bright half of the Bhadrapad. Gauri is believed to be the mother of Ganapati. It is chiefly a festival of a women. On the festival day a clay image of Gauri is installed in the house of the well to do man of the tribe, where all the women living in the locality go to worship. After worship, womens sing and ance before the deity to the accompanyment of the Dholki, men also take part in the dance. The image is immersed on the next day.

**2.** *Pitru Amavasya*—Pitru Amavasya is observed in the memory of all dead ancestors. It falls on the last day of Bhadrapad, cooked food is offered to crows in the name of the dead.

**3.** *Sakad-Chauth*—It is celebrated on the fourth day on the dark half of the Bhadrapad, women and bhagats fast during the day, worship the moon, after it is raisen and then take food. No other rite is performed.

**4.** *Diwali*—Among the Malhar Kolis Diwali is restricted to the last day of Ashwin and first day of Kartik. On these days they take bath, put on new clothes, eat sweets, decorate their and houses. Drinking country liquor and dancing are the other important features.

**5.** *Holi*—It is observed as a community festival by all castes and tribe, in the month of March/April.

**(VII)** ***Festivals of Dhodia***—This tribe is found in Thane District, and South Gujarat.

**1.** *Divasa*—The Divasa festival falls on Ashadhi Pournima. It is celebrated by organizing mock marriages of dolls, on a large scale. It is festival of unmarried girls. Married men and women however do not keep aloof from the celeration. The girls prepare male and female dolls and marry them in a small pendol which is specially erected for this purpose. This marriage is performed from most of the detail observed during marriages. The dolls are made-up of cloth, when it is eve these dolls are ceremoniously carred to a river in palas or teak leaf cups and immeresed. This mock marriage is not performed separately in each house, it is performed jointly. If the village is small, that is only one celebration. In big village, a group of marriages are arranged in one or two of its hamlets.

2. *Narali Pournima:* Narali Pournima falls on the full moon day of Shravan. The chief activity of the day is to throw coconut into the rivers excepting these, this no other rituals are performed on this occasion.

3. *Sakad Chouth*—It comes on the fourth day of the dark half of the Bhadrapada. A married man or women preferably the head of the household fasts during the day and worships the moon on the moon rise by drawing an he image of the moon on the moon on the path (stool) in a sandal wood paste a few persons draw a circle of rice flour (kumkum and haldi) on a path, keep a tulsi plant on it and walk around it after the same is worshipped.

**(VIII)** ***Festivals of Bhil***—Bhils are found in Nasik, Dhule, Jalgaon, Thane, Raigad, Ahmednagar, Pune, Satara and Sangli Districts.

1. *Akaji*—This is a day for celebrating visit of one ancestor to the village by offering cooked food to him. It falls on vaishaka and it is also known as Akhatri. On this day the Bhils worship an earthen pot and feed a man belonging to different clan as pitar (ancestor) and offer cooked food to crows in the name of ancestors in the family. They regard the day to be an auspicious one and believe that any work started on this day, that work will turn out well.

2. *Nagpanchami*—The festival is celebrated on Sharavan sudh five, in honour of cobras. The worship of waruls (ant hills) with an offering of milk it its main feature, only a few Bhils observe this festival.

3. *Dasera*—This festival falls on the tenth day of the bright half of Ashwin on this day the Bhils worship at the usual fixed place in the village with offering of a coconut, arecanut, beetle leaf, liquor, a few grains of rice and a hen, farms impliments are also worshipped. Some people feed a mon of tribe as a pitar. They take processions in the villages. The procession is led by a Bhagat, who walks in front with a long bamboo pole in his hand to which are tied a garland of flowers a piece of cloth and a peacock weather a goat is them taken around the village, and village gate. Its four feet and horms are cut and buried ceremonialy in ground by the side of fire. It tail is cut and kept hanging from the roof above, later-on the remaining portion of the goat is cooked and distributed as prasad.

4. *Pola, Diwali and Gudhipadva*—These festivals are observed like caste of the Hindus.

5. *Waghdeo*—Waghdeo is observed in the honour of Tigergod and it is believed by doing so they are protected from the tigers roaming around the village. The Bhil observe this festivals on full moon day of Shravan. On that day one tribesmen becomes a tiger and the one put him with clods of earth. To avoid these clods, he starts running for a few minutes. On coming back milk is offered to him. All the tribesmen then go on the neighboring forest and worship the place where a tiger is believed to be found with a offering of cooked rice, milk and a vegetable dish of Tandla leaves. After distribution this as prasad of the tiger god, a portion of it is kept in the house on a teak leaf as it is believed that by doing so they are protected from the tigers. The Bhils of Dhanora observe this festival on the Sunday prior to the full moon day of Shravan. Early that morning they go into their village and fixed their five or six branches of pulas tree on coming home a branch of the same tree is fixed in the compound of the house and at the place where the cowdung is stored. In the evening they enjoy a community dinner or on the bank of the river or any other convenient place. Before that a man of the tribe who becomes a tiger is offered milk to drink. This man then starts running and children pelt him with stones. The man who becomes tiger on this occasion observes the fast and takes his meal only at evening at the time of the community dinner.

6. *Nilchri or Nanduradev*—It is observed on any suitable day preferably a Sunday in Jyeshta after the rains are setting. The day is fixed by the panchas, on the day of festival they keep from impliments in the field near the village boundry and worship them with an offering with a coconut, eggs, liquor and handful of rice and wheat.

(IX) ***Festivals of Korku:*** Korkus are found in Amravati, district.

1. The Korkus celebrate Dasera, Diwali, Holi and Nagpanchami. Pola is celebrated in Shravan Amavasya when their bullocks are washed, decorated and given rest.

2. Three important fairs are held in Melghat in honour of (a) Mahadev (b) Meghnath (c) Dhoroba (all Hindu Gods) which are attended by hundreds of Korkus.

**(X)** ***Festivals of Gonds***—Gonds are found in Melghat, Gadduchi, Chandrapur, Yavatmal and Aurangabad Districts.

**1.** *Bhavaicha Sal*—It is celebrated in June. Small boys tie a frog in the centre of pestil and more about from house to house singing songs. Housewives throw bucket full of water at them and then give them some grains, chillies etc. These boys collect the article of food till mid-day. Go to a place outside the village site cook the provisions, they have collected and consume the food this festival is essentially for boys (Raj Gond).

**2.** *Bada Dev*—Another Raj Gond festival is known as Motha/Bada Dev. The hair of Neel Gye (wild cow) is put in a silver socket and the socket is pressed so that a chamari like shape is given to it. The socket is them kept in a new earthern pot after wrapping it in a Kharwa cloth, the earthern pot is tied to Mauha Brandi. The bhagat who is also known as "Katola" worships it. On the festival day the son-in-law or a guest of the Katola climbs the tree on which the earthern pot is tied and throws it down. The Katola washes the feet of the person and collects the socket which symbolizes the Dev. The Dev is placed on a woolen blanket and carried in a procession to the village with music.

From there, the Dev is taken to the river bathed in its water and worshipped by the Katola.

A goat is sacrificed. The Dev is taken back in procession tot he Mauha tree by the Kotola's guest or son-in-law and restored to the brandy as before. The Dev is again brough in the month of Bhavai. The Katola mormally worships the Dev twice a month, on full moon day and new moon day by standing below the tree, but the Dev is not brought down.

**3.** *Diwali and Holi*—Diwali and Holi are the most important festivals. Diwali is observed for ten days. They sing songs to the accompaniment of flute and painjans. Men and women participate in singing. They move from village to village, sing songs and collecting money as grains. On the last day they light a small earthern lamp and worship the deity of Akhadi. They also worship buffaloes and other cattle on the outskirts of the village.

**(XI)** ***Festivals of Kolam***—Kolams are found in Yavatmal, Gadchiroli, Chandrapur and Amravati Districts.

Kolams observe all Hindu festivals and observe few tribal festivals as well. During Diwali, they decorate their huts and arrange the Dandar dance. Only men take part in this dance, they wear saris and cholis while dancing. They put on masks made up of paper. These are Ganapati, tiger etc. at the time of the dance. They enjoy Holi by feasting, singing, dancing and drinking liquor.

Holi is also known as Simga. When the fire is lit every person from each house comes with a piece of bread, and a port of water, and moves around the stacks for once in an anti dock manner. The bread is offered to the fire. Rest of the night they sing, dance, and drink.

## Kota-Mandos

Kolams associated this festival with new year as it corresponds to the Gudi Padva festival of Maharashtra. Villagers keep their houses and village premises clean. From this day their new agricultural season starts. Fowl sacrifices are offered to the village deities. Tappate (drums) and Vas (flutes) are played at night by men folk.

## Goan Bandhani

Kolams refer to Goan bandhani as Sati festival. It is the greatest festival of the Kolam. Relatives and friends are invited on this day. The village boundaries of a Kolam settlement are worshipped so as to prevent evil, misfortune and epidemics in the villages. Village deities and the boundaries are offered fowl and/or goats blood. Communal feasting takes place. Shamans perform the rites of Kassa pakad (rite of prevention). Every house hold participates in this festival.

## Vitanal-Vanga Kad

It is a festival of productive magic for Kolams. They celebrate it before the sowing operation. Seeds are offered to village and Clan deities, in order to get their blessings for a successful harvest during that year.

## Polum

This festival is meant for bullocks and other cattle in the house. Kolams bathe their bulls. Their horns and body is decorated with paint and give them good fodder. They are not employed in any agricultural work that day. Anthropological interpretation of Polum would be that it is a festival celebrated to thank the bullocks for their precious contribution in cultivation and of course production of cows and bulls.

Some of the other festivals of Kolam associated with harvest are Dasera and Diwali. Sita dali is yet another festival celebrated by Kolam cultivators before growing cotton. They worship village and clan deities before harvesting the cotton crop.

**Concluding Remarks**

Out of the 47 tribes of Maharashtra an attempt has been made to provide glimpses of festivals celebrated by major tribes of the state. Tribal celebrate festivals to express their joy over good harvest, sound health and change of seasons. Rituals associated with tribal festivals are productive, preventing and curative in nature. I would call them the rituals of survival.

**REFERENCES**

1. Hazra D, 1983, The Kolam of Yeotmal, A.S.I., Calcutta.

2. Rao K. Mohan, 1990, The Kolams, A primitive Tribe in Transition Book Links Corporations, Hyderabad.

# 10

# Nyokum: The Festival of the Nyishis of Arunachal Pradesh

***Ms. Indra Mallo***

Nestled among the foothills of the Eastern Himalayas of Arunachal Pradesh lie the Dafla hills. The Nyishis or Daflas as they were earlier called, occupy the south central part in the state of Arunachal Pradesh. The Nyishis tribe is mostly found in four districts of Arunachal pradesh ie.. Papum Pare, Lower Subansiri, Upper Subansiri, and East Kameng districts. The Nyishis are the single largest tribe of Arunachal Pradesh, comprising about 30,000 souls.

Nyishis speak the Nyishi dialect belonging to the Tibeto-Burman language family. They don't have a script. Generally, the Roman script is used for communicating. As is commonly found among other tribes, the Nyishi people also have a rich oral tradition of folklore, tribal history and folk wisdom. "Nyokum", the annual festival of the Nyishis is an example of this rich oral tradition when for days together the story of creation is narrated by the head priest and his assistants, regaling the common folk with their treasure of knowledge about their ancestors and their feats in creating this world.

## SOCIAL ORGANIZATION

The Nyishi tribe follows a clan based system of kinship relations. Lineage is traced through the male members only. The lineage of the clan can be traced to the first ancestor i.e., "Abotani" or Father Tani. Members of a clan are considered brothers.

They are distinguished by their surnames. During marriage, clan exogamy is the rule. Any marriage between two persons belonging to the same clan is considered incestous.

The family system is both patriarchal and patrilocal. Authority vests in the eldest male member of the family. There is also the practise of polygyny i.e., one husband and many wives. During marriage, it is the groom who has to compensate the bride's family by paying bride price. Bride price takes the form of both cash and kind. Usually "mithun" or traditional cattle is given as bride price. Incase of divorce, the bride price is returned to the groom. Thus marriage is seen as contract between two individual families.

## NYOKUM

It is the annual festival of the Nyishi tribe. It's held in the month of February (23$^{rd}$-26$^{th}$). Interestingly, till the late 1960's, Nyokum was celebrated in an individual manner, i.e., limited to a village area. But with increasing awareness about ethnic tribal identity, Nyokum became the symbol of a united tribal identity. Soon it was recognised as the major festival of the Nyishis of Arunachal Pradesh.

The word Nyokum comprises of two distinct meanings-nyok or land and kum or people. Nyokum is the invocation of the spirit forces in nature to ensure the harmony, well being and prosperity of the people who have observed Nyokum.

The main prayer structure of Nyokum is made of bamboo, called the "yugin". Alongside the 'yugin' sacrificial animals are tethered. Like, cows, mithuns, and goats. Often one finds small chickens hung from bamboo poles of the 'yugin". The "nyib" or the traditional priest specifies the number and kinds of animal for sacrifice, or any other offering to be made. There are no idols in this worship. Neither is there any permanent structure. Besides the animal sacrifice, beer made from millet seeds and rice paste is used.

People turn up wearing their traditional clothes during this time. The men dress in a cotton 'eri' robe draped from the shoulder and reaching the thighs. From their neck hangs a variety of bead jewellery necklaces. Often semi precious stones like turquoise adorn these necklaces. The men's attire is topped by a bamboo woven cap on the head. This cap is decorated with feathers or furs of wild animals. The beak of the hornbill is a favorite ornament for the traditional cap. The women also dress in their finery of 'par ej', earrings bead necklaces, topped with a headdress made of finely scraped bamboo. All in all, it is a real fine sight to see Nyishi men and women celebrate Nyokum in the way their ancestors had celebrated it before them.

Both men and women take part in the festivities equally. There is singing and dancing before the head priest or nyib comes with his attendants to perform the main ritual. Guests are welcomed with rice paste powder, and 'opo' or millet seed beer which is scooped in dried gourd ladles. The song and dance are performed in a group. Usually men and women hold hands in a circular form and sing and dance these lines.. "Nyokum bo tapa debe".. And sometimes men dance mock fights with 'dao' (short sword) and shield made of animal hide. In between all this, the children of course are all over the place and join in the fun. The community participation and spirit of brotherhood make Nyokum a true celebration of life itself.

Nowadays, Nyokum is celebrated each year in a different place within the Nyishi inhabited region. This has greatly aided in raising the consciousness of the people and helped in mobilising them towards community participation. Nyokum is usually held in community grounds of the area. The proceedings of the festival is open and welcome for each and for all without distinction of high or low. Besides the traditional part of the festival, during the evenings, cultural program competition are also held. These have become especially popular with the youth that get a chance to display their artistic talents and inclinations. These competitions encourage the traditional art forms to flourish. It has become a means to reach out to the young to make them feel proud of their tribal heritage. State dignitaries like the Governor and the Chief Minister are often invited as chief guests to such occasions. The active organizations of the Nyishi community are, the All Nishi Students Union (ANSU), the Nishi Elite society, and The Native People's Committee (Capital Complex).

## CONCLUSION

I have attempted in this paper to give an overview of Nyokum festival. However, as I am aware, this paper doesn't deal with the larger anthropological and sociological aspects. I have attempted a brief descriptive record of the festival and the changes it has witnessed over the years. Serious study of the ritual aspect found in the oral tradition and the changing nature of the organization of the festival will contribute to study of the processes of social change through consciousness of identity formation and it's implications.

The Nyishi tribe has not really been the study of any serious theoretical research so far. But there has been documentation undertaken by the Research Deptt. of Arunachal Pradesh. These are valuable as monographs of the changing face of the tribe.

❑❑❑

# 11

# Tribal Festivals in Kalhandi, of Orissa State

*Kunj Bihari Nayak*

## INTRODUCTION

Festivals are an important part of the cultural life of Kalhandi-district in Western Orissa. The role of environment is so dominant here that the people, specially tribals must always bow before, it in humility and reverence. This is expressed by them through their festivals. The seasons have played a dominant role is shaping the festivals of Kalhandi. Every season has it is own appropriate festivals, each being largely influenced by the climatic needs or other characteristics of the particular season. The whole appearance of the hilly-forest, land-scape changes with the seasons, so does it transform the activities, interests and rituals of the tribal people of Kalahandi in western Orissa.

Infact, fairs and festivals of Kalahandi offer a most frank an untinted glimpse of its people, their cultural heritage and social background, their love for the present and their hopes and aspirations for the future. We would find teeming multitude of people .... young and old like ..... in their traditional clothes, lost to the rhythmic beats of drums and music in dances and songs. The charm of music is so deeply blended in their veins, that even a faint breeze of music would make their feet restless in ecstatic frenzy wherever they are, be it in field or forest. The fields and forests here do not only grow grain and wood, these also weave music. Toilsome routine of the people in fields and forests is thus blended here with songs and dances, and that is why people in pleasure even in hard and laborious living. We would find here sowing-songs and harvesting- songs as well as songs of jungles besides many other forms. Similarly there are numerous dances. All these faculties fund collective expression in the tribal fairs and festivals.[1]

The fairs and festivals of Kalahandi are, thus, not simply the crowd-gathering of people for mundane objective, but these are the spontaneous expressions of their social integrity and cultural coherence.. and occasion for collective rejoicing. Nevertheless, festivals serve to mitigate, and more positively soften the otherwise severe feelings of struggle with the elements around the year. These provide occasions to display their joys and jovial sentiments, renew social contacts, strengthen community relations and finally in Durkheimian words, maintain social solidarity.

Moreover, the tribal festivals of Kalahandi are also educative in nature. The elements of social orientation and religious cultivation are inherent in them. The local Gods and Goddesses around whom these festivals are organized, some of them like Manikeswari, Stambhesvari, have little written records about their origin (Padhi H.S.: 1996 & M.S.A.: 1991).

Thus, the development of some cults is shrouded in mystery, while that of others in traditionally transmitted myths and legends. However, those festivals serve the need or social co-operation not only for economic sustenance of the people, but for their cultural survival as well.

According to R. Briffault (2), festivals generally represent collective ritual, specially for the primitive people, who through different social groups like the family, clan or tribe participate in them for the welfare of the entire community. As the agricultural operation is collective among the tribal peoples, they perform community festivals which represent the rites variously called as fertility rites, vegetation rites, productivity rites etc. Naturally, the festivals of agricultural people, resembling religious rites, have the social urge of fertility, fecundity, generation and all that is connected with the very existence of such people (Mukhopadhaya S., 1975:75).

Correspondingly, in various regions of Kalahandi, any religious or cultural festival is called as Yatra while the term Yatra, means folk-drama as popularly known in the north eastern regions of Orissa. However, there are mainly two patterns of festivals in Kalahandi. 1) the community festivals observed by tribals are based on their religion, agriculture and livelihood; and II) the other pattern is derived or evolved from the Aryan religious ideology and praxis, for instance the festivals like Ratha-Yatra (Car-festival), Holi, Shivratri, Maker Sankranti etc. which are observed throughout Orissa.

It is believed that most of the festivals in Kalahandi, whether based on agriculture, livelihood, entertainment or religious orientation, have been evolved form the tribal communities. Even if in accordance with customary rules, different festivals are observed throughout the year. At each phase of agricultural and livelihood activities for instance in the beginning of ploughing, sowing, weeding, transplanting, reaping, hunting or food-gathering and collecting the mother Earth or village deities are worshiped with offering of all the Nature-give fruits and crops. The main purpose behind these festivities lies in the predominant interests of tribals or other local people in this region for earning livelihood, for security of jungles, for success in hunting and procuring forest products, for protection of ones body and health, for rain and higher agricultural products, or to be saved from epidemics and other diseases.

Among religious and entertainment festivals in Kalahandi, the most important common ones are: Chait -Parab, Dashehara, Toki Parab, Podha-Puja, Holi etc. Besides, a number of festivals are celebrated by some specific caste-groups and tribes, for example: Chait-Yatra, Mati-Yatra, Akshyatritiya, Asharkhena-Yatra, or Rani-Parab of Paraja tribe, Kendu-Yatra of Kutia-Kondh tribe, Dhami-Yatra of Lanjegarh, Budha Raja Parab of Ampani, Shemi Yatra of the Kondh tribe and so on. All these festivals are celebrated under a big tree and in a wide ground near each village deity. During festival, the most common social fact that observed among village communities involved is the "we-feeling" or solidarity for successful planning and organization of all activities. As a common rule, no one in the village takes fruit or food without offering it to the deities in such community festivals. Even agricultural or any other seasonal routine activities are allowed to start unless and until such activities are initiated during certain specific festivals. For instance, until the Chaul-Dhua Parab (rice -washing) festival comes, people continue in cooking unwashed rice. Similarly, until the rain-festival is passed, the agricultural activities like weeding, transplanting etc. are not started.

In the following pages, some important festivals of the tribes in Kalahandi are described in detail. (3).

1. ***Chit—Parab Or Chaitra—Yatra:*** On any Tuesday falling between the new moon of dark fortnight and the full moon of bright fortnight in the month of Chitra (March-April), the village deity is worshiped with traditional geity. On this day, the deity called "Boel" is carried in a procession to move around the village. In this procession, unmarried girls carry on their heads small pitchers (Kalasi) filled with turmeric water and visit each house-hold,

the deity Boel and the accompanied auspicious pitchers are worshiped with full devotion and respect.

The local people in Kalahandi consider this procession as "Chaitra-Yatra". But in some areas of the old kalhandi like in Thorampur, Kalampur, Jaya-Patana, and Koksara, the Chait-parab of some tribal communities are observed as entertainment based festival since this festival falls in the month of Chaitra (March-April), it is popularly known as Chaitra festival.

Generally, the livelihood of tribes in Kalahandi revolves round two aspects i.e. agricultural and forest products. The agricultural activities goon between the Akshi-Trutiya festival in he month of Ashadha (June-July) and the Pousa-Purnima festival in the month of January. After the agricultural production is over, half of the year is spent by the tribals in collecting food and other items from the forest. During this period, the tribal in Kalahandi get plenty of leisure time. Since there is a tradition of living merely by means of collecting fruits-roots and hunting-gathering in the jungle, the young tribals in this region enjoy their time in merry-making, dancing, singing and making hearty union of couples. Therefore, the symbols of hunting dance and romantic, love-making are observed as distinct features in this Chitra festival.

On the day of festival, the priest-cum-astrologer (Disari) standing near the village deity (called Semal Mdua) announces the "Chait-Parab". All the villagers, young and old gather together there. A sacrifice of hen or goat is offered to the village deity. Then having a community feast the villagers pass the whole night in dancing singing and merry-making.

In the early morning of next day, on the request of village women, all the men-folk carrying arrows in their hands travel into a nearby jungle in quest of hunting. Thus, as a custom, this festival initiates a traditional activity of tribal livelihood as hunting and gathering once in every year. Since both struggle for livelihood and the romantic love-making for entertainment are two important aspects of tribal life, the programmes of hunting, singing, dancing and merry-making becomes a part and parcel of this festival. Besides, one more distinctive feature in this festival is that young boys and girls are offered a change to exchange and communicate their hearts to each other by means of singing romantic songs and dancing hand-in-hand and finally to select their respective life-partners for marriage.

2. ***Mati—Yatra or Bihan—Chhinna—Yatra:*** In the dark fortnight of Chaitra (march-April), the village priest or astrologer (Jhankar or Jani), announces

an auspicious day for Mati-yatra. This festival basically symbolizes the worship of Soil (Mati) that is the cultivating land for the purpose of expecting higher growth of agricultural products. Thus, in this festival, a small-ball like clay is kept on the alter of village deity. The priest (Jhankar) collects a basket of sowing-paddy from the villagers.

While offering a hen-sacrifice to the deity, the priest dedicates that basket of sowing -paddy and prays for the higher productivity of land in the year. After this ritualistic function is over, the priest equally distributes that basket of sowing-paddy among all the farmers apply a bit of the worshiped clay on their foreheads as a symbol of blessing.

This customary ritual is in wellknown in sociological sense as a "fertility rite" which in other words signifies a desire for higher fertility of the land in the coming year. After the village farmers come back home with handful of that auspicious sowing paddy, the women at home devotionally worship that paddy and preserve it till the day of "Akshyatrutiya" (3rd day of paddy-sowing month that is in June-July) comes. On the day of "Akshyatrutiya" that worshiped paddy is again ritually mixed with larger amount of sowing-paddy and then taken to sow them in cultivating field.

However, as this festival (Mati-Yatra) ritually begins with\a symbolic worship of a ball-like clay, this, festival is also called as "Kadhuo-Yatra". On this festival day, every house-hold sacrifices the blood of a hen to the soil-deity (mati Devi) or to the mother earth for the hope of higher productivity and enjoys the day in feasting and merry-making.

3. ***Akshyatrutiya or Paddy-Sowing Festival:*** This festival is known as agricultural based festival throughout Orissa. It is observed on the 3rd day of bright fortnight in the month of Ashadha (June-July). On this day, the village farmers mix the worshiped paddy with the larger amount of sowing paddy and then they carry it in new baskets veiled with new red clothes to the cultivating field where after worshiping the land they start sowing. On this day, the tribals in kalhandi worship their ancestors called as "Duma". Baring differences in their rituals, all Aryans and tribals consider this festival as a agricultural one since it symbolizes the "fertility rites" for higher production of food crops.

4. ***Ashar—Khena Yatra Or Gangadi—Yatra:*** This festival is observed in-between the 11th day of bright-fortnight and the full-moon day in the month

of Ashadha (June-July). It is also called as "Gangadi-Yatra" because the Hindu deity Ganga is worshiped as a village deity in each and every village of Kalahandi. After the earlier sown paddy got sprouted, the land needs weeding and transplanting, which are initiated after this festival. That is why this festival is considered as transplanting festival (Ashar-Khena Yatra).

A few days before the festival, the village priest (jhankar) calls a meeting of all the villagers and selects an auspicious day for the festival. On the day of festival, the village farmers again bring rice and hen to offer to the village deity. After performing a ritual, the priest smears the blood of the sacrificed hen on the alter and weapon of the deity. After sacrificing every hen and returns the rest to the respective villagers who cook it at their home and eat as "Prashad". The next day onwards the weeding and transplanting activities start in the field. If any farmer has already transplanted before this festival, he is bound to offer an extra hen to sacrifice before the deity for the purpose of satisfying her. Infact, this in a sociological sense, a socially sanctioned penalty for the committed sin.

5. ***Rani-Parab:*** Rani-Parab is one of the most important festivals of the Paroja tribe in Kalahandi. Besides Paroja, Bhatara, Kondh tribes and other people co-habiting in the Southern part of kalahandi also observe this festival. It is celebrated on any auspicious day of dark forthnight in the month of Shravan (July -August).

This festival is similar with "Ashar-Khena". In the month of Ashadha (June-July), the tribal farmers sow paddy and after it becomes transplantable they bring those to worship before either home-deity or village deity. While offering puja on this day of festival, those plants are dedicated in the name of their ancestors and a goat or a hen is sacrificed just to satisfy the deity. People enjoy the night in feasting. In the next day morning, the farmers again carry those plants to their fields and after worshiping the mother land they start transplanting.

6. ***Harali—Unas Parab:*** The new moon of Shravana (July-August) is called as "Harali-Unas" in Kalahandi. This festival is specially celebrated to convey greatness to the Mother -Earth, just after the corns in the field get turned green. This festival is also called as "Harial Simbonga Parab" by the Santal tribes.

On the day of festival, all the farmers in the village again offer a puja (ritual) in the cornfield with unboiled cow-milk, turmeric branches, valia, khaens, devadun or satawari etc. After pouring milk on the land the farmers plant the turmeric branches. On this day, the black-smith (Lohora) plants a iron pin on the door of each household and after chanting a hymn for the purpose of protecting people from evil forces and beings on the same day, a village leader of servant (Nariha) also keeps some branches of forest turmeric, Devadun, Khaes and Valia on the door of each house-hold. Infact, all these branches, leaves and roots have some Ayurvedic medinal value to protect people from the poisonous snakes and scorpions. Thus, here the beliefs and rituals of the tribes co-opt with their social psychology and which have been consciously designed for the sake of their health and security.

7. ***Donsara or Belsara yatra:*** The new-moon day falling in the dark forthnight of Bhadrab (August-September) is called as "Saptapuri Amawasya" in Kalahandi. This day stands as an important auspicious day for the Hindus in Orissa. However, the festival observed on this day is called by the tribals in kalahandi as "Pora-Unas". It is because, during this period a deep red-coloured bunches of followers blossoms in the jungle which are known as "Pora-Phool".

This festival is specially meant for the children. Thus, on the day of festival, parents or other guardians after offering a puja (ritual) to the village deity, make playing carts (made of wood) for their children. On the cart, they decorate various toys like pistols, bullocks, elephants, horses etc. with that "Pora-Phool". Children wearing new dresses and enjoying sweets at home come out in groups to play with the carts on the village road. This play is known as "Gedi-Khel".

In the evening, this play is discontinued in the village until the same day comes in the next year. Children burry all their toys (Gedis) in a white-ant hill lying outside village, which is called as "Duker-Kheda". The "Duker" is a deity of diseases. Infact, behind this play, there is a traditional belief among people that if that deity (Duker) goes out of the village with those playing toys, all the diseases affecting villages also disappear. After all, this festival stands for the entertainment of villagers in general and of children in particular.

8. ***Nuakhai or Nawarnna Parab:*** This is a agricultural based festival observed through out Western Orissa. It comes on an auspicious day falling between the 3rd day and the 13th day of bright fortnight in the month of Bhadrav (August -September). The day is fixed by a decision taken by the village priest, astrologer and some other village leaders. If there is unfortunately any

case of impurity as associated with birth or death threads, the festival day is post-poned to some other auspicious day in the same month. This custom has been infact till today.

This festival is named as (Nuakhai or Nwarnna) because it initiates to take new food, made up of new rice grown in the field. All the villagers follow him. The husked new rice is called as "Nwarnna" and the feasting of a food (Khir) made of that rice, cow-milk, ghee and sugar is called as "Nuakhai". After the priest offers this food to the village deity, all the villagers wearing new dresses are allowed to take the food as "Prasad".

Although each family in the village prepares its own nwarnna, as a customary norm all the families of a clan are supposed, to come to the house of their kin-head just to offer that nwarnna to their original ancestors and then to collectively enjoy that food as a traditional custom. In the end all respectfully bow head before the kin-head and after greeting each other come back to their respective home. Besides, there is also a custom to enjoy Nwarnna in every joint family, in case it is impossible to arrange such programme in the house of kin-head. But the pattern of feasting is that all irrespective of age and sex in the community, rich and poor, ruler and ruled dine together that Nwarnna only on the leaf-plates. Thus, it symbolizes equality of all before their ancestral Gods.

The specific time to enjoy Nowarnna is between morning and noon. In the afternoon, all the villagers, wearing new dresses, come out to visit the village deity and convey regards to each other. The young boys play different kinds of rural games i.e. Dodo, Kaluadi, Wadi-ghicha, Koko, Kusti, etc. While the girls move around the village in groups, joke, play hide and sick each other. In the evening, all join in a special programme of songs, music and dances.

The next day is observed as "Nua-Khai-Wasi" The main significance of observing this day is that the plenty of sweets, cakes and khir (Nawarnna) prepared on the previous day gets finished on this day. Besides, the non-veg food is prepared and enjoyed with plenty of country or local win known as".

The second day of Wasi is observed as Tiwasi that is the 3rd day of Nua-Khai festival. Again on this day, people enjoy a lot of liquor and meat and pass time in singing collective songs and dances.

As a customary rule, during these three days of festival, bonded laburers (Goti), agricultural workers, ploughers (Halla) and some tribals of paroja and Bhatia are donated rice, pulses, salt, turmeric, vegetables, clothes and money by their respective landlords (jamindars) and money-lenders (Sahukars).

In fact, this festival is a agricultural festival. It is most distinctive features are that, firstly it bridges the gap between the culture of Aryans and tribals, secondly its symbolic programmes of collective dining on leaf-plates, Juharan (greeting each other). Ancestral worship, Arna-Puja (rice worship), festive songs and dances etc. maintains unity and integrity in the village.

9. ***Bali-Yatra:*** This festival is observed by the Dora, Paroja, Desia-Kondh, and Gond tribes in the Rampur and Karlapatna regions of Kalahandi. The festive day falls on the bright fortnight of Bhadrav (Aug-Sept), just before Durga-Puja. It is celebrated near the Khandual temple off Karlapata where a special ritual is offered by respective communities. It is observed two days. On the second day of this festival, the Dhangari-Dola ceremony is held. It is a socially and religiously sanctioned programme providing and encouraging full freedom and security to young boys and girls (Dhangara and Dhangari) facilitating their open love-marriage. This marriage is distinct from all other types in a sense that is a love marriage between partners is held on this day, no objection arises from their parents and no dowry (Haraja) or bride-price is entertained. It is sanctified by strong religious faith. As a religious festival, it is main objective is to worship the temple deity with full religious fervour and traditional geity.

10. ***Dashehara Parab:*** This festival is held on the 7th and 10th days of bright forthnight in the month of Ashwina (Sept-Oct). It is one of the festival in the tradition of Shaktaism. But, on praxis, it amalgamates the ancient land-nature worshiping (Dharani-prakriti puja) tradition of the tribals with that of vedic Aryan Shakta religion. Western Orissa has been considered as the land of both Shaktaism and Tantrism, in its mythological history. Thus, Matru-Shakti (the female deity) is worshiped in different forms and names during various festivals of this region. For instance the deities like Manikeswari, Stambheswari etc. are most popular deities in Kalahandi. Besides, each village has its own deities called by different names. Tribals in this region are most accustomed to worship female deities.

However, there is a myth that every village deity is meant atleast once upon a year for a collective "Shastriya or Loukikya Shakta Puja". Thus, the month of

Dashehara festival that is "Ashwina" is often called as "Dehilia-Mas" (the month of deities). During Dashehara festival, it is also believed that all the deities freely move around in the village. Therefore, together with Durga Mata, all other deities are worshiped in the village. Every devotee expects blessings of the Mother deity called by different names. There is no single village in Western Orissa where Shakta -Puja is not held. Hence, the tribal or folk religion in this region is well-understood as "Shakta-dharma".

The Dashehara festival is observed in a ritualistic manner for four days and from 7th day to 10th day of the bright fortnight in Ashwina. On the 7th day Durga-mata or Dashehara (the deity having ten hands) is taken from her temple to her original birth place (where the Devi-Shakti is convened ) and offering a puja (ritual) there, the deity is again brought back. The to and fro of the deity is accompanied by a grand procession of devotees singing and dancing together. This procession of devotees singing and dancing together. This procession is known as "Chhatra-Yatra". On this day, all devotes including Jhankar (priest) and astrologer observe a fast and devotionally worship the deity in the temple. The ritual continually goes on till the end of this festival. Animal sacrifices are also offered to the deity.

On the 10th day, the deity is colourfully decorated on a big chariot and is carried in a grand procession to visit each house hold in the village. The whole region echoes with the recitation "Mata-Shree" hymn, invocation songs and obeisance accompanied by various types of music. Women standing at the door-steps of each house hold worship the feet of the deity with flower, milk, rice, dhup, deep, chandan and sindur. In the procession, the female servants of the temple (Sheera or Kalishi), colourfully decorating their bodies with various ornaments and garlands, carrying weapons of the deity in their hands and opening their long head-hair, dance with the rhythm of drum and other musical instruments. It is believed that the Sheera or Kalishi is endowed with the deity power (Devi-Shakti). Thus, they are also worshiped by the villagers at each house hold during procession. When people sacrifice goat or hen to offer blood to the deity, the Sheera or Kalishi covering their faces with red cloth imitate as if drinking it.

While being worshipped by the villagers, the Sheera or Kalishi, lightly blows by mouth in their ears for the purpose of saving them from all diseases. In case, any person has been attacked by certain ghostly spirit, sheera tribes to control that spirit by means of her endowed deity power. Furthermore, if any house is believed to have been habited by ghosts, then she moves around that house and controls the ghostly spirits. She displays her power by cutting some part of their body or by walking on fire. Such type of practices in termed as "imitative magic" in the mainstream social Anthropology.

Although this festival is chiefly religious in nature, but it provides a lot of entertainment to various communities in the village. All the communities participate in different types of folk-dance and folk-song competition held for three days during festival. Among dances, the Dhangra-Dhangri dance of the Paroja tribe in Jaya Patana and Koksara, the Kutia-girls dance in Madanpur and Lanjigarh, the Gond-girls dance are some of the most enchanting tribal dances in Kalahandi. People also enjoy the festival with feasting and fasting.

11. ***Budha-Raja-Parab:*** This festival is observed on the next day of Dashehara Parab. It is held in a open field near a jungle situated by the Ampani village of Koksara block in Kalahandi. A deity known as "Budha-Deo" of the Gond tribe is specially worshiped in this festival. The nomenclature of this festival is derived from a myth. It is believed that a powerful old king of the Gonds (popularly called as "Budha-Raja-Deo") left a metal of his horse (Khoger or Ghoda-Jin) on that spot in the long past. Subsequently, that spot was named as the alter of the old king and the festival was followed after devising him. While offering puja (ritual), people sacrifice goats, sheeps, cocks etc. in front of the alter and pray for blessings.

This festival is observed only one day and tribal people from all walks of Kalahandi and its adjoining districts join in it. The village priest, astrologer and leader (Jani and Jhankar) observing a fast worship the deity. It is also believed that at midnight, the Budha-Raja disguisedly in the image of a tiger comes to the alter and without harming anyone takes away his food. Thus people wait till midnight and enjoy that night in feasting, singing and dancing. Various types of dance competitions and fold-dramas like Ghumua dance, Ramlila Yatra, Nata-Swant (melodies) etc. are organized to encourage the people to sleeplessly enjoy the night.

12. ***Chaula-Dhua Parab Or Diel-yatra Or Pitori Yatra:*** The month of Kartika (Oct-Nov) is called in this region as "Diel-Mas". It corresponds to the Hindu festival Diwali. In this month and on the same day, people observe "Chaula-Dhua-parab" (rice-washing festival or "Pitori-Yatri" (cake making festival).

From Nawarnna festival till Diel (Diwali) people usually cook unwashed boiled rice at hoe. But, after the Diwali new moon, the village priest (jhankar) on any auspicious day of the bright fortnight announces the festival. At first, he grinds the washed rice and offers the prepared cake or cooked rice (Khichodi or Khir) to the village deity. All the villagers follow him. On this day also women, in each house hold, through away their old cooking earthern bowl and replace it with new one. So, this programme at home is called as "Handi-Phika".

Besides, this festival is also called as "Pitori-Yatra because on this day, women after grinding the dried unboiled rice, make white liquid out of it and artistically draw various kinds of colourful pictures on the alter or temple walls of the village deity as well as on the walls of their own houses. Moreover, in order to worship "De-Duma" (home deity) or ancestors, people sacrifice goats, sheeps, cocks etc. before the deities and enjoy the day in feasting of both vegetarian as well as non-veg food.

13. ***Charu-Puja Or Khala-Puja:*** In the country side, an open field is arranged to systematically separate paddy from the corn-straw by a traditional method called "Bengata". In this technique, a number of bullocks are tied by a rope in a line and driven then to move around a central pillar. In this process, while moving around the central pole, the bullocks continuously trod on the paddy corn, as a result by pressure the paddy get, separated for the corn. This field where the paddy is processed is called as "Khala".

On a special day during harvesting in the month of Margashirsha (Nov-Dec) field (Khala) is worshiped by the farmers before processing the paddy. They perform a ritual called "charu Puja" and sacrifice cocks in the field. Then, after reaping the paddy, the farmers again worship the paddy pockets or baskets at home. At night, they enjoy perform feasting.

14. ***Shemi Yatra:*** In the bright fortnight of Margashir (Nov-Dec) the Shemi Puja or Shemi Yatra is observed by the Kondh tribes in Kalahandi. The Kandh people dedicate all the beams collected from their field before the village deity "Dharani". After offering beams, country-liquor and sacrifice of cocks tot he deity, they collectively eat that food (prasad). There is a folk-belief that if the beam is taken before this festival, then there is possibility of diseases in the village. Even if, the co-habiting people of other castes living in the Konth village do not cook the beam unless and until the beam (shemi) is ritually offered to the village deity in this festival.

15. ***Push-Puni Or Chhera-Chhera Parab:*** The Push-Puni-Parab is named after the full moon day falling in the month of Push or Pousha (Dec-Jan). This

festival is observed through out Orissa, but is called as chhera-cherra-Parab in Kalahandi. Farmers of Western Orissa after continuously working long during agricultural season (from June to January), become restless and tired. People get plenty of leisure time from this month till the Akshi-Trutiya Parab falling in the month of "Ashadha" (June-July) when the agricultural works start again. Thus, after reaping the agricultural products, people like to relax their long hardships in this festival.

In the early morning of the day of this festival, young boys and girls carrying baskets go in groups from door to door in the village to collect food-grains from each house-hold. As a custom, people never hesitate to contribute them for the festival. While collecting food-grains from each house-hold, the group of boys and girls go on speaking only "chhera-chhera" and singing collective songs. That morning echoes the sweet songs and recitals of young children. Children irrespective of rich and poor, age, sex and caste join in this programme of food grains collection.

Infact, behind collection of foodgrains lies a dominant symbolic value of socialism that is equal contribution according to one's ability ad collective enjoyment of the feast in this festival. There does not arise neither any feeling of inferior complexity among the collectors (children) nor that of superior generosity among the contributors or donner, as it happens in the case of begging. People consider it as a customary duty to voluntarily contribute for the festival and collectively enjoy it.

As an entertainment based agricultural festival, people like landlords, money lenders and big farmers do not hesitate to donate grains and only on this day take accounts of their annual expenditure and also prepare a budget for the coming year. Thus, this festival recalls the traditional system of exchange relationships in rural Kalahandi, popularly known as "Jajmani-system. On this day, people belonging to the service castes, i.e. barbers, washerman, fishermen, blacksmiths, carpenters, ploughmen and others get their yearly payments. In exchange of their service throughout year, from their respective land-lords, money-lenders and other big farmers, their payment is either in the form of money or in kinds (food grains).

On this festive day, a special kind of sweet cake known as "Manda-Pitha" (made of rice, sugar, coconut and ghee) is prepared as a tradition and is exchanged among different families or communities in the village. Like the "Nua-Khal" festival, people enjoy various kinds of cakes, khir, khichodi and other non-veg food items and sweets in this festival. People also enjoy the day after this "Push-Puni" like that of

"Nawarnna" by taking plenty of meat or chicken and country-liquor. As a final-agricultural festival in the year, it ends with collective or community songs and dances in every village or Khalhandi.

16. ***Toki-Parab:*** One of the most popular events among the Kandha (Kondh) tribes of Thuamul Rampur block of Kalahandi district is the "Toki-Parab". This festival is otherwise known as " Push-Parab" or "Maria-Parab". It is celebrated in the month of Pausa (Dec-Jan), on a Sunday falling between the 7th to 14th day excepting the 8th day of the bright fortnight.

During Pre-British period, human (son) sacrifice in the Kondh tribe was known as "Maria", while the human (daughter) sacrifice was called as "Toki-Mara" in the Kondh-Paraja tribes of Kalahandi and Koraput was performed. The difference is that ghose kondh people who observed "Maria" (sone sacrifice festival) were not observing "Toki-Parab". (5).

The evidence about human sacrifice (both maria and Toki) during 200 years back was found in the reports of British officers. (Mahanty Gopinath 1971, P. 331). It is also seen in the report of a British officer Kyambel that the land-lords of Th.Rampur, Mahul-Patana (Jaya-Patana) and Karlapat were selling their prisoners to the Kondh people for the purpose of "Meria" practice (6). Thus, human sacrifice was a customary tradition in Kalahandi. But this custom was strictly banned by the then British Government, rulling over old Kalahandi estate of the Sambalpur provice (Das Kunja Bihari, 1977). Because of such restriction, the Kondh people substituted sheep sacrifice for the human sacrifice in their most popular festivals like Maria and Toki. But, today the manner of celebration of these festivals has more or less remained the same.

The main reasons behind the sacrifice of one's own purchased daughter in the Kondh's Toki Parab was the socio-economic problems i.e. acute poverty, customary tradition, and strong commitment to their orthodox blind religious beliefs. (Orissa Review: Vol. XXXV, No.5, 1978, PP 44-46). This "Toki-Parab" is closed related to the Earth culture. Even today, the Goddess Earth is worshiped every year by one or other villages of kalahandi as she is considered as the supreme source of all necessities. Thus, during such festival, the offering of blood of a sacrificed animal (human child in earlier periods) is meant to satisfy the Dharani deity (Mother Earth) for fulfilling all necessities of the Kondh community. (7)

The decision for organizing the "Toki" festival is taken during the month of Dushehara (Durga-Puja). The Raja (Ex-zamindar here) of Kabblapat (Thuamul

Rampur block) is consulted on the day of Manikeswar Puja ( a ritual held in the Manikeswari temple at Bhawanipatana). The approval of the king arrives through a "Kundi" to the village priest "Jani". After this, the Jani calls a meeting of all his "Pata-Panchura" (associate priests and astrologers of other Kondh villages) makes arrangement for the festival.

This "Toki-Parab" is observed for seven days. On the first day, all the kondh people go to collect wood, leaves and other necessities for the jungle. It is known as "Aka-Tala". On the second day a fast is observed by all to worship their ancestral spiritual teacher (Guru Puja). All the mountains of Kalahandi are called as "Guru-Danger" because it is believed that the "Guru-Budha" (old teacher) lives on there. On the third day, the sacred axe of the village deity is taken out and is given to worship at each house of the village. This day is meant for gathering and feasting. People enjoy a lot of meat curry and liquor.

The main Toki-Parab (Toki-sacrifice) is observed on the fourth day. A tamed Toki (female sheep) called as "Rasamuana" is brought from the priest's house to central place of the festival. On this day, the village road is kept neat and clan and the festival ground is decorated with leafs and colourful flowers. With a customary ritual, the Toki is sacrificed before the Dharani deity. The liver of toki is preserved with rice, water and chaff in an earthen container which is known as "Mupen". At midnight, the priest shoots and arrow towards East direction and the Mutpen is worshiped before the village deity.

On the fifth day, a buffalo or goat is sacrificed and then the dead body of Toki is carried from the festival place to the "Dharani-Khala" (a hollow meant for burring dead bodies) in a grand procession. During procession, the "Mutpen" is secretly carried with strong security. A group of people constantly keep watch on it being armed with their weapons. The main reason is to protect it fro the forceful attack of other village groups who may steal or snatch it away. Since the kondh-paraja people of all other villages in Kalhandi, are invited in this festival the people of the celebrating village strictly control the procession. This period is most dangerous because there is possibility of creating violence by others for their own interests.

After successfully reaching on the spot of "Dharani-Khala", one more ritual is held. The priest chants hymns and the astrologer recites invocations songs which are aimed for the wellbeing of the Kondh community and the country as a whole. People pray for better crops, sound environment, free from diseases and calamities and sound health for all. After burry thing the mutpen and the dead "Toki" in the Dharani-

Khala, an announcement is made for the end of the toki festival. On this day no song or dance programmes is arranged because the whole day is dedicated in the name of "Dharanki" deity.

On the sixth day, a socio-cultural celebration known as "Dhangari-Dola" is held. This day is socially sanctified for the free marriage between young lover and beloved in the Kondh village. No objection arises from their parents. Even if, dowry or bride-price is strictly prohibited in such kind of marriage. During celebration of the "dhangari-Dola" programme, young boys and girls select their life-partners according to their own choice and mutual understanding. The priest blesses each couple before the village deity. This kind of love-marriage is called as "Udulia" marriage. The whole day is happily passed by community songs and dances. Thus, this day is known as the day of merrymaking "Brlupata".

On the seventh day, again a "Guru-Puja" is observed on the top of a hill or mountain. All the newly married couples after offering a puja and enjoying a collective feast, songs and dances there, come back home in the early evening. After all, a last ritual known as "Tangiulen" is held in the village temple. The sacred axe is ritually submitted to the deity by the priest. The whole festival ends here.

17. ***Podha—Puja:*** When the "Toki-Parab" is observed only by the kondh-Paraja tribes, the "Podha-Puja" is celebrated by all other kondh tribes including Kutia-kondh, Dongria-Kondh and Desia Kondh. This festival is observed in-between the 10th day of bright fortnight in the month of Pausa (Dec-Jan) and the full moon day of Magha (Jan-Feb). In this festival, a buffalo (podha) is ritual scarified before the "Dharani-deity" (mother Earth). It is observed once in twelve years. One year before the celebration, a decision is made by the concerned villagers in a meeting called by the village priest "Jani". On the day of "Shemi-Yatra" falling in the month of Margashira (Nov-Dec) that year, a Babe (rope) is tied by the priest on a pillar of the village temple. It is meant as a symbol for the wellbeing of villagers observing such festival. A prime duty of each Kondh tribe is to join in the rope-typing ceremony.

This "Podha-Puja" is another substitute for the past Meria bali (a custom of human son sacrifice) in Kalahandi. Thus as a customary rule one year before the festival, a priest known as Khunta-Jani buys a young male buffalo and adopts it as his son (Jani-podha). But it is tamed by another priest Yoga-jani. One month before the festival on a pillar is erected and the Podhais tied with a rope on an auspicious day and the hair of the Podha is out or shaved as a symbol of sacrificing. Since then till the festival day, various musical programmes are held every evening. Just five days before the festival, the "Yoga-Jani" (who tames the Podha) is invited to hang the two white gourds on a swing over two pillars. It is called as "Kenda-Khunta" or "Yoga-khunta".

On the day of festival, the "Yog-Jani" (who tames the Podha stands as a mediator between the "Khunta-jani" (who purched the podha) and the "Gova-Jani" (the original priest who offers the ritual of "podha-puja"). The podha is taken through each house on the village road to sacrifice before the Dharani-Devi (Mother earth deity) whole after is situated on a broad space in the middle of the kondh village. This deity is also called as "Jaden-Budhi" because a stone is divinised as the mother deity. A small thatched room is constructed around the sacred stone. While offering ritual, three eggs are laced on three small heaps of handful rice at the feet of the deity. These three eggs, perhaps, represent three Hindu Gods i.e. Brahma, Bishnu and Maheswar. A number of weapons like, the sacred axe, knife, arrow etc. are kept on the alter. An umbrella of the deity called "Dharani-Chhatar" is brought for the village of "Yog-Jani".

The Kondh people of other villages are invited who come to join the festival in different groups of procession, carrying the sacred weapons of their village deities. This procession starts from the afternoon of the previous day. Since then, the festival ground increasing by gets crowded. in their procession, the kondh people of other villages come in groups with playing various kinds of music, reciting invocation songs or hymns and dancing war-dances. The main priest together with all the villagers ritually welcome the "Sheera" (two women assuming themselves as having "Devi-Shankti"- the power of their respective village deities, keeping their head-hair open, wearing red clothes and various ornaments of their village deities and dancing with the rhythm of music) and the accompanied groups of procession.

In the evening of the festival day, the real {podha-puja" starts. The chief priest (Gova-jani) offers the ritual, narrates the "Gova-Uttara" (the history of the Dharani-deity) and recites the ritual songs and hymns, while his associates (including astrologer and other priests) follow after him. Ali the villagers and observers take interest in attentively listening the myths, legends and folk-tales regarding the origin and history of the whole kondh tribes and their deities. A long series of dialogue and discussion between the priests and the village folks goes on whole night. Such an event of the "Gova-Uttaha" ends in the next day morning. It is mainly held for the sake of descending the Devi-Shakti (deity's spiritual power).

Moreover, while offering the ritual of "Podha puja" that night, the "Khunta-Jani" at first strikes on the neck of the podha by a sacred axe with the help of a specific kutia or Dongria kondh group who systematically control the buffalo inside a wooden frame. Increase the "khunta-jani" is not successful in separating the podha-head from its body by only one stroke, then it is blindly believed that the Kunta-Jani will die in one year. During this process of sacrifice before the dharani-Deity, a group of strong villagers holding sharp weapons and other arms surround the puja-place to safe guarding the flesh of the podha. They believe that other villagers may snatch away the sacred flesh which is an unauspicious sign. Thus, in order to protect the podha-flesh, the armed villagers watch carefully.

After sacrificing the "Podha", the "Gova-jani" offers its head and blood to the Dharani-deity and distributes the rest part among all the villagers. People cook it at their home and enjoy the "Prasad" as a graceful sacred food. Besides, during "podha-Puja", a packet of 5 kg. paddy is kept near the deity. After the ritual gets over, that packet of paddy is again measured. As a blind belief, its quantity (either increased or decreased) is assumed as a determinant sign of indicating the success or failure of crops in the coming year. Moreover, if some white ant or their carried soil is found in that paddy-packet, it is also believed as an auspicious sign of good fortune for the Kondh people. Finally, one more sacrifice of "Boka or Godara" is offered to the deity just for the purpose of cooling her anger. The Podha-puja, in this manner, ends after seven days and during this period, ploughing and other agricultural activities are strictly prohibited.

## CONCLUSION

Tribal festivals in Kalhandi, are observed by the tribal society have their own distinct culture and way of life, although there are many cases where the mainstream culture and its symbols have been manifestly or latently integrated. Nevertheless, this paper has highlighted how various kinds of tribal myths, and legends, cultural norms and values, and the age-old traditional customs and life-style are very much reflected in different types of tribal festivals in an underdeveloped society of western Orissa. Above all, it points to the fact that the tribal people of Kalahandi in this region have upheld their rich cultural traditions through festivals, in spite of modern forces of change.

## Notes

1. For understanding the relevance of tribal festivals in kalahandi, it is suggestive to have an overall idea about tribal life and culture of Orissa. For

this purpose, see Mahapatra Sita Kanta: The Tangled Web- Tribal Life and Culture of Orissa". Orissa Sahitya Akademi, Bhubaneswar, 1993.

2. For a definition on the festival, particularly of the primitive people, see: Briffanlt, R: "Festivals" in Encyclopaedia of the Social Sciences, ed E.R.A. Seligman, Vol. V, New York, 1951, P. 198.

3. I am grateful to Dr. Mahendra Kumar Mishra for his book "Kalahandira Lok-Sanskruti", friends Publishers, Cuttack 1996, PP 82-117.

4. See Panda Ajit Kumar: "Toki-Parab" in Kalahandira Adivasi Sanskruti, ed by Mahabir Sanskrutik Anusthan, Bhawani Patana, Orissa, 1993. PP 70-89.

5. Mishra Mahendra Kumar 1996. Ibid.

6. Ibid.

7. Also see Panda A.K. Ibid.

**REFERENCES**

**Das Kunja Bihari:** Loka Galpa Sanchayan, O.S.A. (Orissa Sahitya akademi, Bhuaneswar, 1977.

**Mahanty Gopinath:** "Adivasi Ek Drustikshepa", Banaphool, Upendra Mishra, Cuttack 1971, p. 331.

M.S.A. (Mahabir Sanskrutik Anusthan) "Maa Manikeswari-The Tutelary deity of Kalahandi", M.S.A. Bhawani Patana, Orissa, 1991.

**Mukhopadhaya Sankarananda:** Austrics of India-their Religion and Tradition", K.P. Bagchi and Company, Calcutta, 1975. PP 75-76.

Orissa Review Vol. XXXV, No.5, 1978, PP 44-46.

**Padhi Himansu Sekhar:** "Stambhewari Cult in Orissa" in Utkal Historical Research, Journal, Vol VII, P.G. Department of History, Utkal University, Bhubaneswar, Orissa, 1996, PP 26-36.

# 12

# Influence of Kali Puja Festival on Tribals of West Bengal

***Sumita Mukherjee, & Dr. Robin. D. Tribhuwan***

## INTRODUCTION

The worship of Shakti, or female is a popular concept in the Hindu religion. Goddess Durga, a form of the mellow goddess Parwati is the "Shaktiship" who has evolved by the combined forces and strength of Brahma Vishnu and Maheshwar (shiva). Goddess kali is the angry form of goddess Durga, and is also considered the goddess of Destruction.

## SOME MYTHOLOGICAL CONCEPTS ABOUT GODDESS KALI

In the Hindu scriptures, the tales about wars between gods (Devtas) and Rakshasas or Asurs (Demons) are quite Common. It actually symbolizes the battle between the good and the evil and the victory of those who are good and honest. It was in one such war, that, all gods failed to control Mahisasura, which led to the creation of female power-Durga. Durga overpowers Mahisasura and destroys the evil. Then came the "Raktabijas," a type of Asura, whose , one drop of blood falling on the ground produced hundreds of asuras. The killing of one Raktabija would produce several evil characters like him. It was during this battle that goddess Durga assumed the form of godess. Kali, and became known as "Rana Chandi, she wons the battle against asuras. She got so engrossed at the destruction of evil, that at one point of time, gods felt, that the Asuras would become extinct. This is where Lord Shiva, Kali's husband, lies beneath her, feet and, Kali sticks out her tongue red and blood stained.

**A Scientific Outlook:** A more rational interpretation of Raktabija would be overpopulation of demons would have been a threat to the Devtas or the good folks. Goddess Kali evolved with all her inner strength and destroyed the huge evil population in the fierce battle. Here, she became the goddess of destruction. If goddess kali continued her random killing of Asuras, the latter would have been wiped off the face of earth. This is where lord Shiva intervenes and stops her from bringing about total extinction. This highlights the effort of preservation of bio-diversity by mother nature. The Hibiscus flower, an essential item of Kali puja, particularly in West Bengal has natural contraceptive elements, which signifies the lowering of same.

***The Form Of Goddess Kali:*** Goddess Kali, as the name complexion, large eyes, a third eye on the forehead, which is open, red lips, tongue sticking out (both are blood stained) and long black hair. She has four arms, one holding a snake, one a chopper, one the hair of a beheaded demon and the last, a thunderbolt on a spear. Beneath her feet is Lord Shiva lying on his back. She wears a huge garland of demon heads and a skirt of demon hands.

Even goddess kali, has a milder form and expression in places, where she is considered a deity. In some cases, she has a bluish complexion. Which indicates a non- destructive form of the goddess. (TARA)

## THE WORSHIP RITUAL IN WEST BENGAL

In the eastern worship of "Shakti" is prevalent. The worship of goddess kali, takes place daily in the temples and at home. Temple rituals are very different from daily home worship rituals. At home, only pictures of the goddess are kept, and small offerings like fruits, and sweets, and flowers are made and Vedic mantras on goddess Kali are chanted. But in the temples, the rituals are very rigid. The temple puja is also carried out, as community puja or individual house hold puja, in the Devi Paksha 15 days after Dushera in the "New Moon Night."

***The Vedic Ritual:*** Worship, according to the Vedas is considered very auspicious. First, life is instilled in the idol of the goddess by a recognized priest. This life becomes permanent in the idols of temples. The rituals have to be carried out by fasting people. It begins with chanting of Kali stators and status in Sanskrit, where the deeds of goddess is praised. Moreover, these stators also have directives for human beings-where emphasis is on good conduct. This is followed by the description of battles between goddess and demon and the lessons learnt from these battles, follows this ritual, and after this, animal sacrifices takes place. In the present times, a goat, (ram), which is spotlessly black to offered in the sacrifice the animal sacrifice is followed by a "Yagna" for which, of all things, 108 pieces of lotus and "bel leaves are essential.

In the Kali Festival, which is either a community or household affair, the puja rituals are preceded by decorating the house with oil lamps (replaced by candles in cities). One day before the puja, fourteen different kinds of leafy vegetables are eaten by the people, which is believed to enhance the longevity of the next fourteen generation. At night, lamps (candles) are lit, in rooms and corner of the house, which is an attempt at scaring away the spirits of the preceding the generations. On the Kali Puja day, (which falls only a day before Diwali), five crackers are burnt, to scaring away the spirits of the proceeding the generations. On the kali Puja day, (which falls only a day before Diwali), five crackers are burnt, to scare away all evil spirit, while, scientifically, the tiny insects, which fly about night from the monsoon season are killed by the sulphur fumes of the crackers.

Another important feature is that, no one pities the animal which is being scarified, as it is being offered to god. Ancient records show that, previously, human sacrifices were also common. Such offering are made, in cases of wish fulfillment, and creatures offered, are said to be reaching goddess kali, after their life on earth. The animal on human sacrifice pleases the blood- thirsty goddess Kali the most. In many places, however, bloodshed is avoided by offering vegetables, like gourds bananas a sugarcane staff etc. Whatever is placed on the alter frame, should be cut, in one stroke by the chopper, on else, it is considered as bad luck on disaster to the family on community on the whole.

In important person (other than the priest and the person who carries out sacrifices), is the Dhaki" on the drum player, who holds on the spirit of the Puja. This role is the greatest during the sacrifices, where, he plays his drum very loudly to make the creatures inandible. After the sacrifice, the women folk, cross the ring finger of their right hands on the blood, to evade all evils from their family members.

Last in the ritual list, is the Yajna, after which, the ashes of the burnt wood and all that is offered to the flames is pint as a long mark (Tilak) on the foreheads. The following day, the meat of the sacrificed animal is prepared without, onions and garlic and eaten by the people as "Maha Prasad". This kind of Ritual is common in the cities and rural areas. In some places, in rural areas, buffalo sacrifices are made, but human sacrifices have stopped everywhere.

***The Tribal Ritual Of Kali Puja:*** Kali Puja the Vedic ages, and it is limited in case of the tribals. But certain tribals who are influenced by Hinduism, do practices kali puja ritual. In West Bengal, particularly, the Munda and Murmu tribe, inhabiting the Ayodhya hill region of Purulia district, (P.O. Balrampur) have faith in goddess Kali. Kalipada munda, a resident of Kiyri rekka village said, that since they worship lord Shiva, goddess Durga and Kali have to be worshipped as his "Ardhanginis". The increasing faith in goddess kali, has been brought about by people visiting calcutta and other such nerve centres. Almost, all the household have pictures of the deity in their houses. The elaborate processes of the puja are not practiced, but she is worshipped as the other gods and goddesses. According to the Murmu tribe, the mother goddesses, such as the earth, Parvati, and Kali, have great strengths and capacities. The women folk on the earth are representatives of these strengths. It is the reproductive capacity and the inherent power of endurance in women, which have made them god-like.

Goddess Kali, among the tribals is the goddess of destruction, and so, she has to be pleased time and again. The tribals on Ayodhya hill, are enthivators, so, in case of rain-failure, they make several offerings to different gods and goddess to make them happy. Goddess kali keeps evils and evil spirits at bay. So, she has to be made life offerings, and here too, buffaloes and goats are offered.

"Annapurna" the goddess of fortune (who is also the daughter of Shiva and Parvati) is worshipped by the tribals, when they are successful in their agricultural ventures. Basically, all goddesses are derived from "Shakti," they are different in forms, by one in their spirits and execution of justice a faith that is so fundamental in the Hindu tribal areas.

## THE TANTRIK CULT

Tantra vidya is a very strong and those, practising tantra vidya are known as tantriks. Tantriks essentially worship Kali. These people, after long meditation and penance, gain power and turn into faith healers and destroyers. A tantrik kali temple, most commonly has skulls and bones of humans offered to the deity. The tantrik cult, if practiced by time Yantra-yojis, can in some cases bring about results, but it makes, child sacrifices common. It is actually a form of witchcraft and black-magic, practiced in the name of goddess Kali.

A milder form of Tantra vidya is found in the tribal areas, among whom witches and sorcerers are common. The power of witchcraft instills fear among people, and children and women become targets of sacrifice and destruction. Tanriks now require license for practicing their cult, and of course, human sacrifice has been banned by the government. Trapith in West Bengal (Birkhum District), has the largest number of Tantra Yogis. An interesting fact about Kali Puja, is her great fear and awe among the dacoits. The Dacoits of almost entire India, worship goddess kali.

'In Calcutta, the temple of a 24 handed kali idol is present in the heart of the city, which before the colonial rule was meant for decoits. In Maharashtra, the kali temple at Kuradi, near Nagpur was especially frequented by Dacoits, even during the British period? Several such small temples of Ma Bhawani (Goddess Kali), are found in the savories of Chambal, which is still the den of Dacoits. To them Bhawani Ma is the greatest Symbol of power and strength.

Goddess Kali, reflects the other side of female, which is very destructive. In many of our Hindu epics, the anger of women, caused by their insult has brought about massive destmetion. Goddess Kali actually represents female anger, and her inner power, which is maximam in adverse times. To many people Kali is a living goddes, but gust and impartral. She is worshippped in some form on the other in entire India.

## Concluding Remarks

Worship of goddess Kali is common among tribes residing close to Calcutta and other major cities of West Bengal. This is due to the impact of hindu influence on tribals. Among the Bhils of Rajasthan Kali or Parvati is known as "Gorja Devi" and is worshipped for nearly a month. Among the Dhodias of Maharashtra and Gujarat Parvati is worshipped during a festival called Divasa. Thus, wherever acculturation between hindus and tribals has occurred for a long time and especially in West Bengal, tribals living close to the cities have taken up Kali worship.

❑❑❑

# 13

# Festivals in India: A Theoretical Consideration

*Kunj Bihari Nayak*

## INTRODUCTION

In the traditional societies, where the monstrous tentacles of the hybrid modernism have not yet affected the life style of people, their fairs, and festivals are the core indices of their socio-cultural inheritance and the collective psychological response to the challenges of the world around them.[1] Today, the modern world is tending to become too serious to foster the spirit of popular gaiety because a good deal of our troubles can be ascribed to the neglect of this festive spirit. The superfluous energies of people, if not diverted into harmless channels like the celebration of festivals, are likely to find expression in political upheavals, violent conflicts, wars and other destructive activities.[2] Infact, festivals are among the most attractive and memorable features of a tourist itinerary, is not yet to answer the question of their importance for those who celebrate them. Festivals as special performances of complex of performances, at special times-provide vital insights into the religions, aesthetic, social, economic and political values as well as concerns in the societies of communities in which they occur.[3]

Fortunately, India is old fashioned enough to appreciate and cultivate the festive spirit and it is doubtful if there is any country in the world at present where so many festivals are celebrated with zest and traditional gaiety. Unlike many other countries, religion is still a living force in India and institutionalized religions have, from time immemorial encouraged the spirit of festivals and pilgrimages.[4] India is an agrarian country with an ancient heritage. It's past lives on in its splendid monuments, varied cultural life style, religions, cults and rituals, traditional arts and crafts, and an amazing variety of colourful festivals based on an enormous number of myths and legends.[5] Majority of festivals and fairs in India, whether those of Hindu, Muslim, Sikh, Zoroastrain, Christian, Buddhist or those of Jain are spiritual in nature. Besides the wellknown and universally observed festivals, there are innumerable and largely unheard of festivities which are steeped thousands of years of customs, whose formalities are still observed in remote villages and tribal areas.[6]

In this paper an attempt has been made to understand the concept of form sociological angle festivals. For this objective, according to Marcel Mauss. The aim and principle of sociology is to observe and understand the whole group in its total behaviour" (Maus 1954:79). Following this method in his study of ritual prestations, he stated that, "We are dealing with something more than institutions divisible into legal, economic, religious and other parts. We are concerned with wholes with systems i their entirety. It is only by considering them as a whole that we have been able to see their essence, their operation and their living aspect and to catch the fleeting moment when the society and its members take emotional stock of themselves and their situation as regards others." (Mauss 1954:77-78).[7]

Since this paper takes interest to focus primarily on a sociological approach to festivals in India, we need to have a glance at some ideological standpoints of sociologists, social Anthropologists, philosophers and others on festivals in general, before going into delineating meaning, nature and scope of festivals particularly in Indian context.

## IDEOLOGICAL TRADITIONS OF FESTIVALS

In Sociology, the classic analysis of festivals goes back to Emile Durkheim and his notion of "collective effervescence" as the supreme moment of the solidarity of collective consciousness. Mechanical solidarity only, since it concerned with the festivals of "primitive" people. Franz Boas and Marcel Mauss adopted this idea "The Elementary Forms of Religious Life",[9] in which Durkheim introduced the concept of a "Living Social Whole". Once the unity of everything social had been postulated, Durkheim with his proceeded to divide it up into abstract categories based on binary oppositions: the sacred and the profane, which became the ontological poles of the social drama.

The sacred delirium is actualized in the festival and reaches beyond itself: collective conscience is sublimated, magnified, adoring the dramatic form of it's own substance in dance, agitation; confusion, transvestism etc. However, Durkheim's positivism managed to reintegrate the sacred with an almost mystical twist, into the enlarged positivism of "Mana". He remained profoundly Kantian identifying the "essential" principle of everything social with that "transcendental apperception" of which we have a glimpse in the "Mana", the "spirit".

This interpretation exercised a lasting influence on various schools of sociology and anthropology through the work of Marcel Mauss, who formulated in "Erquisse dunne theories generate de la magic", te explanation of dance in terms of an exaltation of "Mana". Although Mauss was dominated by Durkeimian doctrine at that time (1903), but his analysis was more phenomenological than positivistic in a sense that the substance of the festival evokes that which is non-existent, discovering a "sur-reality" which alters the cosmic order. The itentionality of the phenomenon surpasses its actuality. Mauss characterised this "dynamic totality" and its creative "effervescence" as the whole social body . . . vibrating to the same chord. In the momentum of intense participation" individuals melt away. They become so to speak . . . the spokes of a single wheel whose magical gyrations, dancing and singing, would appear to constitute a perfect image". The creativity of the festival stems from the groups realizing in common an experience that lies outside of it.[10]

The classic doctrine of the festivals is transposed and enriched in the essays of Roger Caillois's work captioned "Man and the Sacred" states that the group no longer comes to merge with a fixed image of what is sacred, on the contrary, it has "recourse to the sacred". The paroxysm of the festival can not be mistaken with the "region of the sacred". Its "frenzied activity", and the excesses it provokes us to undoubtedly seek to restore the "primal chaos", the "mythical era" of a "bygonetime" regarded as a paragon of purity and collective communication, but also attempt to recreate the cosmos through the dramatic representation of its myths. At its most intense, the festival becomes a ceremony of perpetual creation and re-creation of embodied beliefs, dramatized and played all at once, producing and reproducing culture from one generation to the next. The myths would be refined and enriched by means of these "fertile out bursts".[11]

Caillois perceived that the festival relies on different motives from those governing the rules of collective order. He used the term "Transgression " to "suspend" the norms and rules of everyday life. It implies that the disorganization is perceived as a full and blasphemous experience. Commercial and sexual relations are intensified during the festival, the classes, or rather segregations which divide groups, disappear, and the prohibitions scoffed. But the awareness of this destruction constitutes an integral part of the trespasses, fleeting though they may be. Caillois is so conscious of the negative and destructive aspects of the festival that he compares it to the destruction and exuberance of war.

Georges Bataille alone deals with the idea of destruction on its own ground. For Bataille, from his "La Part mandite to L erostisme", the idea of an "expenditure of energy" without a practical goal dominated his thought. The vain depletion of energy, an unused force-awareness of which is merely pretense of subterfuge-certainly recalls the term "consummation", the Unwhlistic will that Schopenhaner placed at the basis of existence and which Nietzsche treated in his first essays. But Bataille treats this theme in a subjective and individual horizon. While Mauss, in his work entitled "The Gift" says that transgression and destruction stemmed from the idea that every society perpetuates useless forms of exchange and consumption. The principle of gift involves sacred destruction, even in the economics of modern countries.

However, the concept of is more than merely a festival and that modern analyses are simply part of a much wider obsession continuing to raise doubts for our civilization. What is ironic is that the festival is assuming interest today, just when commercialization, market economics and increasing industrialization with politicization (added) are crystallizing the social conditions for eliminating such manifestations, which remain the privilege of non-historical societies or those which are not dominated by concerns of productivity (and politics).

In this context, Rousseau's reflection was highly indicative of a wider social insecurity. Going beyond his "Letter and Alembert in considerations sur le government de La Pologne (1972)", Aoussean encouraged the new nations, over throwing the yoke of tyranny to discover the existential reality of their "Social Contract" in festivals embodying the spirit of their union. Roussean might have considered supplanting all social institutions with festivals, the best activity for elaborating the "general will". In opposition to organized society Roussean advocated perpetual changed based on the principle of the festival, dissolving private life into a general and intense communion. This "cultural revolution" excluded the use of imaginary representation, a distorted sign of the state of slavery and arbitrary division.

By the way, the importance of Roussean's teachings was modified by the ideologists of French Revolution, who sought to institutionalize the festival, overlooking the fact that for Roussean the festival was contrary to all institutions. The "quarrel of festivals" was actually much more than a politicians debate which concealed the ideal definition of civil society and that of the revolution itself. Where as Mirabean, Thoret and Talleyrand pushed through the idea of commemorative ceremonies aimed at rekindling civic spirit, of Rousseaus conception whether it was to be embodied in Reason, the Nation or some other model. Even Saint Just left some curious texts identifying "Mass upheavals" and the "national war" with festivals, for the eradication of tyrannical institutions.

The festival seems to rekindle a dynamic activity in the people, a power capable of swaying the whole of society into an act of innovation. History in the making, as it were, and fully conscious of it's development. It is as it before "thinking out" history and discovering it's laws, men had experienced it in the festival. In fact, it is too difficult to discover the "essence of the festival" common to all civilizations. For while Roussean and certain revolutionaries have seen and remain fundamentally conservative.

## NATURE AND TYPES OF FESTIVALS

There are several different types of festivals of tribals, diorganization, symbolic hallucinations, festivals of prestige and competition, festivals involving unbridled consumption, commemorative ceremonies and the intense exaltations of sects or groups. He needs to compare different types of festivals and observation their role and latent meaning change in different societies and civilizations. Some of them have inherent destructive or subversive spirit which involve a real awakening of individual consciousness.

### I. Festivals Of Tribal Disorganization

Ever since L.H. Morgan, Anthropologists have focussed their studies on the social system or code of archaic societies and have discovered order throughout the world precisely because all societies have rules which divide human groups from nature. Festivals constitute a paroxysmic phase of collective life during which nature is apprehended, as both creative and destructive. Thus, most ritual behaviour is seen as a defense of collective life against the great moments of disorder and destruction: death, sexuality, hunger. According to Paul Sartre (13), such behaviors might be regarded as magical and the ritual perceived as a gigantic conjuration of nature. Yet all observers agree that the festival involves a powerful denal of the established order.

It is perhaps this capacity for self-destruction, which we misunderstand as a sign of weakness or inferiority, that has allowed archaic societies of survive much longer than historical ones.

## II. Festivals of Prestige and Competition and Consumption

Festivals of prestige and competition are of an entirely different nature from those of tribal disorganization, although they may sometimes co-exist. Bronislaw Malinowsk, Marcel Mauss and Franz Boas have each given accounts of these "agonistic" encounters in which rival groups engage in the disorderly and destructive consumption of accumulated riches of provisions. But, for Bataille, such "consumption" probably constitutes the dawn of economic activity. At the very least, the act of destruction repeats the nature of the cosmos, which consumes more than it produces, as Darwin puts it. However, agonistic festivals indicate the positive influence they have on social and economic activity. When scarcity is the echo of abundance, this consummation invariably has a corrosive effect on some other group, whether it's purpose is to make an impression, to dominate it, or simply obtain it's symbolic allegiance. For instance a matter of dominating psychologically, symbolically and finally socially other men, are observed in royal appearances and urban ceremonies".

## III. Festivals Of Symbolic Hallucination

While the festivals of "symbolic hallucination" corresponds to a wish for imposing a mystical, symbolic order which is at odds with social reality. In this regard we may refer to the religious festivals of middle ages in Europe. It represents an imaginary space in which man is freed from the constraints of economic and social hierarchies.

The "mysteries" and liturgical performances of the festival create an image of man different from the reality of the social system a living utopia. For Duvignaud, these festivals are neither identical nor equivalent. They are not opposed but diverse. They co-exist but never clash; they may be mingled but never confused. They simply are, one next to other, and each equally inspiring.

## IV. Commemorative Ceremony

The commemorative ceremony only appears when societies and civilizations are sufficiently established to recognize what they have acquired and how to define themselves in relation to the past. The whole picture seems to be modified when an active consciousness engages in the festival confident in it's power to modify its own structures and consequently, conscious of history. Roger Caillois and Mircea Eliade[14] observe "uchronia" gives life to history. Commemorations are not destructive. They do not possess the negative forces of nature since their goal is to reconstitute social life and instill it with a positive force. George R. Kernolde in his book "From Art to Theater" observe that commemorations are essentially conservative having a desire for stability and conservation.[15]

## V. Festivals of Intense Exaltations

While the festivals which take place in sects or small tightly-knit groups, held together by religion, mysticism, politics, or identification with a sage or Guru, are of a different nature. For instance, the warm and intense gatherings of primitive Christians during the Roman period. Alfred Metraux, Roger Bastide or Michel Leiris have studied microscopic groups separated from the rest of social life or even the groups which are accused of witchcraft and cruelly decimated by Inquisition. These restricted groupings which maintain a separate reality zealously guarded from the "public" also concern puritan Sects, ideological and political sects, clandestine groups, the rallies of sports or artistic fanatics. Technological societies induce a proliferation of sects whose mystical motivation resides in a deceased or powerless "Leader" a sports or movie star or an artist.

It is undoubtedly significant that an intense participation characterizes these sects, as well as an atmosphere of permanent festivity: the members gather around the mythical image of a personality which by magic, removes them from the surrounding world. The same intense festival dissolves the individual personality and the environing social order. In this context history itself, as a collective movement, is rejected in favour of another history, that of the group and its mystical order. Evidences from millenarists, utopists, fanatics or sectarians in all civilizations remind us that there exist some restricted festivals which abolish the official status and role of men to make way for fantastic participation.

A final aspect of the festival is perhaps represented by those frightening, intense, but short-lived social explosions, disdained by historians and politicians alike. For instance, the explosion of 1848 and the Paris commune. These types of explosions are never intended to be political, though they are invariably perceived as a political event when industrialized and technological societies base the organization of their collective life on an ideology of rationality, which exerts a generalized constraint at all levels of society. These explosive movements, then, are not simply a reaction against apparently stifling conditions, but also a necessary ephemeral attempt at creating another world, a separate reality inside a fixed and rationalized world.

This "other world" implies intense participation and a communication of minds and spirits normally precluded by the banalization of organized collective living. It exalts the somolent powers of exchange between minds, acts and styles of behaviour. It also tends towards the negation of society, just as tribal festival abolishes the rules of culture when it discovers the destructive power of nature. But such apparent nihilism is an affirmation of the capacity men have to discover and realize in common an experience, which some regard as imaginary.

Finally, festival is not be treated as a game. Huizing[16] in his "Homo Lundens" mentions that some human activities are not meant to fulfill a function or pursue an efficient goal as in a game. He includes the aesthetics of the festival in this category. But festival is not a useless or non-functional activity. Such non-functionality would, in any case, have some structural utility, depending on the type of society in which it appeared. What distinguishes one human activity from another resides in it's manifest or latent project. The project of the festival is not necessarily to maintain or preserve society, despite the confusion and disorder. The perishable and transitory character of the festival is not proof of weakness and insignificance, but on the contrary, constitutes evidence of an intense experience, destroyed by its very intensity.

However, the festivals of archaic societies became objects of scientific investigation at the end of the last century-Just when technological society was about to kill them off. But the explosion of the festival carries with it the seed of experience that human progress is achieved more by those brief and necessary "fleeting" illuminations than by the methodical discoveries of the work day world. Ever since Roussean, who foresaw its anti social character (like Nietzsche and later Antonin Artand), the festival has raised doubts for European culture and the self assurance of its systematic rationality. Though technological societies no longer accept those student flashes of a apprehension, it is probably because they are more fragile than archaic societies, which periodically destroy themselves, fearless of the abyss that is then revealed.[17]

Under this background we proceed to focus on the distinctive meaning, nature and scope of Indian festivals in terms of their historicity and contextuality.

## MEANING, NATURE AND SCOPE OF INDIAN FESTIVALS

Indian concept of the festival or "Utsav" is evident in India's traditional philosophy. It acknowledges truth that we keep neglecting in our day to day life.

Festival stands for reunion. No one here celebrated a festival all by himself. Festival, the truth in reunion, is total celebration. It is anand, it is rasa and it is love. It does not only satisfy the intellect, it also fulfills the heart. The strength in the union and the invincible truth in love are inherent in Indian festival.[18]

In the daily humdrum of life, a man invites all men to festivals to share the moment of bliss (anand). On this occasion his behaviors is unusual. His home is no more limited, a narrow entity, but it assumes universality. He spends his money and wealth on others. On such a day, the wealthy honours the poor, the learned offers seat to the fool. All dine together under one common umbrella. Because on that day, 'mine' and 'thine' are bound by mutual love. On the day of a festival, the assembly of people gathers in the name of truth with mutual love for the spiritual bliss (anand). Festival transcends mutuality and all purpose. There are innumerable days in life when poverty reigns. Festival is the day of glory, of beauty, a source to enhance the meaning of life, of enrich the language of love, of amity and friendship.[19]

This ecstasy is the basis of festival. We decorate the day with colourful leaves and flowers we garland it with lamps and make it melodious with music. By such an unity, abundance and beauty, we crown the day of the festival, make it extraordinary, symbolizing immortality in the universe. On a festival day, the man realizes that he is not small and dismembered; that the universe is his abode, truth is companion; that everybody belongs to him; that piety and sacrifice are natural acts for him and that death does not exist for him.[20]

Festival is a major part of Indian life. It occurs throughout each year bringing delight and joy to all classes of people and compensating for life's hardships and inadequaties to any Indian, there is no better way of reflecting on one's civilization that to relive old customs through traditionally significant celebrations. The popular Indian saying "Thirteen festivals in twelve months is in practice an understatement. Every Indian observes a number of festivals in every month, India's attraction for outsiders derives not from being one of the world's leading industrial nations, but from it's rich cultural diversity, extravagance of expression, and myriad cultures and creeds, all interpreted through a year long continuous process of festivals. In short, a celebration is for every season and for every reason. The high degree of esteem in which every Indian holds the soil that is closest to the country's heart, the crops that fill her land, the tools that provide her with work the culture and arts, that offer enlightenment and the sacred rivers that are the source of her very existence, is visually reflected in gratifying celebration.[21]

Festivals of India, took birth with a promise of spiritual strength not to relapse to the past, when face to face;; rather to look forward with an undying freedom replenished with the sanctity of each moment. The Indian culture acknowledges it's festivals as a means of enrichment. Monier williams observes that "There is not an object in heaven and earth which a Hindu is not prepared to worship sun, moon pools and rivers and soon. Behind this worshipful attitude lies the faith in sanctity of moments and periods of festivals when notable psychic experiences are linked with the cardinal Hindu tenet that one divine intelligence pervades all and joins all forms of life, past and present.[22]

The Indian Hindu mind carved out three categories of festivals. They are vrata, parva and tyohar: the first being essentially an occasion to have fast for purification, the second being commemoration of the sanctity of notable events; and the third as sheer celebration. This categorization has a unique and some underlined similarities, though different communities observe in a more or less different way. Each of them is dedicated to gain spiritual or mental prowess, to purify the soul, to strengthen the will power, to deepen the faith in God, to cleanse the environment, to clarity one's own thought processes and to enhance health and vigour. Mahatma Gandhi divided Indian festivals into two categories i.e. Kmaya an Nitya the first presupposes specific desire while the latter having no desire but love and devotion. He attributed much more importance to the later.[23]

Festivals in all the three forms demolish segregation of all types. The high and low are equally accorded welcome women, old and young, children and grown-up people belonging to all castes including untouchable are given equal place in this human exericse.[24] According to H. Daniel, Indian festivals have histories and more important, are frequently based on ritual traditions. Even if, oral myth often links festival.[25]

Buddhists, Jain, Zoroastrians etc. have a fewer number of festivals, compared to the Hindu faith, with its innumerable Gods and Goddesses and it's myriad festivals devoted to them.[26] In the context of Hindu festivals are revealed excellent metaphors in the form of Gods and Goddesses which link up social unity in all caster and creed. Through these metaphors, the ageless unity manifests itself with ever newer content. However, festivals of Indians provide various religious and ethnic groups the freedom to be themselves and at the same time to acquire accents of universality.[27]

Life is composed of joy and fear. Festivity takes care of both, especially when the festival is ritualized. Ritual is believed to appease the powers that be, there by putting an end to fear, or is supposed to attract the attention of the benevolent forces being invoked so that they may suppress the evil that haunts the devout. Invocation seeks fulfillment of a cherished desire that the God can bestow, while the celebration of the affair itself results in joyous festivity. Festivals generally celebrate the seasons, the exploits of legendary heroes, birth anniversaries of myths or historical personages, other events close to the heart of devotees, or may be for their own sake. All the same, all festivals include a factor regulating life-style, enjoining the devotee to do or to retrain from doing certain acts for the sake of spiritual rewards. Rituals thus ensure performance of certain duties by raising them to the order of a sacrament[28] festivals But each festival is different from other. Several religious elements are exposed in large-scale festivals and are also integrated by national identity. The religious rite, in some festivals, is best understood against the background of traditions about the deity for whom it is performed. Observation of ritual behaviour should be complemented by the consideration of relevant texts and historical records.[29]

Apart from festivals there are sheer funfare, sport, fund and frolic, the great bulk of them are essentially based on seasonal and agricultural myths and legends, shifting the focus to themselves. A single festival may have numerous legends explaining it, some simple variations on the same theme, others that are entirely separate. It is these legends that lend a quant charm to most of the festivals of this country. But, at the root of a large number of festivals is the force of the seasons.[30]

## TIMING OF FESTIVALS

When festivals are observed, there is distinctive meaning of "special time" which is set apart from the ordinary. That special time is meant for creativity, spontaneity, and meaningful activity. During this time, anxieties and pressures of daily life are relieved.[31] From people's point of view the two heavenly bodies, sun and moon revolving round the earth, the moon has been chosen to afford convenient periods for timing of festivities in India. The full moon has always been the prototype of all sacrifices prevalent in India. Remaining all the fifteen phases of the moon called "Tithis" (lunar days) as distinguished as occasions for particular ceremonies. But it does not mean that the dark nights or the sun are left out. For instance, the festival of light (Diwali) is celebrated on the darkest of the moon. Solar worship is not in the least neglected. Both spiritual and material are two brightest jewels in the crown of Indian festivals.[32]

However, some festivals are anniversaries, falling on birthdays or founding days and the like. Other fall on auspicious days associated with religious myths and legends.

But, because of seasonality, festivals of the Hindus have the habit of clumping together. For geographical reasons, there are variations in the way festivals clump-up in North India and in the South. The reasons in the South come earlier than in the North. A festival can fall on two days, beginning at a moment on one day and stretching into the following day. In such cases there is utter uncertainty leading to great confusion for the celebration. Therefore, it is difficult to follow any one calender in organizing the festivals into a list.[33]

Despite the apparent trivializing of festivals in many places, it is not clear that any festival has utterly lost either its role or its meaning. If there are quintessential displays. If there are epitomes, if there are true cultural microcosms, then they are to be found in festival performances. However, festivals confirm to social structure or dissolve it. Something is affirmed while other thing is denied or tabooed in the festival. Thus, in a sociological sense, guiding societal norms and values are back bones of festivals in India. But festivals are not blind, superficially interesting commemorations or displays. On the contrary, they are complicated and multivalent occurrences at the heart of social and religious life. There are different ways in which festivals can function to resolve or to intensity social conflict and to restructure social status. Hence, festivals can be adequately understood only when they are holistically analyzed in the context of total festival sequence or cycle.[34]

More interestingly, festivals of India have counterparts and complements in communities living in or out of the country known as Greater India professing any of the religions that originated from here. The people having faith in Jainism and Buddhism, no matter where they live, draw near and mingle while in celebrations. Sometimes and in some places, te liberal Hindu embrace to some of the significant Islamic festivals and vice versa. It is an attempt to further extend frontiers of a composite Indian culture. Besides, there are a number of affinities and points of contact which prove the kinship of communities, a common ethos and a mental atmosphere shared by them. A connected vision of these festivals underlines an ethnological significance furthering glimpses of unity in diversity. In observance of these festivals India pays here homage to the makers of the nation in the past and draws periodical inspiration from recital of their achievements in the realm of the spirit.[35]

The cultural genious of India have never failed to utilize every place of fascinating beauty and grandeur as a perennial source of inspiration, affording supreme peace and consolation to the care-worn hearts. From Himalaya to Cape Camorin, from Dwaraka to Assam there are thousands of places that are considered as sacred without distinction of caste or creed. As a general rule, every such a place has grown out of countless legends and traditions having served as an incentive to religious and cultural feelings. In course of time, they became places of pilgrimages, attracting reverence for other sects on account of innate Catholicism of Indian culture. Neither Idle curiosity nor blind faith can account for the unique phenomenon, for most of pilgrims have to undertake long journeys involving physical discomfort and heavy expenses. It is the cultural-religious moorings of the people responsible for their great long journey. Even commercial enterprises grow around these places giving impetus to various arts and crafts. Indian architecture, sculpture and painting received ample encouragement during festival periods. Temples represent cultural philosophy in brick and stone. Worship in temples was in a way responsible for the astonishing development of all fine arts. Thus, pilgrimage has been the fore-runners of national unity, transforming the country into a vivid and visible reality with all its parts deemed equally sacred and lovable.[36]

Owing to it's chequered history and the tolerant spirit of the natives, all major religions of the world are fairly represented in India so much so that it can be called a variable land of religions. Following their own styles and worshiping their own Gods, the people of numerous indigenous and immigrant faiths live in close harmony, barring some occasional politicised communal riots and violence. However, secularism grew out of the social intercourse between diverse faiths of communities, born of need and nature, far before it was enshrined in the he constitution. In keeping with the spirit of secularism to which a the country is avowed, the Union and State Governments recognize the main festivals of all the important communities of Indian as public holidays.[37]

## DYNAMICS OF FESTIVALS AT MICRO LEVEL

At the micro level of sociological analysis, fairs and festivals are inherently inter twinned in the social structure of village India. In Indian villages, time is generally counted in terms of an annual cycle of festivals. The periods of each year are defined by a series of breaks in the usual routine during which agricultural and business responsibilities are temporarily set aside so that villagers can prepare special foods, attend feasts, organize processions and exchange gifts with friends or relatives. In van Gennep's and Turner's usage, these are "Liminal" periods, or times when time itself stops for a while.

Festivals can also include dramatic ritual events with elaborate performances and many have marveled at the splendor of such rituals as the Jagannath at Puri or

Ganapati in maharashtra. Such events as these present a sociologist or anthropologist with great challenges, from both, analytic and a physical point of view. Sheer complexity and force of numbers should convene us that if we are to capture the "style" of a culture, it is in such dramatic events, as Ortiz has pointed out. But, they are especially difficult to study, because of their frequency duration, or complexity in nature.[39] A number of studies have attempted to focus on some changes which have occurred in the festivals, or one or more villages together with other social and economic changes. They highlight recent social transformations, which provide the background for understanding the outcome of festivals in villages.[40]

While some other studies have attempted to focus on little traditional festivals in particular villages and how they are related to great traditional festivals.[41] (Reddy P.M., 1985)

Suzanne Hanchett, in his study of Ganapati and Narasingh festivals in Bandipur village of Mysore through ethnographic procedure observes that Ganapati festival was developed in direct competition with one other village level festival in the annual cycle: the harvest time festival in honour of the God Narasimha. Neither of these is completely independent and unaffected by the village political events on the basis of its socio-economic structure. On the contrary, these festivals represents symbolic contexts in which compromises are made and the organization of the village is annually negotiated and confirmed unlike the Ganapati festival the financing and management of the harvest festival is a prolonged one and is primarily from the upper caste and upper class community particularly Brahmin community.[42]

Ritual events during the festival period are structured in terms of a purely supernatural order for favourable results and not consciously in terms of any natural or secular social order. However, it is not only the success of the crops that is symbolically prefigured in a village level festival, but as such festival are systematically organized in terms of symbolic relationships between major village groups during the year in which they are performed. Further more, these village rituals can be organized and reorganized, as if to periodically reading social relationships in changing times. Besides, in the village numerous castes of the village, each has specific roles in festival events. The temple committee pays a small honorarium to each caste for contributing its effort, but each group considers such service to be a privilege as well as an obligation castes are generally protective of their rights in processions and other events, since they acquire favour with the God by performing their customary duties.[43]

There are certain mechanical characteristics of the temple cart procession which are seen as mysteries. The procession is organized according to specific sociological principles. The miracle is associated with the movement of the cart. For diverse and conflicting groups must join together to perform a task in unison once a year. Thus, this procession is an annual test of the viability of the village as an organization. If the procession moves at all, the "socio-mechanical" principles which motivate it are valid otherwise not. The increasing importance of the Harijans in the village land economy (and the Brahmins increasing dependence on them) is emphasized in the contest of the procession.[44]

But, on the contrary, according to Joan Mencher, Harijans have no role at all in the Madras card festivals of Brahmin villages with which she is familiar, in chinglepet district. Speaking of another Brahmin village, in Tanjore District, Madras. Andre Beteile states that, "Once a year when the deity of the main Kali temple is taken around the village, even Adi-Dravidas (Harijans) "Join the procession". (Beteile 1965:101).[42]

In the case of Bandipur village, the relations between the major groups of castes are changing. The introduction of a new festival event at Ganapati represents an attempt to legitimize and confirm the position of a newly independent and powerful caste group- the Non-Brahmins. However, the village level festival event is the one time during the year when representatives of all significant local groups undertake a co-operative venture. It is at this time when relationships during the year to come are identified and established symbolized symbolically. Such festivals provide significant and decisive interludes for other villages in this culture area of Bandipur.[46]

Thus, while discussing a village in Tanjore District, Madras, Kathleen Gaugh[47] states that "The festival, more than any other event, is crucial for the maintenance of the traditional more order. For in it all the castes give dramatic expression to the ritual ranking and distance between them, yet to their mutual interdependence and exclusiveness as a village community". (Gaugh 1960:51). Nur Yalman[48] observes that in Cylon annual processions, called Perahera, "display the entire superstructure of caste and service". (Yalman (1967:17). In Coorg, M.N. Srinivas [49] describes the ways in which descent groups (Okka) divide ritual tasks among themselves in the village deity festival. He also mentions that competition and conflict appear on the occasion of this festival and during the harvest festival as well. (Srinivas 1952:171).

However, such festivals in India, rather being performed in the same way each year, can be changed as social units manipulate their elements, in order to communicate or negotiate with each other on crucial matters. From a "functionalist" point of view, it is important to note that festival event may either socially dissolve villages or unify groups and "reflect" social structure, depending on the outcome of important events. Neither outcome is inevitable and results depend on total social processes pertinent to the case in question. A static framework is not adequate to describe the role that these events seem to play in village social life.[50]

Indian festivals are not static in nature. It is a process of evolution that is manifestly at work to bring out new festivals and to wipe out some of the old ones. The mode and spirit of observance of some festivals have undergone significant changes. Some new festivals have cropped up in analogy of some other festivals. In fact, the dynamicity of festivals in India differs from place to place and from community to community. But there is underlying commonality among most festivals. However, in course of time, different cultures have coalesced through the medium of festivals.[51] Keeping with the spirit of the time, a number of festivals like the Independence Day, Republic Day, Gandhi Jayanti and soon have sprang up since Independence. The expanding horizon of festivals is provided by the recent growth of public functions organized in connection with birth and death anniversaries of the great persons of our country. Thus some festivals have assumed profane or secular character.[52]

Indian festivals do not merely involve associative processes i.e. assimilation, adaptation and competition. Sometimes dissociative processes like conflict, dissention and violence disrupts the observance of festivals. Besides the exuberance of the festivals sometimes inspires the revelers to indulge in some unseemly practices. As for example, some of the processionists, who take out the images in motor, trucks, and lorries in the immersion day of any puja festival, are often seen to dance grotesquely while singing vulgar songs and throwing rice or colour on the pedestrians, particularly females, Sometimes, the victims of the frenzy stain injuries. Similarly the indiscriminate sprinkling of colured water on the Holi festival, reckless bursting of crackers on the Diwali night verge on vandalism. Even sometimes community festivals in villages and cities give rise to different intensity of conflict and violence only because of conflict of community inerests.[53]

## FUNCTIONS OF FESTIVALS

Inspite, of such criticisms Indian festivals have their salutary effects on the minds of people. It is a source of immense joy and pleasure for all sections of people living in a society. Festivals serve to mitigate and more positively soften the otherwise severe feelings of struggle with the elements round the year. These provide occasions to display their joys and jovial sentiments, renew social contacts, strengthen community relations and maintain social solidarity. Besides, the observance of festivals is a potent factor for the development of artistic talents and activities of the people. In celebrating a festival care is taken to present dance, song, music and other literary and cultural items.[54]

Moreover, festivals are also a source of income to many people in the villages and towns. The priestly class largely depend on the income from these festivals. Many professional parties like operas earn their livelihood mainly on these occasions. The making of images, which fetch usually high prices, gives the artisans a good means of livelihood. The community worships, such as Durga Puja, Ganapati Puja, Kali Puja etc. have been a occasion of the big business boom particularly for the business class. However, the economic aspect of the festivals is not always bright for all. People are sometimes compelled to go beyond their means in meeting the expenses of their household. Time has perhaps come to put a curb on such excesses and extravagances.[55]

## A GLANCE AT TRIBAL FESTIVALS IN INDIA

A large percentage of the population of India inhabiting in the wild regions of hilly and forest areas, cannot be strictly considered as Hindu or other. Their traditional uninhibited gaity still finds expression in tribal celebrations and rituals. Those spectacular festivals are of particular interest not only to tourists but also to scholars in general and social anthropologists in particular. The folklore and legends of festivals may supply a key to understand the origin, migration and past fortunes of the tribes.[56]

Specially for the primitive people like tribes, festivals generally represent collective ritual, who through different social groups like the family, clan or kin participate in them for the welfare of the entire group.[57] As agricultural operation is collective among the tribal people, they perform community festivals which represent the rites variously called as Fertility rites, vegetation rites, productivity rites etc. Naturally the festivals of the agricultural people, resembling religious rites, have the social urge of fertility, fecundity, generation and all that is connected with the very existence of such people.

There are also individual festivals in which the entire society takes part. These take place when an individual passes from one stage to another, from one occupation to another. Primitive people are used to perform such ceremonies because to them no act is entirely free from sacred character. In their societies every change in an individuals life involve actions and reactions between the sacred and the profane, and that life requires to be guarded and regulated so that no harm is caused to the society as a whole. Such rites are known as "rites of assuage which the Hindus call as "Samskara"[59]

While the festivals centered upon an individual, a clan, or a family speak of social solidarity, the communal festivals are mostly propitiation of Gods of Goddesses in the hope that they bountiful to the entire society or that they may save the community from some continuing or impending dangers. In some places, festivals are observed as a sort of fertility magic for greater production of food. Such magic known as "initiative magic" with regard to food production is expected after each successive harvest when the soil becomes exhausted and requires to be fertilized through fertility rites.[60] Such festivals or rites may ethuse sexual abandon with the intention of having magical effect on the fertility of the crop and the community.[61] For instance Santals have a number of community festivals connected with different agricultural occupations. On these occasions they sacrifice cocks and goats and make a community feasting. The Mundas, the Birhors, the Hos, the Kondhs and many other tribes too celebrate such festivals under various names.[62]

Dancing and singing occupy important roles in tribal festivals. For instance, the bear dance, pigeon dance, pig and tortoise dance of the Junags as noted by Dalton E.T. represent mimetic magic on the part of these people. Tribal dances are mostly connected with festivals celebrated in honour of Gods and have magical expression through movement of hands and the body. Further more, festivals originally are designed to activise Nature by sympathetic magic for rain-making through dances and other similar sports.[63] Tribal festivals are culturally and socially significant because through them contacts are established between different classes of people. Festivals generally take place in the open. Though celebrated on a grand scale and having interesting legends about it's origin, the festival may be a vegetation rite common to all people living in the aforesaid area. Some tribes like the Santals and the Mundas have borrowed such legends from the Hindus.[64]

In some festivals, cow-sheds are cleaned and cows are given good food and allowed rest. On this occasion, bull sports called Khuntan are held by Santals.[65] Frazer has shown how the bull, cow or ox is treated as the corn-spirit in different European countries.[66] However, other animal sacrifices are common among different tribes in India, for cessation of drought and death. The festivals of tribals in India would appear lifeless if no reference is made to the practice of drinking on these occasions.

Drinks are named differently in different regions. These are locally made and sold in chapter rate. Today, the tribals have started adopting foreign liquor. On festive occasions, all tribals in a community enjoy in drinking, singing and dancing.[67]

Tribals in India observe several festivals and religions ceremonies through out the year. They are mainly agriculturists and their life is confined to land and spirits. They believe that natural objects exercise a beneficent influence on their life and happiness. All their festivals are invariable components of their lifestyle. The natural environment in which they are born and brought-up compels them to believe on certain omniscient powers who reveal themselves through several deities. Since time immemorial tribals worship certain deities their own. But it would seem that their religious beliefs and practices have undergone change during last six or seven decades only because of influence of Hinduism and other religions. Even it, they propitiate the spirits of their deceased ancestors on festive occasion and whenever confronted with a critical situation. Since their tradition culture moves around Nature, so also their owes and amusements moves around it. In course of life, they have developed a life-cycle based on seasons and months in which their amusements and sorrows, works and leisure have given birth several religious beliefs and festivals. [(68)] (Alok Kumar 1986).

Tribal festivals in India are not always religious. Some of them are seasonal and entertainment oriented. For instance, Karam festival in a Munda village is one or merriment, dancing and drinking beer. It takes place after the agricultural activities reach an end. From the point of view of functionalism this festival perhaps is a hallmark of integration in the Munda culture (Das D.N., 1954) [(69)]. However, religion is an integral part of tribal social structure. Many studies reveal that trial from the benevolent spirits and on the other hand, to deprive the malevolent ones of their evil influences. The secular aspect of their rituals is to provide entertainment and diversion, to give them confidence and security and to strengthen social solidarity. The expressive aspect of their spirit worship is especially manifested in the rites and rituals of festivals related to the annual agricultural cycle and also during the rites of passage of their life cycles (J. Troisi, 1978) [(70)]

## CONCLUSION

India is a popularly known as a melting pot of second largest popular country of the world, consisting of multiple languages, religions, castes, creeds and races alongwith their respective distinct cultures. Inspite of this, there is unity in diversity. For India composite culture". Has always attracted and fascinated people from far and wide. Tourists have gone through the length and breadth of the country and left rich accounts of their impressions. Each and every unit of her culture is so deep-rooted and variously complicated that it often assumes strange to foreigners of outsiders. It is therefore, not an easy task to write justifiably on the fairs and festivals of India without having comprehensive knowledge of the socio-cultural background of her people, their manners and customs and the faculty to feel and regard the folk-sentiments in right earnest. However, with much difficulty an attempt has been made in this paper to delineate the nature and scope of festivals in India. While focussing on their processual and composite character in line with ideological traditions.

## REFERENCES

1. See forward by Dr. O.C. Handa in "Festivals, Fairs and Customs of H.P. "ed. by: Main Goverdhan Singh: Indus Publishing Company, New Delhi, 1992.
2. Thomas P.: "Festivals and Holidays of India", D 8. Taraporvala Sons & Co. Ltd., Mumbai, 1971.
3. Welbon, guy R and Glenn E. Yocum: "Religious Festivals in South India and Srilanka" See (Preface), Manohar Publications, New Delhi, 1982.
4. Thomas P. Ibid
5. Sanon Arun: "Festive India", Frank Bros & Co., New Delhi, 1987. (See Introduction)
6. See Leila Ghosh and Daha Roys: Festivals of India", India Book House, Spain Print Pvt. Ltd., Mumbai, 1986.
7. Mauss Marcel, 1954 "The Gift", The Free Press, Gleneoe, Illinois.
8. For detail see Jean Duvignaud "Festivals: A Sociological Approach" In Cultures Vol. III, No. 1, 1976 PP. 13-25.
9. Durkheim emile ; "The Elementary forms of Religious Life", trans by J.W. Swain, Glencoe, I11:Free Press, 1954, See Jean Duvignaud Ibid.
10. See also Mrcel Mauss "The Gifts, Forms and Functions of Exchange in Archaic "Societies, trans by Ian Cunnison (New York: W.W. Norton 7 Co., 1967, P. 128 (In Jean Duvignaud Ibid).
11. Roger Caillois, "Man and the sacred, trans by Meyer Barash, (Glencoe III: Free Press, 1969), 190 PP (In jean Duvignaud Ibid).

12. For detail see Jean Duvignaud 1976 Ibid.
13. Jean aul Sartre "The Emotions: outline of a Theory", trans by Bernard Frechtman (New York: Philosophical library, 1939) In Jean Duvignaud Ibid.
14. Mircea Eliad, the Myth of the Eternal Return, trans by Willard R. Trask (New York: Pantheon Books, 1954). In Jean duvignaud Ibid.
15. George R. Kernolde, "From Art to Theatre (Chicago University Press, 1944) In Jean Duvignaud.
16. Johan Huizinga "Homo Ludens-A study of the play Element in Culture" (various editions) see Jean Duvignaud.
17. The reference on tis whole discourse has been made to the comments by Jean Duvignaud 1976 Ibid.
18. Tewari Udai Narain, 1987 "India: A Cultural Voyage" Chapt. on "Festivals: Accents on Truer Lights". Gian Offset Printers, Old Rohatak Road, Delhi, PP 135-44.
19. Ibid P. 136.
20 Tewari, udai Narain, bid P. 137.
21. Leila gosh and Daha Roy, Ibid.
22. Ibid.
23. Ibid P. 137.
24. Ibid p. 138.
25. Wlbon Guy R & Yocum G.E. Ibid.
26. Sanon Arun Ibid p. 3.
27. Tewari U.D., Ibid.
28. Sanon Arun Ibid.
29. Welbon Guy R & Yocum G.E. Ibid.
30. Sanon Arun Ibid P. 4.
31. Welbon & Yocum, Ibid.
32. Tewari U.D. Ibid P. 139.

33. Sanon Arun, Ibid P. 4

34. Welbon and Yocum Ibid.

35. Tewari U.D., Ibid P. 142.

36. Ibid P. 143.

37. Sanon Arun Ibid P. 2.

38. Hanchett Suzanne: "Festivals and Social Relations In a Mysore Village-Mechanics of Two Processions", Economic and Political Weekly, Special Number August 1972, P. 1517).

39. Ibid (Turner, Victor W. 1969 "The Ritual Porcess" Aldine Publication Co., Chicago, Ortiz Alfonso, 1970 "Challenges in Anthropological Study Ritual Drama & Festival").

40. For understanding the dynamics of festivals at Micro (village) level, also see: Harsha N. Mukherjee "Ritual Structure of a village in West Bengal", Man and Life, Vol. II No. 1& 2, 1985, Pp. 1-16: P. Munirathan Reddy "Little Traditional Festivals in an Andhra Village, Venur"-The Eastern Anthropologist, Vol. 38/ 2.1985 PP. 69-7; Indra Dev "Feasts and Family Celebrations in Northern Indian Society", Cultures Vol. III. No. 2, 1976 PP. 59-71 and others.

41. Reddy P.M. "Little Traditional Festivals in Andhra village, Venur", The Eastern Anthropologist, Vol. 38 No. 2, 1985 PP. 169-71.

42. Hanchett Suzanne, Ibid.

43. Ibid, P. 1519.

44. Ibid.

45. See also Beteille Andre: 1965 "Caste, Class and Power",, University of California Press, Berkeley.

46. Hanchett Suzanne, Ibid P. 1521.

47. Gough, E. Kathleen, 1960 "Caste In a Tanjore Village" In "Aspects of Caste In South India, Ceylone and North-West Pakistan" E.R. Leach (editor) Cambridge University Press, Cambridge, PP. 11-60.

48. Yalman Nur, 1967 "Under The Bo Tree", The University of California Press, Berkeley and Los Angeles.

49. Srinivas, M.N. 1952 "Religion and Society Among The Coorgs of south India" Asia Publishing House, Bombay.
50. Hanchett Suzanne, Ibid P. 1522.
51. Sharma Hemant Kumar, "Socio-Religious Life of The Assamese Hindus" Daya Publishing House, Delhi 110006, 1992, p. 231.
52. Ibid P. 240.
53. Ibid P. 241-242.
54. Also See Sing, Mian Goverdhan "Festivals, Fairs and Customs of H.P.," Indus Publishing Company, New Delhi, 1992.
55. Sharma, Hemant Kumar, Ibid P. 241.
56. Thomas P. Ibid.
57. Briffault R. "Festivals" in Encyclopaedia of the Social Sciences, Ed. E.R.A. Seligman, Vol. V, New York, 1951, P. 198.
58. Mukhopadhaya Sankaranana: Austrics of India", K.P. Bagchi & Company, Calcutta, 1975, P. 75.
59. See also Gennep, A.V.: The Rites of Passage, Trans, M.B. Vizedom and G.L. Caffe, London, 1960, PP. 2-3 (Phoenix Books).
60. James E.O.: "Seasonal Feasts and Festivals", London, 1961, P. 38.
61. Hulton, J.H.
62. There are a number of studies on this issue of feasting and festivals of Indian tribes. For instance see: S.C. Roy and R.C. Roy "The Kharias" Vol. II, Ranchi 1937, P. 335: D.N. Majumdar, "The Affairs of a Tribe" Lucknow 1950, P. 221 and also S.C. Roy: "The Mundas and their Country", Mumbai, 1970 (reprint) PP. 263-76.
63. Mukhopadhaya S. Ibid P. 79. See also Sachidananda "Culture Change in Tribal Bihar: Munda and Oraon, Calcutta, 1964. PP. 73-74 and Briffault R. Op. cit P. 199.
64. Mukhopadhaya S. Ibid, P. 80. Also se S.C. Roy, op. cit PP. 263-A detailed description of the festivals alongwith the legends and rites, seen from a folklouristic point of view, has been given in S.K. Karan, "Simanta Banglar Lokayan" (In Bengali), Calcutta 1371 BS. PP. 100-28.

65. C.L. Mukherjee "The Santals", Calcutta, 1962, P. 255.

66. Frazer, J.G. "Golden Gough", Vol. II, PP. 600-12.

67. Mukhopadhaya, S. Ibid, PP. 81-83.

68. Kumar Alok:"Tribal Culture and Economy-the Malpahhias of Santal Pragans". Inter India Publication, New Delhi. 1986, PP 223-25.

69. Das D.N.: "Karam Festival in a Munda Village", Vanyajati, Vol. 2, No. 1, Jan. 1954, PP. 22-25.

70. Troisi, J: "Tribal Communior with the Supernatural-An Analysis of Santal Flower Festival". Social Action, Vol. 28, No. 2, 1978, PP. 149-64.

# 14

# Bohada: The Mask Festival of Bharsatmet

*Dr. Robin D. Tribhuwan & Dr. Laurence Savelli*

## WHERE IS BHARSATMET?

Bharsatmet village is located about 16 Kms away from Jawahar tahsil, of Thane district, in Maharashtra State India. The village is predominently inhabited by the Koknas with few Warli houses. The total population of Bharsatmet is 1600, as per 1991, census.

This village is one of the popular villages known for "Bohada"—the mask festival. People from Nasik, Bombay, Gujarat, Sylvasa, Daman etc. come to see this tribal festival. Primary data collected from the villagers of Bharsatmet and Ramachandra Bharsat—the master mask maker, revealed that this tradition is as old as the village. They were however, able to take back their memory 300 years ago. Today there is a mask made out of wood by the grandfather of Ramachandra. This mask character is called "Ghuba Devi" and is 200 years old.

Ramachandra's forefathers were mask and copper motif makers. Infact it would be appropriate to make a statement that Ramachandra is the best mask maker in tribal Maharashtra and is among the few craftsman who makes copper, alluminium and brass motifs without using moulds. He along with the village head's family have been responsible to preserve and promote this traditional art. He takes active interest in organizing the Bohada festival, which takes place for three days.

## ORGANISERS OF BOHADA FESTIVAL

As mentioned earlier the key role to organise the Bohada festival is played by Ramachandra the mask maker, the village head and at least 30 village elders. These 30 village elders represent those families which keep mask characters at home, maintain and preserve them. They are given the responsibility of taking care of these masks. Each family owns a mask. This mask is covered in a sari and safely kept on the loft of their house. It is removed only 10 to 15 days before the festival, in case of re-painting or decorating the same. These mask owners pay Rs. 100-150 to the organising committee. This committee works on the preparation and management of the festival.

## PREPARATION PHASE

Bohada festival usually occurs after holi. When we attended this festival it was on 5th, 6th and 7th of May 2000. We observed all the phases of the festival.

### A. Fund Raising by the Villagers

Every house hold of Bharsatmet is concerned about fund raising. As mentioned earlier all the families owning a mask pays Rs. 100-150/- per family, towards the organisational fund. Besides this, other families donate between Rs. 10-50. The Warlis who have been converted to 'Malkari' cult, do not pay anything. Malkaris are people who refrain from drinking, eating non-vegetarian food and narcotics. They have also taken up worshipping hindu deities and hence do not participate in the festival. On an average the villagers of Bharsatmet are able to collect Rs. 5000 to 8000/- every year, on their own.

### B. Contribution by Traders

Since tribals and non-tribals from far and near attend the festival, traders also come to sell their goods. The organising committee receives Rs. 50 to 150 depending on what kind of goods are sold by the trader. This money is considered as tax. The villagers called it "DÊr Patti".

### C. Contribution by the Visitors

Visitors who come to watch the festival from other villages are approached to contribute voluntarily for the festival. We contributed Rs. 500/- during the year 1999.

## D. Purchasing Material

Once an amount of Rs. 10 to 15 thousand is gathered then the members of the organising committee discuss on purchasing material and also payment of people who contribute to the making of the festival. Individuals are send to buy the material, summon musicians, decoration contractor etc.

## E. Expenditure

Major expense of the festival can be categorised under following budget heads.

*(i)* Paint, brushes, colour paper, bamboo, etc. for renovating masks;

*(ii)* Painting and cleaning the Hanuman temple in the village;

*(iii)* Purchasing coconuts and other items of puja;

*(iv)* Honorarium of Katkari/Mahar musicians. Kathkari is another tribe, while Mahars are a backward caste community, traditionally assigned to play music for Bohada processions;

*(v)* Expense in lighting and decorating the streets of the village;

*(vi)* Expense on alcohol;

*(vii)* Expense for Kerosine and latterns;

*(viii)* Food expenditure;

*(xi)* Costumes purchase;

*(x)* Miscellaneous expenses.

## F. Painting Masks

Responsibility of painting, decorating the masks is fully bestowed upon Ramachandra—the chief mask maker. He starts his buisness one month before the festival.

## G. Assigning Places to Traders

Asigning places to vendors and hawkers depends on first come first served basis. Traders come one month in advance and book their places. Thus, money is collected one month in advance from the traders.

## H. Rehearsal of Participant Actors (Mask Characters)

It is the responsibility of the village head and Ramachandra to supervise the rehearsal sessions of Bohada. Every mask owner comes for the practice or sends his son. These guys are asked to enact the whole scene and their individual roles during practice sessions.

## I. Village Head: The Co-ordinator

Luxman Pandu Bharsat, the traditional head of Bharsatmet pours in his entire experience and potential to make the festival a success. He co-ordinates, monitors, and checks every activity of the festival.

## J. Role of Ramachandra

Ramachandra Bharsat the chief mask maker and a master craftsman is the soul of the festival. He dedicates his time, talent and energy without charging a single peny to make the festival a success.

## K. Co-operation of the Villagers

Not to forget the honest and sincere efforts put in by the villagers of Bharsatmet. Their active participation too contributes to the success of the festival.

## BOHADA FESTIVAL IN ACTION

First signs of Bohada in Bharsatmet are scenes of tribals and non-tribals in groups and families moving towards Bharsatmet. On 5th of May 1999, we witnessed tribals walking towards this historic village to participate in the festival. People seemed relaxed and happy as they marched on.

As they enter the village there is place to park their bullock-carts outisde the village. We also witnessed a number of two-wheelers parked outside. Maximum tribals had walked all the way to the village, while some came in buses, trucks, tractors, and rikshaws.

### (a) Scene in the Village

As soon as you enter the village, you witness crowdedness. People take their positions on the countryards. Few stand, while most sit. They wait for the festival to begin. One also gets to see traders shouting to attract the attention of buyers. Children make noise, run around, shout and play. The main street of Bharsatmet is just crowded. By six, in the evening they put on the lights.

## (b) Village Head Welcomes the Musicians

Musicians who are hired for three nights are welcomed by the head. They are offered liquor, bidis (cigars) and tobacco. By eight in the night after their dinner musicians start tunning their instruments. By now Bharsatmet has over 10,000 people gathered to witness the festival.

## (c) Headman's Party Comes Out in a Procession

By the time it is 9 in the night, the first event of the festival starts with musicians playing durms and clarenets. There are two drummers playing (Sambulas) two triangular sets of drums and two tribal musicians play clarenet, while one exclusively plays a base clarenet.

While the music is on the "Pahily Pati"—the first procession starts. It is led by the musicians from the headman's house to the Hanuman temple. The members include village head, his wife, Rama Chandra, his wife and other family members of village head.

The women folk carry 'aarti' and coconuts in plate and basket. The first lady of the village, i.e. the head's wife offers a puja to Hanuman—the monkey god. She is followed by other women who offer 'aarti' to Hanuman. This is followed by breaking of coconuts starting off with the village head, followed by Ramachandra and then other male members of the headman's family. Once this in done, mask characters are brought in procession from the village head's house uptil the temple of Hanuman. Every mask is worn by the owner or his son and is accompanied by the musicians in a procession.

## MASK CHARACTERS

Tribals of Jawhar, Mokhada and Peth tahsils of Thane and Nasik districts have revealed that there are as many as 52 characters of Bohada festival. However, when actually observed in Bharsat met—a village of the Kokna tribe, it was discovered that there are 30 traditional mask characters, possessed by 30 clans. These 30 characters are:

| | | | |
|---|---|---|---|
| 1. | Naran dev | 16. | Bakasur |
| 2. | Masa or Fish | 17. | Ravan |
| 3. | Sarjadevi or Saraswati—Peocock | 18. | Vishnudev |
| 4. | Ganapati—or Ganesh | 19. | Chanddev |
| 5. | Mahadev | 20. | Suryadev |
| 6. | Indradev | 21. | Bhim-Bakasur |
| 7. | Khanderao | 22. | Raktadevi |
| 8. | Kaloba | 23. | Ghubadevi |
| 9. | Niloba | 24. | Agnidev |
| 10. | Bhairoba | 25. | Londhya |
| 11. | Kalbhairi | 26. | Narsihva |
| 12. | Ram Tati | 27. | Satwai |
| 13. | Kaurav Tati | 28. | Kumbha Karma—Brother of Ravan |
| 14. | Hedumba | 29. | Bibisan—Brother of Ravan |
| 15. | Mhaisasur | 30. | Krishna |

**Other Characters (Used in Bohadas by the Warlis, Thakars, Kokna etc.)**

| | | | |
|---|---|---|---|
| 31. | Charnin | — | a female herder |
| 32. | Top | — | a man with a cap |
| 33. | Balantin | — | new mother |
| 34. | Gavalani | — | a female herders |
| 35. | Garud | — | Eagle |

*(Contd. ...)*

| | | | |
|---|---|---|---|
| 36. | Waghoba | — | Tiger |
| 37. | Sinhva | — | Lion |
| 38. | Kasav | — | Tortoise |
| 39. | Dait | — | a male demon |
| 40. | Bhil Tati | — | A mask representing-Bhils |
| 41. | Ekadas | — | one headed mask |
| 42. | Duvadas | — | Two headed masks |
| 43. | Zakati Tati | — | small bamboo mask |
| 44. | Vithoba | — | hindu male god |
| 45. | Rukhmai | — | hindu female goddess |
| 46. | Vetal | — | An evil forest spirit |
| 47. | Gajasur | — | long faced Ganesh |
| 48. | Ghoda | — | Horse |
| 49. | Evana | — | mythological character |
| 50. | Dhavloba | — | Mask with white face |
| 51. | Maha Laxmi | — | female goddess |
| 52. | Shivaji Maharaj | — | a Maratha king |

Bohada festival celebrated in Bharsatmet village in Jawhar block of Thane district displayed 30 characters. Each mask character is enacted by a male member of a family. For instance the character of Satvai—the goddess of fertility is enacted by Chandrakant Govanda. Earlier his father, grandfather and great grandfather enacted the same. This family has to permanently take care of that mask. Every year it has to be decorated and maintained by the same family. During Bohada festival people of Bharsatmet send each character in a sequence. These are as follows:

**Sequence of Mask Characters Displayed in Bharsatmet**

| S. No. | Mask Character | | | Name of the Actor |
|---|---|---|---|---|
| 1. | Naradmuni | — | — | Yashwant Pawar |
| 2. | Saraswati | — | — | Narayan Barsat |
| 3. | Ganpati | — | — | Ganesh Gavli |
| 4. | Maruti | — | — | Shashi Kant Barsat |
| 5. | Satvai | — | — | Chandrakant Govanda |
| 6. | Bhim and Bakasur | — | — | Lahu Bhusar |
| 7. | Kalbhairi | — | — | Namdev Pawar |
| 8. | Trimurti | — | — | Hari Raghu Dalvi |
| 9. | Vishnudev | — | — | Subhash Dalvi |
| 10 | Kaurav Thati | — | — | Jayant Shanker Barsat |
| 11. | Indra dev | — | — | Bhasker Khirari |
| 12. | Ramtati* | — | — | Devram Bhusar |
| 13. | Brahma dev | — | — | Vijay Dalvi |
| 14. | Raktadevi | — | — | Suresh Maule |
| 15. | Agnidev | — | — | Ramchandra Barsat |
| 16. | Sri Krishna | — | — | Ramchandra Barsat |
| 17. | Kaloba | — | — | Bhaurao Bhole |
| 18. | Khanderao | — | — | Luxman Barsat |
| 19. | Hedumba | | | Ganpat Gavit |

(Contd. ...)

*Character No. 12*

Ram Thati has three characters namely Ram, Laxman and Sita.

| *S. No.* | *Mask Character* | | | *Name of the Actor* |
|---|---|---|---|---|
| 20. | Vetal | — | — | Sadashiv Barsat |
| 21. | Narsivha | — | — | Vasant Raghu Dalvi |
| 22. | Ravan | — | — | Ram Pawar |
| 23. | Dait | — | — | Dasrat Bharsat |
| 24. | Jagdamba | — | — | Magan Ramu Barsat |
| 25. | Mhashasur | — | — | Govind Raju Pawar |
| 26. | Londhya | — | — | Bhauram Parshuram Maule |

## EVIL OR DEMONIC CHARACTERS

1. *Bhim Bakasur*—Bakasur or a demon popularly known as 'Rakshas' who fought with "Bhima" is named as Bhim Bakasur.

2. *Ravan*—The demon who lived in Lanka', currently known as a Sri Lanka situated, towards the south of India. Ravan had ten heads. He fought with Ram and Laxman, when they were in exile for 14 years. Ravan is said to have captured 'Sita' i.e. Rama's wife, hence the fight, took place.

3. *Hedumba*—is believed to be the sister of Ravana.

4. *Narsivha*—is yet another male demon.

5. *Dait*—a male demon, belongs to the family of demons.

6. *Vetal*—a male forest spirit, that usually moves in the thick woods.

7. *Mhashasur*—a male demon who is killed by Jagdamba on the last day of the "Bohada" festival.

8. *Londhya*—After Mhashasur the dreadful demon is killed, another male evil demon comes out of his stamoch. He is known as Londhya.

## GOOD OR HOLY MASK CHARACTERS

1. *Narad muni:* A form of Brahmans who act like brahmans.

2. *Saraswati:* Sits on the peacock. Peacock to the tribals is "Hirva" a clan deity. Here again it is a fusion of Hindu and tribal deities. The dance shows more action of peacock flying than the goddess.

3. *Ganpati:* The son of Shiva and Parvati is taken in a procession.

4. *Maruti:* The monkey god and a devottee of Ram.

5. *Satvai:* Mother earth who writes the fortune and life span of every human being. That is why whenever a child is born, on the fifth day, it is offered to Satvai for her to decide his life span. Most tribals in Maharashtra worship Satvai on the fifth day after the child is born. They place a child in a basket. A basket is half hemisphere or half part of mother earth in this situation. This basket is a symbol of earth's womb called 'oti'. So they thank the womb of mother earth who is productive and fertile for making the new mother fertile.

6. *Bhim and Bakasur*: Bhim is one of the characters in Mahabharata. He is one of the brother of Panch Pandavas. Where as Bakasur is a demon. Bhim fights with Bakasur in the play and defeats him.

7. *Kalbhairi:* Kalbhairi is a black faced mask with a green crown. He is suppose to be protecting tribals from snakes. If someone is bitten by a snake, ash is applied on the forehead of the patient in the name of Kalbhairi. This socio-ritualistic treatment has an impact on the psyche of the patient. It helps him to come out of the fear that he is going to die.

8. *Trimurti:* As the name suggests "trimurti" is a three faced god, none other than Brahma, Vishnu and Mahesh.

9. *Vishnu Dev:* One of the characters of the trinity, i.e. Vishnu is displayed separately by the Kokanas of Bharsatmet.

10. *Kaurav Thati:* Kavravs are 100 brothers, all characters from the Hindu epic Mahabharata. The Kokanas of Bharstmet make either 10 or 100 small masks on a bamboo mat and is displayed during the Bohada festival. This is done to recreate the mythological scene from Mahabharata.

11. *Indra Dev:* The God of fire, is shown with yellowish or light pink face.

**12.** *Ramtati*: A bamboo mat on which figures of Ram, Laxman and Sita are displayed is called Ram tati. In Bharsatmet Koknas display two types of thee characters.

1. *Ram tati*: the Bamboo mat with three statues of Ram, Laxman and Sita, the heros of Ramayan epic.
2. The living characters of Ram, Laxman and Sita enacted by the Koknas. Three men dress up like Ram, Laxman and Sita and act while they are taken on the streets of Bharsat. The procession is lead by the musicians.

**13.** *Brahmadev*: One of the characters from Trimurti, is Brahma—the creator.

**14.** *Rakta Devi*: Rakta refers to blood, and Devi to godess. Tribals worship the goddess who requires animal sacrifice.

**15.** *Agnidev*: Agni refers to fire, hence the god of fire. The tribals associate him with sun, and not Indra Dev.

**16.** *Sri Krishna:* Is the famous hero of Mahabharata of the Hindu epic. He is usually enacted by a small boy, who wears the mask of Krishna and walks in the procession.

**17.** *Kaloba:* The black faced mask is yet another clan deity of the Kokna.

**18.** *Khanderao:* Yet another Hindu deity, mostly worshipped by the people from middle and lower caste groups.

**19.** *Jagdamba:* Jagdamba or 'Ambadevi' is the most important mask character of "Bohada festival". Its procession is taken out on the third day at 11° clock. People offer her (mask character) coconut, poultry birds, goats etc. The term "Amba" refers to mango. One of the respondents said that since her festival occurs at the time of mango season, she may have got the name "Amba". All the tribals, however say she is the symbol of mother earth—the goddess of fertility, good grains, trees, vegetation, fruits, water, life. She is considered to be their sustainer. They say we are able to survive because of "Jagdamba".

The Non-tribals in the vicinity however associate her with-Kali, who kills Mahishasur—a demon on the Dasera festival. The Koknas however enact the scene of "Amba devi" killing "Mahishasur—a wild buffallo mask bearer" in the play. We feel 'Amba devi' is a cyncritized symbol of tribal and Hindu myths.

The last character in the play is Londhya—a demon, who is given birth to after the death of Mahishasur.

Bharsatmet people also have other mask characters such as "Ghuba Devi"—the goddess with bulging cheeks. This mask is a wodden mask, nearly 200 years old. This was made by Ramchandra's great grandfather. The people of Bharsatmet, who belongs to the Kokna community worship all the masks with aspect and reverence. They believe that these masks are representatives of actual gods and goddesses. It is like all the gods are with them, to protect them from disasters and other calamities.

Another interesting aspect of the Bohada Masks of Bharsatmet is that all these masks are made by one family of artisans, i.e. Ramchandra Pandharinath Bharsat. Other than the above mentioned 30 masks, Koknas of Bharsatmet do not display other characters.

## OTHER MASK CHARACTERS

Bohada is also celebrated by tribals in other parts of Thane and Nasik. These places are Mokhada, Dahanu and Jawhar in Thane and Peth and Surgana in Nasik. Different villages display different mask characters. Some of the other mask characters not discussed in the book are:

1. *Charnin*—A female forest spirit and care taker of the cattle. She is the goddess of tribal cow boys. She protects the cattle from tigers and other wild animals;
2. *Top*—is yet another character of a man, wearing a long cap. Top is another word for cap;
3. *Balatin*—the goddess who presides over the process of delivery. She ensures safe delivery of a new born;
4. *Gavalani*—are seven planetary spirits, believed to be sisters of mother earth. They are spinsters. They visit a human body in the form of hot air, this erupts skins and causes chicken pox, measles boils and Visitation of Gavalani is considered to be auspicious;
5. *Garud*—Is the eagle, referred in Hindu myths as a vihicle of gods.
6. *Waghoba*—The famous tiger god of the tribes in western Maharashtra. The Warlis and Thakars have him as a village god;

7. *Sinhva*—The Lion god. His maks is made and worshipped during Bohada;
8. *Kasav*—Tortoise god is suppose to be a clan deity. It is has medicinal properties;
9. *Dait:* Is a demon from the South direction.
10. *Bhil Thati*—A Bamboo mat on which figures of Bhil tribals are fixed. This mat is taken in procession during 'Bohada'. Bhils may have been providing occupation on daily wage labour to the Thakars and Katkaris and hence Bhil Thati. The Koknas who are economically well off, than other tribals, do not make this mask;
11. *Ekadas*—Is a single headed mask either made up of wood or paper masche.
12. *Duvadas*—Is a two headed mask, usually made up of wood;
13. *Zakati Thati*—A bamboo background having few soldiers. Zakti meaning small, bamboo masks having few figures of soldiers;
14. *Vithoba*—Also known as vithal is a male Hindu deity;
15. *Rukhamani*—A female hindu deity, usually shown with vithal. Both vithal and Rukmani are found in a place called Pandharpur in south Maharashtra;
16. *Vetal*—An evial forest spirit;
17. *Gajasur*—Long faced Ganesh;
18. *Evana*—Is a mythological character;
19. *Dhavolaba*—A male god with white face and body. He is a spirit of the forest;
20. *Ghoda*—The spirit of Horse;
21. *Niloba*—God with blue face and blue body;
22. *Mahalaxmi*—The Hindu deity the goddess of wealth worshipped on the second day of Diwali. To the tribals, she is a tribal goddess whose temple is situated in Dahanu;
23. *Shivaji Maharaj*—A Maratha King who worked with the tribals during the Mughal rule. He was instumental in gaining freedom for Maharashtra. The tribals workship him during Bohada;

24. *Masa*—Is yet another character displayed during Bohada. Masa means fish. Tribals occassionally fish but are regularly consumers of dry fish. Since fish forms an important part of their diet, it may have been given godly status;

25. *Surya Dev*—Wooden masks, of Sun are displayed in Nasik during Bohada;

26. *Chandra Dev*—Wooden mask of moon displayed in Nasik, during Bohada.

## ANALYSIS OF MASK CHARACTERS

In all, there are 54 mask characters enacted by the koknas, Thakars, Warlis, Mahadev Kolis, Katkaris, Malhar Kolis, Dhor Kolis etc. of Thane and Nasik districts in the state of Maharashtra. After analysis all the characters we have come to conclusion that the Koknas and Mahadev Kolis who are economically, socially, educationally and politically are better of have a lot of Hindu characters in Bohada clebrated by them. There two tribes being cultivators have been interacting with the Hindus for long and hence have in corporated characters from Ramayana and Mahabharata in their pantheon.

While the Warlis, Thakars, Katkaris, Malhar Kolis, Dhor Kolis etc. who are socially, educationally, economically and politically quite backward have lot of tribal deities, cosmic forces, forest spirits etc in their Bohada masks. This reveals the socio-economic hierarchy among the tribals, as well as their capacity to celebrate 'Bohada' in a grand or less flashy styles.

Keeping mask characters in the village has multiple advantages They are:

1. The belief that gods are with us provides them moral, mental, and spiritual support;

2. That the presence of these deities facilitates good omen for productive magic such as good rains, good crops, people's welfare etc;

3. This is the best cultural method of preserving the tradition of 'Bohada' and more importantly the making of masks and the techniques these of;

4. Mask festival fetches the villagers money by two ways:

   *(a)* In giving out masks on hire to another village to clebrate Bohada.

   *(b)* Collecting taxes from traders who come to sell their goods in the village, during Bohada.

The artist also makes money in the process. Especially when villagers from other villages order new masks or repair the old ones. Thus, the festival of Bohada is celebrated to bring good fortunes to the village by appearing the mask characters.

The Department of Tribal Development and the Ministry of Human Resource Development must encourage such villages so as to preserve, promote and propagate the declining traditions of tribal art. In Bharsatmet we would certainly like to give credit to two families. One Ramchandra Pandhari Nath Bharsat and the second family is of the village head. Currently Laxman Pandu Bharsat is the village head of Bharsatmet.

He has taken maximum interest along with Ramchandra—the mask maker, to organize Bohadas in their village for last 40 years. The Bohada, we witnessed was 38th Bohada organized by these two men. The entire village however supports them. Given below is the case study of Laxman Pandu Bharsat.

## CASE STUDY

### Personal Background

Laxman Pandu Barsat, a member of Kokna, tribe resident of Bharsatmet village, of Jamsar panchayat in Jawhar block of Thane district, is a head of his village. As the head of the village he has been a pioneer in contributing to the preservation of "Bohada Festival", besides binding and maintaining the community together.

### Course of Events

His great grandfather Ramji Patil, who lived almost 300 years ago was an important force in bringing the people of Bharstmet together, so as to preserve the "cult of Bohada" Ramji was in close contact with the king and princess of Jawhar. The king and his royal family belonged to the Mahadev Tribal community popularly known as "Muknes". The king had special interest in Bharsatmet and even other villages of Jawhar celebrating the Mask Festival.

Since Bharsatmet was a village of artists like Ramchandra and Pandurang Bharsat, who were unique, the king of Jawhar may have taken special interest in this village. These and many other factors make the Bohada of Bharsatmet interesting. We have provided an analysis of why we think Bharsatmet Bohada is unique.

## UNIQUENESS OF BOHADA IN BHARSATMET

1. All characters who use traditional masks in Bharsatmet, make new clothes, depending on the character they are palying.
2. Every clan, which has been playing a particular character is responsible for the santity and maintenance of the mask. This includes expenses for clothes as well.
3. The whole village, thereby is involved (Kokna tribe only) in playing these characters.
4. The Head of the village and the Mask Maker's families have to play a key role in organising the Bohada festival.
5. Manachi pati (The Basket of honour) consisting of ten coconuts to be offered to dieties (Masks) comes from the village head's place. Head is designated traditionally as 'patil'.
6. They do not allow drunkards to participate in the Bohada dance and festival.
7. Buisnessman who came to sell different things/commodities in the festival for 3 days have to pay tax to the village. Thus, a sum of Rs. 1000 to 1500 Rs is collected.
8. Every clan which owns a mask pay Rs. 100 to 150 for the festival
9. Besides this, other villagers also contribute money. Thus, a sum of Rs. 10,000 to 15,000 is collected to host the show.
10. They repaint the masks every year.
11. The characters mentioned in this chapter nearly 30 to 35 of them are taken in a procession. Tribals worship them. Some villages display 52 to 54 characters, they also include other Hindu deities common to all the villages, that celebrate Bohada festival is the display of goddess "Jagdamba" or "Ambadevi" on the third day. For the first two days either 30 or 54 characters are displayed in a procession.

On the third day after the family members of the village head and artist bathe, some where at 9 a.m. they bring out the mask of Jagdamba—a female goddess and her procession is taken out nearly for 4 hours for 'darshan'—tribals from other villages offer sacrifices of fowls and goats, including coconuts. This procession is called "Motha Bohada's, because on this day the main goddess is taken into a procession. The Bohada of first two days is called 'Lahan' Bohada. Motha meaning big and Lahan–meaning small. By 4 p.m. in the evening of the third day, Bohada rituals get over.

## WORSHIP OF VILLAGE GODDESS

Seven days before Bohada festival tribals in and around Bharsatmet grow cereals such as rice, millets, etc. in a small basket and keep it in a cool and moist place. By the second day of Bohada there seedlings become six to seven inches. These seedlings are taken in a procession along with musicians to the village goddess (Gaon devi) and offered to her. This ritual in which all the tribal women participate, offer coconut to gaondevi and thank her for foodgrains. Bohada thus, is an expression of gratitude not only to the gaon devi, but all the gods and goddesses, that are displayed and worshipped in the form of mask characters.

12. One of the most interesting aspect of masks of tribals in Thane and Nasik region is the inclusion of hindu gods and goddesses. This is certainly an impact of acculturation. Secondly Mukne Kings who were exposed to modern and urban world played an important role in incorporating certain mask characters, in the process of hinduization.

## MYTHS ASSOCIATED WITH MASKS OF BHARSATMET

Our analysis of the data collected through interviews and observation revealed that two types of myths are associated with "Bohada Festival".

### 1. Recreation of Ramayan and Mahabharata

Tribals through Bohada try to recreate few scenes of Ramayan and Mahabharat. Besides this they also depict important hindu deities associated with creation of universe. This is however done in a tribal way with their limitation.

### 2. Tribal Concept of Creation and Cosmos

Most of the mask characters depict tribal concept of creation, cosmos and their perceptions about the same.

In doing so the older generations reminds the younger generation of the knowledge of myths which is transmitted socially to them by word of mouth, that is oral tradition.

## THE CULT OF BOHADA: AN INSTITUTION IN ITSELF

The cult of Bohada is an institution in itself, because it is a platform to socialize and enculturate the younger generation about religion, art, dance forms, music, social relations, rituals, myths, history, drama, seasonal cycle, social solidarity and so on. It enhances organizational ability of the village and promotes cultural and multi-enthnic solidarity. It is a social force that binds and brings people together. Given below is a flow diagram that demonstrates the same.

From the flow chart given below it is evident that the cult of Bohada Festival Cross cuts other domains of tribal life. It is a platform for enriching the process of enculturation and socialization for the younger tribal generations. In the Bohada mask festival youngsters learn:

*(i)* all about mask characters, their nature and role in sustaining humanity. The powers possessed by these mask gods and goddesses.

### CULT OF BOHADA: AN INSTITUTION

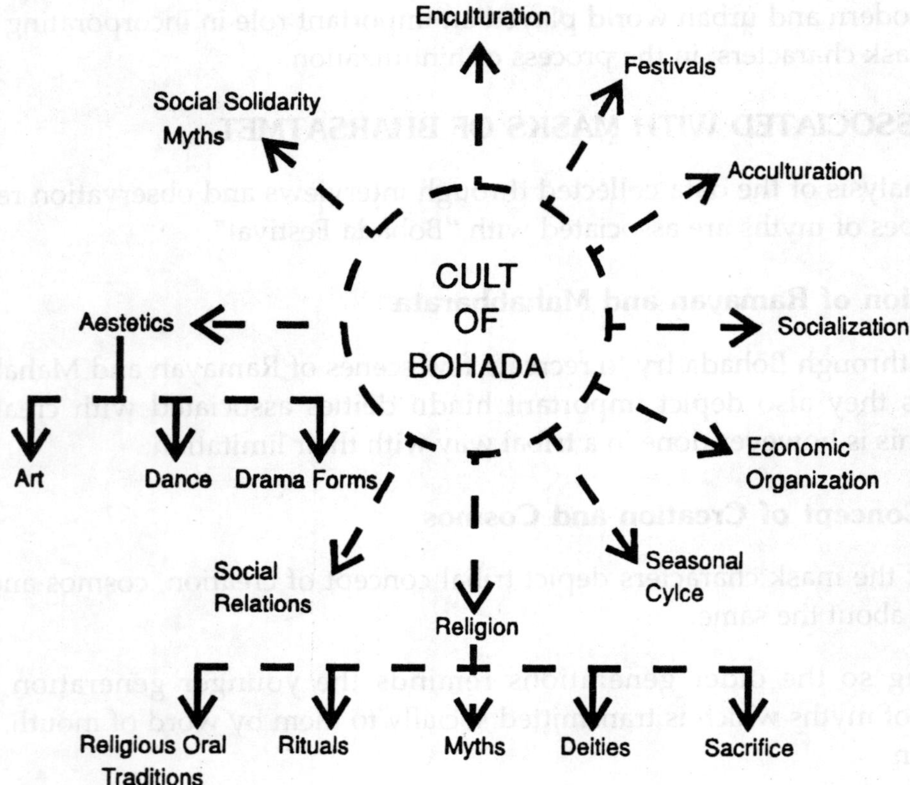

*(ii)* they learn all the processes and sequences of rituals.

*(iii)* study myths associated with masks

*(iv)* learn to organize the festival.

*(v)* enhance their ability to interact and co-ordinate with other tribal and non-tribal communities.

*(vi)* learn to built up their acting, singing and dancing talents.

*(vii)* the Bohada festival teaches them to know more about seasonal cycles and economic organizations.

*(viii)* to stregnthen social relationships.

*(ix)* to stregnthen social solidarity with in the village, their community and with other communities.

*(x)* to stregnthen the need to preserve and promote their traditional art forms.

*(xi)* finally, the cult of Bohada speaks of their cultural heritage, as it is an institution is itself.

❑❑❑

# 15

# Festivals of the Nagas

***Talimenla & Dr. Robin D. Tribhuwan***

## INTRODUCTION

Nagaland is in the north eastern corner of India. Nagaland was proclaimed the sixteenth state of the Indian union on 1st December 1963. It was carved out of the hill district of the former undivided Assam. It covers an area of 16,527 sq. km. and hills between 25º6′, 27º4′ N and 93º20′ 95º15′ E. It borders Assam in the North and the West Arunachal Pradesh in the Northeast, and Burma in the East, on the state of Manipur in the South and runs more or less parallel to the left bank of the Brahmaputra. Nagaland in the past was called as 'Naga Hills'. Nagaland has eight districts namely Kohima, Mokokchhung, Mon, Phek, Wohha, Thensang, Zunhebato and Dimapur.

Nagaland state in the home of several tribes, who still preserve their cultural identity and linguistic characteristics. The tribes occupying different districts of the state are given in the table below.

**Table 15.1: District Wise Distribution of Tribes**

| *S. No* | *Districts* | *Tribes* |
|---|---|---|
| 1. | Kohima | Angami, Rengma, Zeliang |
| 2. | Mokakchung | Ao |
| 3. | Mon | Konyak |

*(Contd. ...)*

| | | |
|---|---|---|
| 4. | Phek | Lhakesang, Polhury |
| 5. | Wokha | Lotha |
| 6. | Tuensang | Lhang, Sangtam, Yimchunger, Phom, Khiamnivungan |
| 7. | Zunheboto | Sema |
| 8. | Dimapur | A. Mixture of all the Tribes |

## I. Origin of the Word 'Naga'

Every term or name originates with a meaning either through an incident or through a story linked with it. The origin of the word Naga is very complicated and is shrouded in mystery.

According to Butlu (1875) the word 'Naga' is derived from Bengali word 'Nanga' meaning Nahed. Another view states that the word Naga is probably derived from the word 'Nok' or Noka meaning floks or people. Another theory States that the word Naga is derived from Sanskrit word 'Nag' which means Hill or mountain and thus Naga means 'Hillman'. Sometimes the word 'Nag' is also referred to a Snake presumably connected with snake Charmer. But the most acceptable or plausible theory in so far as the origin of the word Naga is concerned as opinioned by Shimery (1985) is that "The Naga men and women have the tradition of making holes in the ears for decoration, the Burmese as 'Naha' meaning peiched ear, the anglicized word for 'Naka' became Naga.

## II. Physical Features

Physically the Nagas are predominantly Mongoloid. The Naga's have straight black hair, black eyes, epicanthic eye-fold, yellowish complexion slightly brachiocephalic head and other features of the huge spread of Mongoloid peoples, who now inhabits areas of China and Amazonia. The Naga's are well built and muscular in form or the average the height of the Naga man in 5'5" (163 Cm) and the woman is little less than the man, that is an the average of 5'2" (155 Cm).

## III. Population

According to 2001 census the district wise population of Nagaland is given below.

**Table 15.2: District Wise Male and Female Population**

| *S. No.* | *District* | *Male* | *Female* | *Total* |
|---|---|---|---|---|
| 1. | Kohima | 1,61,702 | 1,52,66 | 3,14,366 |
| 2. | Mokokchung | 1,18,428 | 1,08,802 | 2,27,230 |
| 3. | Mon | 1,38,005 | 1,21,599 | 2,59,604 |
| 4. | Phek | 77,082 | 71,164 | 1,48,246 |
| 5. | Wokha | 83,620 | 77,478 | 1,61,098 |
| 6. | Tuensang | 2,16,888 | 1,97,913 | 4,14,801 |
| 7. | Zunheboto | 79,627 | 75,282 | 1,54,909 |
| 8. | Dimapur | 1,66,335 | 1,42,047 | 3,08,382 |
| | | **10,41,686** | **9,46,950** | **19,88,638** |

## IV. Literacy

The literacy rate as per 2001 census.

| *Persons* | *Male* | *Female* |
|---|---|---|
| 67.11 | 71.77 | 61.92 |

## V. Society

*Social Status and Family*

Naga social organisation is made up of cross—cutting group ties. The individual and the household although, few but are integrated into society by being members of large functional unit *i.e.* lineage, clans age-group, classes, morungs and villages.

The morung or youth's dormitory is typically a huge building which physically dominates a Naga village,.sociologically it is a key institution of a naga society. The morung fulfils various functions, it serves as a sleeping place for young unmarried men as well as a guard house for the warrior. It is in some sense served as school where young people learn about social practices and belief, from their elders. The Naga's are through for bravery.

***Settlement Pattern***—Nagas live in villages situated on the hills or mountains. Their house are made up of bamboos with thatched house.

***Family***—The family types of Naga society are patriarchal and patrilineal family which means the line of succession follow heirs only. The property goes from the father to son and if a man dies without a son, his property will go to his brother's or brother's son's as the case may be. If there is no brother's son. The major share of property goes to the eldest son including the house. Then his younger brother's receive equal shares. However, the eldest son can give up his rightful claim in favour of his younger brothers also.

***Food and Drinks***—The Nagas are farmers and depend on agricultural products with rice as the staple food. The people eat various kinds of meat and fish without any restriction and for the reason animal's are both hunted and domesticated. Various vegetables including jungle leaves are also taken. Bamboo, Shoots, Yam, Soyabeans and dry fish are some important food items. The individual prepare rice beer and it is consumed as the house hold drink. People seldom drink water, but when they feel thirsty they take tea. It is taken lightly generally without milk and sugar.

***Dress and Ornaments***—Formerly the men used to wear only lion cloth and nothing else. To keep warm they used to sit and sleep by the fire. Sometimes traditional shawl is draped on the shoulder. The women use to wear a short mekhala, which hardly covers upto the knee and nothing for the upper part except the many stringed bead necklace to cover the shapely breast. All the tribes have different types of colourful shawls which are used by both man and women. Ornaments like, armlet, wristlet, anklet, necklace, earring, headgear and bracelets etc. are commonly used.

***Marriage***—Marriage is an important event among the Nagas. Different tribes have different systems of marriage. In some tribe there is a system under which the would be groom is required to work in the field of the father or guardian of the would to be bride. The work period last from six months to one year during which the groom should satisfy the bride's father or guardian, his ability to maintain, a wife. Before marriage the groom is to construct a house for his own which is the beginning of being separated from his parents family, as the Nagas follow the system of nuclear family.

In the Naga society they are certain claims a families which cannot intermarry.

## FESTIVALS

### 1. Angami Naga

*Sekrenyi*—Sekrenyi is celebrated by the Angami's in the month of February, with enthusiasm lasting ten days. The ten days festival is also called phousanji, by the Angamis. The celebration intends to invoke the blessing of god. The festival follows a circle of ritual and ceremony but is mostly, marked by full flow of drinks, feasting, singing, dancing and merry making.

### 2. Rengma Naga

*NGA-DA*—The festival of the Rengams, Ngada is celebrated in the last week of November for eight days just after harvest. It is a festival of thanksgiving to the God for his blessing and good harvest. The festival also makes the end of the agricultural year. The spirit is involved for bounty in the coming days. Ritual, prayer feasting, singing, dancing and merrymaking marked the celebration.

### 3. Zeliang Naga

*NGA-NGAI*—The Zeliangs celebrate the Nga-Ngai festival in the last part of December. During this festival thanks is given to god for the year good harvest and prayer is made for more blessing in the days to come. It is celebrated with much, feasting, singing, dancing and fun fare, by all the Zeliang Community.

### 4. Ao Naga

*(i)* *MOATSU*—Moatsu festival is celebrated in the month of May, first week every year just after sowing of paddy seeds. Moatsu is celebrated to appease the deities and to get blessing on the crops. It is celebrated by seeking blessing, peace, health and prosperity from God 'Lyaba'. Moatsu is celebrated by all the Ao's by merry making feasting, singing and dancing.

*(ii)* *Tsungrem Mong*—Tsungrem mong is the second important festival of the Ao's. It is a harvest festival celebrated in the first week of August of every year generally from 1st to 6th August. Tsungrem mong is observed in honour of the God known as Lijaba. By doing so the people believed that they would have good harvest. Tsungrem mong is celebrated in the same manner as Montsu Festival with feasting. Money making, singing and dancing.

## 5. Konyak Naga

***Aoling***—The Konyak celebration the Aoling festival on the first week of April every year. Aoling is observed after completion of sowing of seeds in the new fields, and also to mark the end of the old and to welcome the new year beginning with spring when a riot of flower's in every hue start to bloom. It is a time to ash Almighty God for bountiful harvest of crops in that every year. It is celebrated with great feasting, singing and dancing.

## 6. Chakhesang Naga

*(i)* *Sukrunye*—Sukrunye is the most important festival and it is celebrated on 15th January. This festival marks of sanctification of the boys and girls through religious ceremonies and rituals. This festival is also marked as children's day. Water baptism can take place on this occasion. Dancing this festival the indigenous games, folk dance, folk song's and sports are participated by all the challenging. Sukrunye is a time of joyful celebration and so people do anticipate and flown for the next to come.

***(ii)*** *Tsukhenyi*—Tsukhenyi is another important festival of the Chakesang's which is celebrated every year on the month of March and April. It is celebrated to express thanks for the good harvest yielded and also to invoke the spirit of the God of bounty for the care and prosperity in the coming days too. During this festival the tribals take part in singing, dancing, merrymaking and feasting.

## 7. Puchury Naga

***Yemshe***—Yemshe is the festival of the Peccaries which is celebrated on the first week of October every year. It is the festival of welcoming the new harvest and blessing, peace and prosperity. All the peccaries, young and old, rich and poor celebrate this festival with great pump and gaiety anticipating a good harvest.

## 8. Lotha Naga

***Tokhu-Emong***—Lotha's celebrate Tokhu Emong after harvest on the first of November every year. It is a thanksgiving ceremony for the harvest during which they also seek blessing for the coming year. On these day all the loathes marked the festival by killing of animals, inviting, and sharing of food with relatives, and friends, singing folk song, performing cultural dances, narration of folklore by the villages elders and other forms of merrymaking.

## 9. Chang Naga

***Naknyulum***—Naknyulum is celebrated on the second week of July. It is celebrated to express thanks for the good harvest and to moving more blessing in the coming years. During this festival domestic animals are slaughtered young, and old play games like Tug-of-war, top spinning etc. Young and old all engage themselves in festing and merrymaking.

## 10. Sangtam Naga

***Amongmong***—It is celebrated on the first week of September mainly to appease the spirit dwelling in the three oven stones for bounty, health and prosperity in the days to come. Amongmong is one of the most important festival of the snagtans's celebrated with great pomp and much feasting.

## 11. Yimchunger Naga

***Metemngo***—The Yimchunger's celebrate metemneo festival during the second week of August every year after the harvest of millet. They celebrate this festival for health, wealth, peace and prosperity. This festival is connected with the prayers for the souls of the departed ones. As the festival has a strong agricultural ones, the agricultural upliftments are sharpened and worshipped. During Metemneo festival, the young boys and girls get engaged and those betrothed exchange presents for new born babies. Special prayers's are held and offering are made. On this day friends are invited, gifts are exchanged with great feasting, dancing and fun faces.

## 12. Phom Naga

***Monyu***—Monyu the most popular and biggest festival of the Phom tribe in the month of April 1st week every year soon after sowing season. This festival makes the beginning of monsoon. During this festival the prists on the village elders perform a ritual and predict what the forthcoming festival would be A blessing on a cause Monyu is a time to bid farewell to the ongoing year and held the dam of the new Year. It is also a line of prayers and dictation for the sporting crops that are already sowed. The main feature of the Monyu festival is the occasion when the male members of the family shows lone and affectionate feeling towards their married daughters of sisters by presenting them the present of the rice beer and specially prepared food. This festival is celebrated with pomp and gaiety, singing, dancing and merrymaking.

**13. Khiamnivngan Naga**

*(i)* *MIU*—The Khiamnivngan celebrates min festival on the first week of may every year, and one of the main significance of this festival is to built cordial relations and to forge close knit relations between the maternal uncle and his sisters offsprings *i.e.* nephew and nieces. The significance of this festival is also to mark the seedling in the new field in which all the families of the village go to their fields and perform rituals and prayers to prevent crop damage and mastication of plaque over human and animals.

*(ii)* *Tsohum*—This festival is held during the second week of October. This is mainly observed to give thanks to the almighty deity for giving good crops and safe guarding lives in the family and to invoke the blessing of the god of bounty. The main significance of this festival is to grant permission of right to harvest and test the new crops. It is also during this time that each warrior of the village in the liberty to display his hunted trophies. This festival is celebrated with rituals, feasting and much fanfare.

**14. Sema Naga**

***Tuluni***—The Sema's celebrate Tuluni in the month of July every year. The celebration lasted five days. This day is normally indicated by the medicineman of the village. It is observed mainly to moving the blessing of the God of health wealth and prosperity. Tuluni is a festival of great significance and is marked with feasts as the occasion occurs in the bountiful season of the year. Prayers and rituals are preformed. It is celebrated with great feasts, merrymaking and also Rice beer is served.

All the above mentioned festivals of the Nagas tribes are based on an agricultural cycle. Festivals aim at fertility corresponding to the different agricultural seasons. The people dress themselves in colourful and beautiful traditional thinks on festivals and perform traditional songs and dances during which normal works are suspended.

All the tribal festivals of the nagas are non-Christian festivals. But today Naga people have become cent per cent Christian and so in order to preserve the practice of the last traces of ancient cultural heritage, Christian themselves also observe there festivals unlike the non-Christian, genes are not observed nor sacrifices of animals are practiced nor rice beers is seemed. But they do feasting and partake of meat is plenty. They also take part is singing traditional songs, dancing and merrymaking.

***Christmas***—Christmas is the most important festival which is observed by all the tribes of Nagaland. Christmas is observed on 25th December every year, although Christmas preparation starts as early as 2nd week of December. It is celebrated with great pomp and grandeur not only in the towns but in all the villages of Nagaland. It is an occasion for re-union of families and friends who line apart. Christmas is also an occasion which beings all the Naga tribes together to worship God and to celebrate the birth of Jesus Christ. It is a time when all the tribes meet together and take parts in cultural activities like singing and dancing competition etc. During Christmas all the houses, streets, and churches are cleaned and decorated. All the families hangs Christmas star in bamboo polls high above the roof of the houses or a two remanding every one the very star of Bethlehem as mentioned in the Bible.

## CONCLUSION

The outline of Nagas society explained above is a historical portrait. Today Naga society is evidently pursuing an over all changes and modernization. The impact of Christianity played a vital role in this regard. In terms of social organisation, every Naga is born a member of a clan, which is an important part of an individuals self identity.

There is a huge change in dress habits from traditional attains to modern clothes. But of course the traditional dresses are worn during festivals and special occasions. Education system have improved tremendously among the Naga society. Today Nagaland is the second highest in literacy rate in India.

Morning (which) used to be the most important place of the Naga's but now Churches plays a vital role not only in individuals but also in the Naga society as a whole.

The Naga ethnicity is actively and consciously recommending in the present era. What emerges is a mgorious sense of history and identity, at the level of individual and tribes.

## REFERENCES

Ghosh, B.B. 1979, Nagaland Gazetteers: Mokokchung, District Kohima; Govt. of Nagaland.

Singh, Jai Prakash 1979, Archaelogy of North–East India, New Delhi; Vikas Publication.

Jalobs Julian, 1990, The Nagas, New York; Thames and Hudson, INC.

Mills, J.P, 1926, The Ao Nagas, London; Malmillan and Co. Ltd.

Somare Grata, Vogorelli Leonardo, 1992, The Nagas, Italy.

Hutton, J.H. 1921, The Angami Nagas, London; Themes and Hudson.

# 16

# Festivals of Selected Tribes from South India

*Dr. Robin. D. Tribhuwan*

## INTRODUCTION

This article is based on secondary data. An attempt has been made to unravel the festive celebrations of selected tribes from South India. The tribes selected are Kotas and Kurumbas from Tamil Nadu, Mali, Lambada and Chenchus from Andhra Pradesh. A special mention of Lambadas need to be done here. Traditionally they belonged to Rajasthan, *i.e.* from Western India. They were known as "Banjaras", who migrated to South India, especially in Andhra Pradesh and Karnataka some 300 years ago. Despite of being in South, several traits from Rajasthan have remained intact in their culture. This is an interesting past of Lambadas. The same Lambadas from Andhra Pradesh are known as Lamans in Maharashtra and are categorized as nomadic caste group too.

Well, given below are the festivals celebrated by some of the tribes of South India.

## FESTIVALS OF KOTAS

### 1. Where Abouts of Kota

Kota is one of the primitive tribes of Nilgiri District in Tamil Nadu. According to Thamizoli, Kotas live in seven villages, six of them are located at the upper Nilgiri plateau, and the seventh one is located near Gudalur in the Wyanad on the slopes of Nilgiris.

## 2. Brief Socio-Cultural Profile

As per 1981 census the total population of Kota is just 604. The populations of Kota is reducing gradually. In the first year 1971 they were 832, and in 1961 they were 1112 in number. They speak a dialect called "Emen eau". Men wear shirt and a loin cloth, while women wear sari and a blouse. Kotas traditionally are involved in black smithy, pottery, carpentry and also work as musicians for other groups.

Kota women are efficient potters basket makers. Marriage by consent and elopement are two types found among the Kotas. Family is a basic social unit of the tribe. This tribe exhibits nuclear family types with particularly, patriliny and patrilocal residency as a norm.

## KOTA FESTIVALS

Kotas celebrate a number of festivals. Some of the major ones are:

### 1. The seed Sowing Festival

This festival is celebrated in the month of Kumbam (February—March), on a Tuesday or Friday. For eight days the Pujari abstains from meat and lives on vegetable diet. He does not have sex with his wife.

According to Mr. Harkness (1832) during the seed sowing festival offerings are made in the temples and on the day of full moon, after the whole have taken part of the feast, the black smith and the gold and silver smith. Construct separately a forge and furnace within the temple, each makes something in the way of avocation, the black smith a chopper or an axe, the silver smith a ring or other kind of ornament.

### 2. Kambatrayan and Kambateshwari Festivals

These festivals are held in December and January for thirteen days. The Kotas worship the Kambatrayan and Kambateshwari deities.

### 3. Kannatrayan Festival

Kannatrayan according to the Kotas is a god of rains. In order to appeaser this god, they offer a sacrifice of fowl or goat. The festival is celebrated in the months of June or July. Kotas like the Warlis also worship rain god. The rain god of Warlis is known as 'Naran'.

The Kotas regard Kambatrayar as the Suprome deity. He provides everything that a Kota needs. He is the creator and the lord of universe. Kotas have a temple of this deity. They celebrated the above festivals with reverence.

## KURUMBA FESTIVALS

### 1. Where Abouts of Kurumba?

The Kurumbas are a neighboring tribe of Kotas. They are predominantly found in the Nilgiri district of Tamil Nadu.

### 2. Brief Profile of Kurumbas

The Kurumbs of Nilgiri have been divided into five endogamous groups namely:

*(a)* The Palkurumbas,

*(b)* The Beta Kurumbas,

*(c)* The Jen Kurumbas,

*(d)* Urali Kurumbas and,

*(e)* the Mulle Kurumbas.

The Kurumbas live in geographical isolation and have exclusive settlements. They speak a distinctive dialect which is a combination of Tamil Kannada and Malayalam. The occupation of Kurumba in general is hunting, gathering and small scale agriculture.

Among Kurumba in general wedding is performed either elaborately for four days or in a simple manner by exchanging betel leaves and are arecanuts. Throughout the wedding ancestors are remembered and offerings are made. The whole tribe takes part in the celebrations by going on hunting expeditions.

Ear and Nose boring ceremony is performed for girls just before marriage. Earlier. Earlier even boys would get their ears pierced. Death ceremonies among the Kurumbas is given a lot of significance.

## FESTIVAL OF KURUMBAS

The Kurumbas in general worship ancestral spirits and deities called Karuppdi,

Thaji, and Athivalan. They also celebrated indigenous festivals associated with ancestral spirits and clan deities.

Apart from indigenous festivals like Uchar and Purthari numerous other festivals like the Vishnu, Sankrathi, Onam and Ammanvizha are celebrated in full gaiety. This is due to the influence of neighboring Hindu communities.

## MALI TRIBE AND THEIR FESTIVALS

### 1. Where Abouts of Malis?

Malis are a minor tribe of Andhra Pradesh in South India. The are geographically located in the eastern mountain ranges of Vishakapatnam district.

### 2. Brief Socio-Cultural Profile

According to 1981 census the total population of Mali was, 2,017. Malis are divided into 3 sub-tribes namely *(a)* Bod or Pandri Malis, *(b)* Manzil, and *(c)* Pannera Malis. They believe that the tribe's name has been derived from their gardening occupation. Their dialect is known as "Odiya".

Men wear a simple loin cloth around the waiste and a portion of cloth hangs in front. The women wear a sari without a blouse. Both men and women are fond of ornaments.

Malis mainly depend on agriculture. They cultivate cereals, pulses and vegetable. As compared to other tribes Malis follow advance techniques of cultivation. They are a patriarchal and patrilineal society, with patri local residency as a norm. Divorce is not common among the Mali. Monogamy is common among them, however polygyny is allowed.

## MALI FESTIVALS

Mali observe various festivals throughout the lunar year. In Chaitra (March—April) they observe Cheyeth Parob for which, data will be fixed by local priest ('Disari'). People give food grains and vegetables to "Disari" for performing his job.

In Ashada (June—July) they perform "Ashada Jatra" also called "Takarani" puja. The "Ashada Jatra" is celebrated by the Malis, three days after Jaganath Puri festival in Bhubaneshwar is celebrated.

During July—August months, on full moon day Mali observe "Bandapon" festival for the production of their cattle. "Osa" is yet another festival celebrated in Badrapadha (August—September) by carrying water in a new earthern pot from a near by stream by male members of family and later stump grains from the field and prepare food with there grains in a new pot.

Dasera festival is celebrated in Aswiyuja (October) as observed by plain people Diwali is celebrated in Kartheeka (November) month. In Magham (November—December), they observe "Pondu Palkam," by bringing wild grass in baskets and arranging it in pyramid structures. Sankranti is celebrated by the Mali for a week. They wear new clothes, play 'dimsa" (drum) and perform their traditional dance.

The dimsa dance is performed by the "Malis" during the puberty ritual. When a girl gets her first menses she is dislocated socially from the society for 5 days and then taken to a stream and given bath. This ritual performed to purify her. After this a vegetarian feast is given to the people. The dimsa dance is performed. In Maharashtra there is a caste/group by the name Mali. Where as in Andhra Padesh Mali is a tribe, found in Vishakapatham district.

## LAMBADA FESTIVALS

### Where Abouts of Lambadas?

"Lambadas" also known as "Lamanis" are a versatile and colourful tribe inhabiting most districts of Andhra Pradesh in South India. They predominantly found in East Godavari, Vishakapatnam, Vizianagaram, and Srikakulam districts. They are also known as Lambani, Banjari, Sugali or Sukhali in different regions.

### Brief Cultural Background

Lambadas are the largest tribe in Andhra Pradesh. According to 1981 census their population is 11,57,604. In Maharashtra, however, they have been classified as a "Nomadic caste group". The tribe is divide into five phratries namely:

*(i)* Rathod (Bhukhya)

*(ii)* Jadhav (Vadthiya)

*(iii)* Chavan

*(iv)* Pomar

*(v)* Ade (Banoth)

These phratries are further divided into a number of patrilineal Kin groups called Puda or Jat (clan) in their dialect. Their settlement is known as "tanda". Marriage by negotiation is the only accepted way of performing marriage and sometimes marriage by service is practised. Bride price among the Lambadas varies from Rs. 400 to 1,000, including goats, 1 cow and 150 to 200 Kernel pieces of Coconuts. Both joint and nuclear families are seen the Lambadas.

Traditional dress of men comprises of Dhoti, Shirt, trousers and gaudy turbans. The women folk wear 'lenga' (skirt) and a blouse open on the back. Their dress is studded with embroidery, mirrors and bells. They wear several ornaments.

## 3. Lambada Festivals

They worship "Mathral", a goddess for the welfare of the cattle on either Tuesday or Thursday. Kanakali and Mankali at the time of festivals like Dasera. They sacrifice goats to there deities. The Lambadas also worship and pay reverence to Rupa Sathi, Lakshmi Sathi, Koslai Sathi, Sau Sathi and Somali Sathi who are fertility goddesses.

In the cool month of 'Savana' when the monsoon rains drench the parched. The festival of Teej is celebrated in the beginning of monsoon. It is celebrated for nine days. This festival is exclusively for maidens, who considered to be free from pollutions of birth and other unclean sexual activities. On the eve of Seethla goddesses festival, the Lambadas Propitiate all the seven sisters malevolent deities namely:

*(i)* Rulja,

*(ii)* Dholangar,

*(iii)* Hing bhavani,

*(iv)* Amba,

*(v)* Merama,

*(vi)* Masoori,

*(vii)* Seetala.

Seetala being youngest of them is propitiated first. Apart from the seven sister deities, Banjaras also propitiate a male deity called "Lankadiay". He is the messenger of the seven sisters. The festival is celebrated outside the tanda. Seetala and her seven sister deities are considered to be the goddesses of small pox and there rituals are performed to appear them.

Tulija Bhavani is yet another festival celebrated on any Tuesday or Thursday in the months of Kartika (November-December). They offer individual sacrifices to this goddess.

Some Lambadas also go to Solapur district to visit the main temple of Tulja Bhavani.

## FESTIVALS OF THE CHENCHUS

### 1. Where Abouts of Chenchus?

Chunchus are one of the primitive tribes of Andhra Pradesh, in South India. They are geographically located in the districts of Mahaboobnagar, Nalgonda, Rangareddy, Kurnool, Prakusam and Guntur. (Bhowmick P.K 1992: 11).

The name "Chenchu" has many a alluding references about its origin. Some believe that the name is derived from a person who lives under a tree. Some others believe that these people were in the habit of eating a kind of rat, which is locally known as chenchus and the same term was applied to designate the people. The chunches themselves have several folk tales regarding their origin. However according P.K. Bhowmick (1992: 13) Chenchus have some connection with early stone-age civilization. He makes this statement on the basis of archaeological facts and specimens collected by Vhinn.

### 2. Brief Profile of Chenchu Culture

Traditionally most Chenchus preferred to live aloof from other tribal and non-tribal communities, however due to process of acculturations, over decades, their settlement patterns have changed. Bhawmick classified their settlement patterns as follows:

*(a)* Villages, where in the chenchus live with other tribal groups such as the Sugalis and Lambadas or Banjaras.

*(b)* Villages exclusively inhibited by the Chenchus.

*(c)* Villages of Chenchus inhabited by multi-ethnic population including caste and other tribal groups.

A hamlet exclusively inhabited by the Chenchus is locally called as "Gudem" or "penta". Chenchus are basically a pre-agricultural community. Besides cultivating land, they also hunt, fish and go out for daily wage labour in off agricultural seasons. The material equipments of Chenchus including, cooking utensils mostly made up of clay, wood and recently aluminium. Use of bamboo for making hunting gadgets, household articles, fishing traps etc. is a common feature of Chenchu material culture. Wooden combs are generally used to comb their hair.

Chenchus promote monogamy. A boy pays bride-price in cash or kind to the girl's father. Cross-cousin marriages are preferred. Clan exogamy is strictly observed. Marriage in general is associated with a series of rituals. Both nuclear and joint family types are prevalent is Chenchu culture.

The traditional political organisations of the Chenchus is called Nasab (or Kula Panchayat). It is headed by the head man of the village. Nasab comprises of 4 to 6 members who are called Peddamanusulu representing the clans of the village. This organisation solves problems related family, marriage, property, communal problems etc. The Chenchus bury their dead.

Use of productive, curative, preventive and destructive is very much part and parcel of Chenchu culture. Belief is supernatural and marginal powers is very common.

## 3. Chenchu Festivals

The Chenchu refer festivals to a term called "Panda gallu". On the day of the festival all the members of the tribe get up early in the morning take oil bath and wear clean clothes. The women folk clean the houses and smear them with cow dung. They also draw decorative designs (Muggu) outside the hut. Worship of ancestral spirits, gods and goddesses and clean deities too to done on the festivals. The nature of offering is conditioned by their individual economic status. Some of the major festivals celebrated by the Chenchus are:

*(a)* Nagula Chavithi

*(b)* Maha Shiv ratri

*(c)* Vijayadashami

*(d)* Dasera

*(e)* Deepavali

*(f)* Sànkranti etc.

(a) *Nagula Chavitha:* This festival is celebrated by the Chenchus on Suddha Chavithi of Karthika Masam (October—November). It is celebrated in the honour of snake god. The Chenchus worship Nagula for three days.

(b) *Mahashivratri:* Another important festival is Mahashivratri. Most Chenchus go as pilgrims to worship the Shivling. They carry plantains and boiled horse gram with them for consumption during the journey. They carry offerings and perform the necessary rituals.

(c) *Vijayadashmi:* On this day all of them wake up early in the morning, take bath and wear clean clothes. They then go to the Jammi Chettu (a tree) under which Linggamayya is installed since the hoasy past. The head man washes the deity with water and applies vermilion and turmeric powder. He offers a coconut. On this day the Chenchus worship "Kanakadurga"—the deity of epidemics, such as small pox and cholera.

(d) *Dasera:* This is a Hindu festival celebrated by the Chenchus in the month of Asviyuja (September—October). They celebrated it more or less like the Hindus.

(e) *Deepavali:* The festivals of lights is celebrated by the Hindus. They make good food and worship their duties. They clean their houses. Rituals related to harvested food grains are preformed.

(f) *Sankranti:* This festival is celebrated in the month of January. It is observed by the Chenchus for two days. The first day of the festival is called Bhogi, while the second one is called peddu panduga.

Chenchus seem to celebrated a number of Hindu festivals. This may be due to the long term contact they had with them. Those Chenchu settlements on the plains have accepted more changes in festive rituals as compared to the ones living in the in accessible area. Well, these are the glimpses of festivals celebrated by some tribes in South India.

**REFERENCES**

1. Bhowmick P. K, 1992, Chenchus, Institute of Social Science Research and Applied Anthropology, Calcutta.

2. Sachidananda and Prasad R.R (eds.) Encyclopedic profile of Indian Tribes, Discovery Publishing House, New Delhi.

❑❑❑

# Toranmal Tribal Fair

*Photo Essay by Dr. Narendra Bokhare*

A Lake on the Toranmal Hill.

Pilgrims Getting Ready for the Fair.

Food Preparation.

Bati-flour Balls Being Roasted on Slow Fire.

Tribal Deity of Toranmal.

Another Tribal Deity.

Shiv Ling Being Worshipped.

Madias of Baster (Gad Bengal) Awaiting the Excitment of Cock Fights.

Pilgrims in Que for Darshan.

Devotion with Music.

A Bhil Youth Enjoying the Fair.

Colourful Flute, Producing Melodius Music.

Fairies in the Fair.

Colours in the Fair.

Colours in the Fair.

Colours in the Fair.

Medicine Men Selling Medicines.

Joyous Moods.

Joyous Moods.

Joyous Moods.

Bargains in the Fair.

# Baneshwar Tribal Fair

*Photo Essay by Monica Spolia*

Top View of the Fair.

Dancers in their Costumes.

Dancers Awaiting their Turn.

Musician with his Wife.

Traders in the Fair.

Spectators Watching a Motor Cyclist Perform Tricks.

A View of Baneshwar Fair.

Traders Leaving the Fair on the Last Eve.

# Bhima Shanker Fair: Maharashtra

*Photo Essay by Dr. Robin D. Tribhuwan*

**Bhima Shanker Temple.**

A Mahadev Koli Tribal Priest from the Lokhare Clan, is Incharge of the Tribal Temple.

Tribal Women Purchasing Bangles.

Thakar Tribal at a Shop.

Mahadev Koli Women with Boys of Pulses Which they have Exchanged for Gum.

Oraons Performing Harvest Festival Dance.

Festival Dance of the Bison Hern Madias from Madhya Pradesh.

**Ao Nagas in the Horn Bill Festival.**

**Ao Nagas Celebrating the Horn Bill Festival.**

# PART TWO
# TRIBAL FAIRS IN INDIA

# 17

# Vaneshwar Fair

*Ms. Monika Spolia & Dr. Robin.D. Tribhuwan*

Vaneshvar is commonly known as the Baneshvar fair. In Hindi, Vane means flowing water, i.e. river, and eshvar means god; thus Vaneshvar is god of water. Vaneshvar is located at the trial of three rivers Soam, Jokham and Mahi. Soam and Jokham meet seven Kilometers away from Vaneshvar. Mahi, which flows from east to west, meets with the other two rivers at Vaneshvar. Soam river flows from Udaipur, Jokham flows from Dariavat, and Mahi flows from Chambal in the state of Madhya Pradesh. One has to cross water to get to Vaneshvar. A bridge was built ten years ago to cross the water. Before the bridge, people used to come through water whenever it was low.

The main attraction of Vaneshvar is the five temples. Each one of the temple upholds its own significance and there is a legend and myth related to each one of the temple. Temple of Vaneshvar is the main temple. The others are Radha–Krishna Temple, Valmiki Temple, Brahmas Temple, and Vishvakarma Temple.

## THE TEMPLE OF VANESHVAR

Once a long tie ago, amongst the land covered with forests and mountains lived a community of pastoralists. They herded cattle for living. Once the cattle was roaming around, one cow lost milk after coming back from the fields. People wondered, and of course, their suspicion turned towards the herder. It was figured that the herder was milking the cow in the wilderness behind everybody's back. Some children got together and decided to follow that particular cow in the herd. To their amazement, they witnessed the cow just running away wild from the rest of the cattle. Suddenly, the cow stopped at a particular rock and its milk started to come out. The children reported this is to the community. On second day, the children pushed the cow as it stopped on that same rock. As the cow was being pushed, its feet touched that spot on which its milk ran. And out came a Shivling.

A temple was built around the Shivling. People tried to dug out the Shivling, but it could not be dug. Instead it broke into five pieces which, nowadays, is known as Punchmukhi shivling i.e. five-faced shivling (Punch means five and 'mukhi' means face in hindi).

Around 1200 years ago, the king of Vaneshvar dreamt that Shivji asked him to build a temple around that Shivling. The elephants were used to carry the stones for the temples. About 200 years later Mahu Ji Maharaj worshipped god at that place and prayed. He built a Radha-Krishna[3] temple within one night, right beside the temple of Vaneshvar. Soorpur is a village in Doongarpur Jila (Jila is district). Some pujarees[4] were brought from there many generations ago to perform prayers in the temple. Now it is 12th generations going at present.

Fifty years ago, the curiosity got the best of the king of Doongarpur, Lakshman Sing. He attempted to get the Shivling digged at least 20 to 25 feet. A straight pillar right underneath the Punchmukhi Shivling kept on baring itself. When the workers and the people from round touched the soil of that excavation, they came across snakes, crabs and various other dangerous creatures. Anybody feared digging that place any further than 25 feet. Bhogi lal Ji, the administrator of the king, requested on behalf of the workers to the king that they are feared to death of excavating that place any further; and that they would rather by killed than continue this project. The administrator implored the king to discontinue the dig for it will destroy the estate.

Now the question remarked to repined for feeding the curiosity by committing the mistake of excavating. The king was advised to invite and feast one hundred and twenty five Brahmins. Later, the king rebuilt the temple around the Punchmukhi shivling and called it Akhand Shivling. In hindi Akhand refers to one that can not be destroyed. People donate a lot of money which goes towards building dharamshalas, schools etc. Schools are tended by the local children only. Dharamshalas are the resting place for visitors.

The king of Doongarpur has two brothers, Raj Singh and Dr. Nagandra Singh. Raj Singh is a Cricket commentator. Dr. Nagandra Singh, who is the District judge of Doongarpur, has donated Rs. 1,000,00,00 for the havan-kund of Shivji right outside the temple. Kund is kind of a pool or a pond. Haven is a ceremony that takes place around the sacred fire by repeating mantras. Havan is done for purifying the place where the five is lighted and the ceremony is performed. Basically is it a square hole.

People believe that their prayers will be answered by praying to the Punchmukhi Shivling. One way to test whether the prayers will be answered or not is by leaving a container of water by the Shivling drinks the water, that signifies the answering of prayer. Similarly, if the Punchmukhi Shivling does not drink that water, that means that the prayer has not been answered. In this case, people usually keep on bringing the water until it is consumed by the punchamukhi Shivling. This belief is intensified day by day. This temple started with barely one to two hundred followers and today close to 8 lakh people show up for the festival. On the day of Maha shivratri, nearly 8 thousand believers come. Chanting and praying goes on for all night.

This temple of Vaneshvar is located on one of the highest mounds of the hill near the ghat (beach). The pujarees are taking care of the temple as far as one knows. The king of earlier times, who built the temple, chose this organization of pujaree brothers to look after the pooja, rituals and the other basic requirements of Vaneshvar. One family is picked from the village specifically for this purpose. All the brothers in that family alternate this duty annually. The brothers can be cousins as well.

For instance, during the festival of 1999. Heeralal Jagat Ram Sevak was the caretaker. His turn comes every five years. Here is the list of caretakers.

1. Heeralal Jagat Ram Sevak
2. Shombhoolal Dhoolji Sevak
3. Dhuleshvar Raghunath Sevak
4. Amritlal GangaRam Sevak
5. Kantilal Shankarlal Sevak
6. Gautambhai Asratlal Sevak
7. Durga Shanker Maniklal Sevak
8. Nannu Ram Kachur ji Sevak
9. Dev Shanker Amritlal Sevak

When people come to the temple for prayer or for any healing ritual[5], they usually donate money. This money is the income source for management of the temple.

## THE RADHA-KRISHNA TEMPLE

Radha -krishna are the names of goddess and god respectively in Hindu Mythology. Lord Vishnu follows record in the Holy Trinity. He nurtures humankind. Krishna is the manifestation of Lord Vishnu and Radha is the manifestation of Lord vishnu's wife, Laxmi, during Dwaper time period. Radha was Krishna's beloved from childhood till his teenage. Krishna is always remembered as Radha-Krishna i.e. Radha's name is said before Krishna's.

It is said that Mahu Ji Maharaj built the Radha Krishna temple in one day only. There are no hard records of about two to three generations after Mahu Ji Maharaj. The rest of them upto now are as follows:

Mahu Ji Maharaj

Shivanand Ji Maharaj

Prmanand Ji Maharaj

Kamlanand Ji Maharaj

Devanand Ji Maharaj

Achuayatanand Ji Maharaj

Devanand Ji Maharaj had a sudden heart attack. People or his followers approached Achuayatanand Ji and requested him to leave his worldly life, take Sanyas and replace Devanand ji Maharaj. At the time, Achuayatanand Ji Maharaj was only thirteen years old. Still he took control of the situation and now he has been in change for eighteen years.

Achuayatanand Ji lives in hari-Mandir (Hari means god and Mandir means temple in hindi) in Shabla village. He only comes to Vaneshvar for five days to attend this fair. There is his savari that goes for a couple of Kilometers in the surrounding region of Vaneshvar on the morning of Magh-Purnima[7]. During the Savari, people carry Achuayatanand ji Maharaj and the store horse (horse is better known as the sacred horse of god) in a wooden carriage. The swari starts from a couple of kilometers across the bridge towards Vaneshvar and ends at the Radha Krishna temple.

People donate a lot of money which goes towards building dharmashalas, schools etc. Dharamshala is the resting place for travellers. Inside the temple, there is a container about 5′ x 5′ x 21/2′. Which contains many papers with writing on them. These papers have prophecies written on them which are coming true upto now. The sacred horse of god is made out of stone from Mahu Ji's time. Its three feet are leveled to the ground but the fourth one is slightly lifted. The prophecy about this horse is such that the day this stone-horse will put his fourth foot to the same level as the others. Something drastic will happen. It could be good; Sad; may be everything drastic will happen. It could be good; bad; may be everything will be destroyed; or may be some social or ideological reform will take place among the public. This prophecy is metaphorical. To put down his foot for a stone horse is something drastic nevertheless.

## THE TEMPLE OF BRAHMA

Lord Brahma is the first one in the holy trinity of Hindu Mythology. He give birth to the humankind. A temple of Brahma, vishnu and Mahesh is only found in Pushkar and vaneshvar among the tribals. This was built many years ago by Gaur Brahmans. Along with worshipping and praying to lord Brahma, it was built for the purpose of social-work, dharamshalas etc.

## THE TEMPLE OF VISHVAKARMA

This temple is approximately 12 years old. Vishvakarma belonged to the Suthaar or Tarkhan caste. Tarkhan caste ranks among the lowest, i.e. sudra, according to the ancient Indian varna system. By occupation, the tarkhans are carpenters. Vishvakarma was the best architect designer of his time. He had designed the Shadi-Mundup (wedding -pavilion) for Shivji and Parvati ji. Shadi-Mundup is the square place designed with fire in the center around which the sacred ceremony of marriage takes place. The couple to be wed walk around that fire and take their vows in font of that holy fire. Among the Hindus, the marriage is not complete without this fire.

Shivji is the Lord of destruction, so he mainly resides in forests and takes no interest in materials things. Once Laxmi, the wife of Lord vishnu, was visiting Parvati. Somehow Parvati felt that Laxmi was making for of her because of Parvati's lack of materials elegancy. So, as soon as Laxmi left, Parvati insisted to shivji to have a place built for her so beautiful, extravagant an d elegant that is not heard of anywhere in the universe. Upon her consistent requests, Shivji appointed Vishvakarma to build such a place for her.

For sure, the place was a wonder. Parvati invited everybody including laxmi for the opening day of that place. Shivji also admired that place very much. He propherized that whenever there will be talk of Shivji and Parvati and people will pray to them, Vishvakarmas' name will also be remembered and worshipped just the same.

Thus, this temple of Vishvakarama is the remembrance of his art. Since there is already a temple of Vaneshvar. Shiv Ji, there had to be one of vishvakarma's temple as well. The tarkhan community established this temple.

## THE TEMPLE OF VALMIKI

Adivasis collected money to build this temple. Devanand ji established the statue of valmiki in this Temple. Valmiki Ji was an adivasi by the virtue of his birth. During his youth, he led the life of a decoit. Once he killed a man during robbery. The child of that dead man implored valmiki to bring his father to life, and the child challenged him that if he can not give life, with what right he takes life away. This incidence affected Valmiki deeply.

He stopped his decoit activities. He denounced his worldly life, started to read and write, and became a scholar. Valmiki is the first person to have written Ramayan even before the birth of its man character, Ràm. Thus, Ramayan became a kind of prophetic book as well as historical, political, social, cultural etc.

Valmiki Ji acquired the name of Rishi Valmiki Ji. Rishi means sage in hindi. The prefix, rishi, in front of his name suggests that he is a spiritual being.

## VANESHVAR FAIR

Vaneshvar fair is an annual event which attracts Lakhs of people. It is also one of the major tourist attraction of Rajasthan. This even has been taking place since time immemorial. Before dependence, Rajasthan, Gujarat, Madhya Pradesh and Maharashtra were basically forest areas under monarchy. At that time, the rulers of the surroundings areas used to send the security for this fair. Nowadays, government arranges for the security through police from Doongarpur and Bansvara, districts.

The full event of "Vaneshvar takes five days. The main day for the event is the day before the full moon in month of magh. The morning dip in the water after the full moon is very significant. In the year 1999, the full moon of magh was on the 31st of January, nevertheless, people started gathering from 27th of January.

Other than the tourists and onlookers, the actual participants of this event gather for various reasons. Mostly, adivasis participate in the Vaneshvar Mela. However, a few Brahmins, Banias, Patidars and other castes have been living in the same villages with the adivasis since time immemorial, so they all share this faith and are equal participants of this event.

The adivasis mainly come here for flowing the ashes of their dead ones into the waters of Vaneshvar where the these rivers meet. This ceremony of flowing the ashes in the river is referred to as 'Tarpan' When a community member is cremated after death, the ashes are collected in a container. The families keep the ashes until this event and start dispersing them in water one or two days prior to the full moon of Magh.

The Tarpan ceremony starts with the family visits of surrounding tribals to Vaneshvar about 3 days before the full moon of Magh. They come with their necessary belongings like clothes, blankets, sheets etc. They purchase food and clay-pots from the bazaar in the fair and cook on an open wood fire. Usually, the food is shared among the extended family or even the close community. The water is fetched from the river far away from the place of bathing. The water is also made available through the organizers as well.

After getting the resources together, people sleep at night and wake up very early in the morning. They go to the Abhudra-kind near the ghat. Usually, the women are in the forefront of morning. They cry wholeheartedly expressing their sadness for the dead ones. This is also another way of dealing with their feelings by lefting them out. More often men do not cry.

They bathe in the waters of triad. Among tribals, everybody bathes together. There is no segregation of males, females or children. After bathing, they change into their clean clothes. Then they pour the ashes into the water and pray for Moksh[8] and for their dead ones.

After the Tarpan ceremony, the families return to their sleeping place usually by the ghat. Everybody makes do with personal dressing-up, i.e. fixing hair, putting jewellery for the ladies etc. The usual jewellery for the ladies is garland in the neck, payals (ankle-chains), finger rings, earrings, nose-stud or nose-ring, waist-chair, teeka on the forehead, bindis, lipstick etc. Usually, the large bindis, waist-chains, teekas on the forehead are for the married women only.

Their clothes are very simple. Traditionally, the females wear ghaghra-choli and dupatta. Ghaghea is like a loosely pleated skirt starting from waist down to ankles. Choli is a blouse that reaches upto the upper part of the waist. Dupatta is the long transparent scarf that is usually wrapped around the waist and covers the head. The traditional dress for males is dhoti, baniyan and pagri. Dhoti is about two to three meters long fabric usually white in color rapped around the waist down to just below knees. Baniyan is most often white cotton shirt with buttons only half way down the front. Pagri is anywhere from three to five meters long fabric wrapped around the heard.

However, the use of dhoti, baniyan and pagri is dying with the younger generation. Interestingly, whereas the modernity has influenced females make-up items like the use of plastic bindi and lipstick etc. but not their clothes, the same modernity has rather influenced males' traditional dresses. Consequently most young men wear casual pants and shirt.

While the young ones dress up, the elders prepare the food items like Bati, Saag, Choorma, halva etc. Saag and Bati are everyday use traditional food items. Bati is round bread prepared on open fire; Saag is any kind or combination of vegetables cooked; choorma is prepared by sauteing flour in ghee; and halva depends on its kind i.e. if it is soojee halva then it is prepared by sauteing soojee in ghee and adding sugar and water. Choorma and halva are special items to prepare for occasions like this. Some people also prepare kheer (rice pudding) and such items. People do not tend to prepare very extravagant items to eat since there are very many of these sold in the bazaar. After feasting, people group together in twos, threes, fours or more and set to roam and enjoy the festival. The other most significant ceremony than Tarpan is to visit the Temple of Vaneshvar. People visit the temple at least once during the fair.

A large set of arrangements are done for the market. The small street vendors can be spotted as the bridge starts towards Vaneshvar. A lot of them set up their goods on a sheet on the ground as soon as the bridge ends. The vendors are all along the ways. They could be hundreds in numbers. As food is necessary for living, all kinds of food is sold here. A lot of sugarcane juices are set up on the way. Large amounts of sweets and namkeens are prepared and sold. Usually, these are prepared prior to the fair. By the time fair is about to end, the prices for these sweets and namkeens fall as well as the quality and freshness. There are many dhabhas around for full course measle.

Despite all the readily available food in the fair. Many people, especially the tribals cook their food there. There are clay pots sold in large quantities for cooking food.

People purchase them, cook in them and leave them behind. There is almost no use of plastic there. After the fair is over, water washes the clay pots, ashes and dirt away into the water. It is not so bad from environment point of view.

A lot of stalls are laid in rows which sell clothes, toys, make-up items, animal items. These stalls are usually booked in advance. Some vendors have been coming here for at least fifty years. Some have taken over this business from their forefathers who used to come here. There are at least a couple hundred booths set up.

Obviously, the fair has grown over the years. There used to e only locals involved before. But now with the bridges built, the access to this place is easier. A lot of tourists have been coming here over the years a well. From the last few years, a lot of information booths are added to the stalls as well, for example, water-irrigation for farmers, technological advancements, women and children's health related etc.

The other big attraction of this fair for the villagers is the rides. Large merry-go rounds are always packed with people. The well of death holds wonder to the public. There are magic shows and other rides. People really let loose and enjoy themselves. Perhaps it is a way of lifting free not of their beloved ones only but also of themselves.

The Vaneshwar fair is being used as a platform by politicians these days to gain popularity. Earlier the administration of the fair was people based, but now Government officials and politicians have started intervening. At this rate of interference the Vaneshwar fair may loose its traditionally in near future

**NOTES**

1. Shivling-Statue of Lingham representing Shiv Ji.
2. Shiv Ji-is lord of destruction and underworld.
3. Radha-Krishna-Radha is manifestation of Laxmi and Krishna is manifestation of her husband, Vishnu.
4. Pujarees-priests of temple who look after rituals and ceremonies.
5. Healing Ritual for instance, if someone has a problem, then pujarees can suggest special offering to them and repeat some mantras for the victim etc.
6. Savari-is the ride, in this instance it is parade.
7. Magh-Purnima-Magh is a month in hindi calendar which falls usually in January February. Purnima means full moon in hindi.

8. Moksh-Moksh is breaking the life-rebirth cycles. According to Hind philosophy, a human being goes through eighty four lakh yonis (life cycle) to be born as human. The basic idea is that the first physical birth of a spirit starts from the smallest imaginable insect, something like bacteria, goes through the stages of insects, brids, vertebrae, mamuvals etc. until it reaches the last potential birth, that of a human being. So, praying for Moksh refers to the concept of stopping the birth of the spirit in a physical body and attaining the elevated spiritual plane of soul where the spirit is a free spirit and not bond physically in any way. Moksh is similarto liberation or Nirvana of the soul.

□□□

# 18

# Fairs in Tribal Bihar

*Dr. Pratibha Kumari*

Tribal fairs of Bihar state have a distinguished style and features different from that of non tribal communities. The tribal fairs are not associated with any temple or deity except one or two when a particular deity is propitiated. Fairs are annually celebrated at different regions of Chotanagpur plateau in South Bihar mainly by Oraon tribe. Munda tribe also participates in it and organizes the fair, but Oraon play dominating role in these fairs called *Jatra* (Roy S.C. 1915). Munda and Oraons are two main agricultural tribes of the plateau who have been organizing and actively participating in the Jatras since time immemorial.

The fairs or Jatras have always been a source of unity and extension both on intra and intervillage level. Persons of different Parhas meet during these fairs where they discuss about socio-economic affairs. Parha is a socio-administrative group of villages number of which may be seven, twelve, twenty and thirty. Parha system is an important social institution of Oraons. Each Parha consists of a definite territory, Parha Panchayat and a big tribal organization based on different clan groups. Since the Jatras are the meeting place of the people of different villages disputes and problem related to the socio-economic aspect of particular villages are considered and solved by the group of elderly persons of village councils at the fair site.

Besides Jatra also provides the opportunities for the tribal youths to select their future spouse. Off agricultural season are selected to organise and celebrate a Jatra when the transplantation and harvesting of crops are over and the people have more leisure and rest. Usually *Jatra* is either named after the month of village when and where it is organized such as Jeth Jatra in May and June, Dasain Jatra in September-October, Kartik Jatra in October. November, Paus Jatra, Murma Jatra, Gonda Jatra, Karamtoli Jatra, Kokar and Boreya Jatra etc.

Though Jatras are organized by the Oraon tribe mainly a large number of both tribal and non-tribal people also attend and participate in the Jatras, which usually lasts for one or two days. Locally manufactured commodities used for agriculture, fishing trapping and domestic works, cosmetic goods, hosiery items, clothes stationery, utensils, sweetmeats etc. are sold and purchased during the fair. Tribal folk dances are the main item of recreation in the fair. Tribes of different villages assemble at the site of Jatra with flags, banners and musical instruments. Some of the important fairs are Jyestha Jatra, Buru Mela, Bishu mela and Murma Jatra or Kartik Amawasya Mela.

***Buru Mela:*** Buru is a Mundari word which means hill as the tribes are closely related to the hills, the hill is worshipped for their well being and safety. A shrine of mud is erected under a peepal tree which is named as 'Buru' and the same is worshipped by tribal people with gay and colour. It is an one day fair held at village Kanchi in month of Agrahyana (Nov-Dec) on the bank of river Kanchi in Bundu block of Ranchi district. Thousands of people assemble on the occasion and enjoy folk dance and music. Cock fighting and ram fighting are common recreation.

***Bishu Mela:*** The fair is held on the eve of Chaitra Purnima in the month of chaitra (March/April) in ghaghra Anchal of Ranchi district. Associated with Lord Shiva temple, the fair last for two days in which tribals of different villages participate with their banners and dance in colourful traditional costumes. Thousands of people from different communities assemble during the fair.

***Dharamyatra Mela*:** The fair is annually held at the village Konber of Kolebira "Anchal of Simdega subdivision by the converted tribals of Roman Catholic Mission in the month of Phalgun (Feb/March. The christian tribals of the region assemble on the occasion to listen the religious preaching from the Rev. Father of the Mission. The fair was first started by Rev. Father of R.C. Mission in the year 1895. Colony wise procession in batches is taken out by the Chritian tribals. Tribal dances are performed on the beatings of Mandar. Paush Jatra Mela also held in the same village i.e. Konber in the month of Dec/Jan as a mark of reception of Kharif harvest. Both tribal and non-tribal people participate in this fair.

***Murma Jatra:*** Murma Jatra/fair is the biggest fair organized at the Murma village of Mandar block in the Ranchi district. Murma village is 28 Kms west of Ranchi town.

The fair is held on the eighth or ninth day after the Maha Navami of Dasehera festival. Sometimes the day varies. According to the historians the fair was first celebrated 200-300 years back after the arrival of Oraon tribe from Rohtasgarh and their victory over the local inhabitants. Initially it was a Oraon fair only but later on the local non-tribals also started their participation in it.

Murma Jatra is the meeting place of forty villages of three Parhas where the Oraons enter at the Jatra site with their special Parha flag with particular emblem, beating drums, plying on musical instrument in their traditional costumes. A wooden peg is sunk in the ground known as *Jatra Khunta* around which the dancing tribal group move singing the jatra songs which indicate their victory over battles. Number of villages participating in the Jatra is also indicated in the songs.

The traditional symbol shows the special features of that village and also its cultural importance. In some cases the animal is brought at Jatra site as a symbol of village. Jatra has religion aspects also. Pahan is the sacred specialist and Jatra Khunta is the sacred centre which symbolizes power, victory and unity of the forty villages. It is power pillar made up of sal (*Shorea robusta*) trunk measuring about 8-10 feet in height dug into the earth so that is can stand up without any support. It is not changed until it decays or breaks after weathering. If it needs to be changed it is done by the priest or pahan in traditional way after sacrificing fowl and observing some rituals. No metallic instrument is used to dig the earth. Soil is dug by wood only for placing the pole.

***Ritualistic orbservances:*** Pahan of Murma village first visit the Jatra place with co-villagers having parha flag of particular emblem. He propitiates the wooden pole. Pujar and Mahto also assist the pahan Pole is ammoniated with the paste of creamy soil, the garland of *surguja* (*Guizotia abyssinica*) flower is wrapped around the pole. By offering sweets flowers, burning incense sticks at the pole pahan tries to appease the supernatural power for the successful end of Murma Jatra without facing any untoward events or natural disturbances. After the end of this puja. Pahan alongwith co-villagers return back to the village home with flag where other sacred performances are started at the late hours of night and concluded in the morning of the next day. Rituals performed at the village home of pahan are elaborate and expensive and collectively represented by the members of other village participating in the Jatra.

During initial years of Murma fair the rituals are performed in each village independently, but in present day the religious activities are confined to Murma village only. Village deity, benevolent and malevolent spirits are appeared by propitiation to seek their protection from natural calamities and epidemic.

Puja preparation is started on the previous night of fair/Jatra day. All the community members, young and old, girls and boys contribute their labour at the Pahan house. Earthen pitchers are decorated by the marigold garlands prepared by youths. Net like structure is woven with paddy straws alongwith paddy to be kept at the brim of the pitcher. Raw rice grains turmeric, Doob grass are also put on the strawnet with a lighted earthen lamp on the Jatra day on Jatra/fair day Pahan sacrifices a coloured cock at the boundary of the village. The fowl is first offered rice grains on *sal (Shorea robusta)* leaf when it picks up the grain, then it is sacrificed by the Pahan. Picking up the grains is considered good and auspicious and it is thought that the deities are pleased. It's blood is sprinkled on the leaf. Oblation to the deities is given by water. The Pahan and other persons are offered *Mahua* (*Bassia latifolia*) liquor twice. A white cock is sacrificed repeating the same ritual by the Pahan. Rice beer is taken this time by the Pahan as others collected at the site. Pahan along with the others comes back from the periphery of the village to his home. Five earthen pitchers are filled with rice beer covered with the leaves of jackfruit. Elderly persons of the village do the oblation on the jackfruit leaves by rice beer thrice to the supreme deity of Jatra which is considered as the goddess of power. All the persons present there take the rice beer twice as Prasad. Pahan has to keepfast while doing all these rituals. The decorated earthen pitchers are taken out by the unmarried girls from Pahans house keeping those on their heads. Married women take the pots and dance at the courtyard of the Pahan's house on the beating of drum *(Mandar)* after lunch villagers start for Jatra place. Women move for Akhara site dancing and keeping the pots on their heads from Pahan's house. Akhara is an open space assed for folk dances, meetings and other socio cultural functions of the community. From Akhara ground all proceed for Jatra site. All the foregoing sacred performances are essentially maintained by the Jatra members and the priest or Pahan. Initially parthen pitechers were decorated and brought by the Oraons of different villages independently, but these days the number of such villages has been reduced.

After reaching Jatra around, ladies with pitchers on their heads dance around the Jatra pole with their community members. At night all return back to their village.

## SOCIO-CULTURAL SIGNIFICANCE

The Murma Jatra is of special socio-cultural importance in the tribal life. The fair is being still continue and maintained as an important institution. It serves as a platform to get organized and unite not only the Oraons or Mundas but also other tribal and non tribal communities residing in neighbouring localities. All await the fair eagerly. It is a meeting time of near and far relatives. Most people make provisions for the visitors, friends and kinsmen days before the fair. Different clan members of the tribes meet during the fairs, it provides an opportunity to select one's life partner. Lateron marriages are solemnized by the parents. Different social problems and dispute such as quarrel over hunted animal cases of theft, incest and adultery etc. were also being judged over during Jatra by the councils of village elders and the offenders were changed with fine or feast according to the nature of offense. Elderly members such as Pahan Kolwar, Mahato etc think over the community problems. But these days help of village Panchayat and sometimes Judiciary is also sought for different types of social disputes by the villagers.

Local administration also interferes and extends its help in organizing the Jatra Political leaders of the locality bureaucrats also participate in organizing fair. The Assemblage of different Parha people of all age and sex indicates the unity on community and village level on one hand and their commitment and interest on the other.

## ECONOMIC SIGNIFICANCE

The tribal fair is quite useful on economic sphere also. During earlier days people purchased and sold the agricultural commodities such as seeds, saplings grains, hunting and agricultural implements, tools and musical instruments. Traders from the different districts of the plateau visited to sell their commodities in the fair. But presently the number of such traders has been reduced. Presently different types of stalls such as cosmetic, snacks stalls, hosiery, stationery utensils, metallic trunk shops, sweetmeats stalls are installed in separate areas marked by the administration for different types of goods. Some rent is also taken from the shopkeepers for the areas given to them. People coming from interior villages purchase their required items from there shops or stalls at reasonable price.

## OBSERVED CHANGES

At present the tribal fair or Jatra is not so much serving the purpose as it used to be in olden days in the socio cultural and economic life of tribal communities.

Forty parha villages do not participate in the fair in recent times. The number of participating villages has been reduced to less than half. The Pahan, Kotwar and Mahto etc. who were the socio religious authorities are not given so much importance in comparison to earlier times. Alongwith the district administration, few voluntary institutions such as Sarna Nava Yuvak Sangh, Jatra committee also actively work in the maintenance and successful end of the Jatra. Changes have taken place in the usage of traditional costumes also. Waiste band made of thread, metallic neck ornaments. Pagri or turban, pachhori or wrapper for upper part of body are not being used now a days. All wear modern dresses. Even priest or Pahan also are not wearing their traditional dresses during the fair. Price hike of the commodities used in performing rituals and lack of interest among the Parha members have also effected the Murma fair.

Traditional folk dance or inter Parha dances were a special type performed at different times in harmony with music. Modern impact can be observed in the traditional music and dances also. Many of the tribal youths wear masks and dance on different musical bands. Best dance party gets prize by the local political leader. Jatra dances still serve as the main source of attraction.

Besides these changes which has crept into the tribal fair dues to the impact of urbanisation, alien cultural it cannot be denied that tribal fair or jatra is still unquestionable. Attempts are being made to revitalize the Jatra so that it can be proved more beneficial and fruitful as it was in past.

## REFERENCES

Govt. of India, 1961, Census of India, Bihar part VII B.

Mishra, S.S. and1996, Murma Jatra EK Parichaya, Ashok Prakashan, Ranchi.

Roy S.C., 1915, The Oraon of Chotanagpur, Man in India, Catholic press, Ranchi.

Vidyarthi, L.P. and, 1976 The Tribal Culture of India, B.K. Rai, Concept Publishing Company New Delhi.

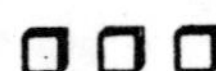

# 19

# Folk Dance in the Season of Fairs and Festivals Amongst the Juangs

*Alok Kumar Kunugo*

## INTRODUCTION

During late evening the Juangs gather outside the *mandaghar* (youth-dormitory)[1]. The sacred fire in the center of dormitory, never allowed to extinguish, bringing warmth and delight to the dancers. The women dressed up in saris, adorned with glass beads and arms laden with bangles and finger rings form a semicircle or a line. The males begin to beat the drums and the hills around reverberate with the tinkling sounds of ornaments and the rhythm of the dancers' feet. Dance flows to its full elaboration and peak during their fairs and festives.

## THE JUANGS

The Juangs comprise one of the major aboriginal communities of Orissa. Inhabiting in the forested districts of Keonjhar, Dhenkanal and Anugul. They divide themselves into two major groups: the *Thaniya* (those who stayed behind) and the *Bhagudiya* (those who did not).[2] According to the 1981 census, there were 30,285 Juangs who claimed to be autochthonous of Gonasika, a hilly region encompassing 12 villages, which is considered to be the capital of the Juang. Gonasika has an elevation of about 1,000 m A.S.L., and is the source of the Baitarani River in Keonjhar District (fig. No. 4). The latter, which is home to most of the Juang, is 8,240 km in extent, and consists of two quite distinct ecosystems. The eastern part has valleys and lowlands, while the west is mountainous with extensive plateaus and peaks reaching nearly 1,070 m A.S.L. (Kanungo: 1999).

## THE LORE OF THE JUANGS

Dance, song and music form an integral part of Juang culture and are an expression of their urge for creativity. By nature the Juangs are peace loving and joyful people. "The development of music and dancing culture has been a way of their life. Not to be forgotten here is the importance of local liquor, which is essential, according to Juang tradition, to make the occasion pleasant.

The folk traditions are the only source to trace the origin and history of Juangs, as there is no textual evidence on hand. Traditions such as folk tales, folk songs, myths, legends, riddles, proverbs, incantations, paintings, bodily decorations, carvings or engravings, dance and music prevalent among Juangs attest the richness of their cultural heritage and to trace their origin.

Many folk tales relate dancing to each other in particular and to prosperity in general. One such tale relating the Juang dance is in the remote past a *rishi* (saint), believed to be the father of Juangs, and his consort enjoyed a sportive life when they had no children. But in the course of time, twelve sons and twelve daughters were born, and it became inconvenient for the saint and his consort to reside in one room with the children. So, they made another room for the children but the frequent quarrels among the children disturbed the saint and his consort at night. In order to keep the children engaged during the night, he devised a ballet in which the brothers and sisters would participate. He taught his children the techniques of the ballet. The boys would play musical instruments and the girls would dance to the rhythm. From thence onwards the dance came to be known as *Changu* dance. Juang word for the drum is *changu*.

Another tale relating to liquor is, during a draught like situation an old man began playing the drum without liquor and an old woman danced for a long time to get rid of their worries. The dance however, bore no fruit. On the next day, the old man drank local liquor before playing the drum, it turned-out that the day was very fruitful; it rained heavily and their crops were saved. From that day, drinks, drum, and dancing became inseparable.

## THE RHYTHM OF THE HILLS

There were many forms of dance among the Juangs, most of which were obviously influenced by their environment. Their dance is mostly animistic in character and can be described as mimetic, based on the behavior of wildlife in a particular situation As such, the dances are modeled on the movements of animals, birds or reptiles, viz: bears, pigeons, tortoises, elephants, snakes (especially the cobra and the python), vultures, cocks, and hens, peacocks, sparrows and crayons (Elwin: 1943a: 31-34, 1948: 81-91 and Watts: 1970: 14 8). Elwin has also mentioned that there are different songs for different dances. Unfortunately at present these dances are limited to folklore. However the most popular and the only extant piece of dance is the Changu dance, for which the Juangs are known to the outer world.

Every year the changu dance begins on the *falguna purnima* (a full Moon day falls in March-April). This is also the day of distribution of plots for the first ploughing (shifting cultivation).

In the Changu dance, the Juangs arrange themselves in two equal rows or in a semicircle with the hands of each girls gripping the waist of the next female. The first and the last dancers keep their hands free, using it to direct the whole group. The right-end dancer is the leader. She maintains the compatibility between the dance and the *changu* (drum) rhythm in the group. The sound of the drum is embellished by the tinkling of the glass beads worn around the neck and the *jhumka mudi* (sound generated by the finger rings).

Generally, the boys move forward and lead the dance, followed by the girls. The first male dancer, acting as a choreographer, leads the drummers' movements by playing the changu. Traditionally dance is performed in front of the youth dormitory: i.e., the school of folk cultures learning and the store-cum-temple for the musical instruments.

## DANCE AND THE ART OF MARRIAGE

During the marriage season there are dancing expeditions. Marriages are performed only between *bandhu* (friendly) villages after an exchange of dancing expedition. When the *kangerki* (boys) of one village develop a liking for the *selanki* (girls) of another village, they give gifts of fried rice, ribbons, combs, etc. to the girls, and invite them to visit their village. In order to convey their eagerness for changu dance, the boys tie the gifts in a piece of cloth on their trip to the girls' village. The girls distribute the gifts among themselves and give a small share to the boys of their own village; likewise when the boys distribute the gifts of their *bandhu* girls, they give a small share to the girls of their village as well.

The teams of girls make the dancing trip to boys' village with gifts of rice cakes (prepared by girls themselves), tobacco and liquor. Some widows and old ladies also chaperone them. During their stay at boys' village the changu dance goes day ad night, more frequently at night, more frequently at night. At night the elders retire to their houses and a strong competitive spirit develops between the boys and girls, with each party trying to defeat the other. The boys try to beat the drum in alternate groups all night and make the girls dance. The girls also split up into two groups and dance intermittently. When the girls try to go away from the dancing ground to sleep, the boys drag them back to dance, and likewise, the girls kick the boys, pull the drums, throw ash and water on them to prevent them from falling asleep.

During the dance, both parties try to play with each other. The girls kick and step on the feet of the boys while dancing and, as it is taboo for girls to sing during the changu dance, the boys use the opportunity to display their wit through songs. Singing competitions take place between group on their way back home from market fairs or while working together on field.

At the dead of night when all the villagers are asleep, the boys get themselves massaged in a group or may pair-off with one girl each to different places, but in no case do they sit apart from each other. While getting massaged a boy may fondle the breasts of the girl, but it does not lead to actual sexual indulgence. On the day the girls part, they are entertained with a meat-meal. The boys go up to certain distance to see the girls off. On the way the girls massage the boys and the boys decorate the girls' hair with flowers.

The groups singing of Juangs is very interesting. The songs are melodic and lend rhythmic support to dance movements. Most of their songs are marriage songs. The bride is brought to the bridegroom's house, where the young sing the songs relating to the bride.

## DANCE AND COSTUMES

There is no special dress code for dancing. In the past, the Juang women put on leaf dresses to cover the lower half of their bodies, the upper half being covered by bead strings. This was how the dancers dressed too. But subsequently, the girls wore saris and ornaments like earring (*noli*), bracelets (*bainsi*), anklets (*kathadi*), head ornaments (*chunri musi*) and brass rings. Nowadays, the men wear dhotis, turbans etc. Traditionally all the ornaments of the girls were designed to generate musical sound- the glass beads around the neck tinkle; the rings, bangles and anklets also create their own music. The commonly used finger-ring during the dance is the *Jhumka mudi*, made up of strings or wire circles with *jhumkas* (hollow balls with stone inside) attached to it. Sometimes the same jhumka attachments are also used with anklets and in other cases, the anklets are made of one side split hollow brasses, with stones placed inside them.

## THE SOUND OF THE JUANGS

The musical instruments are very few in numbers and are locally made. The Juangs use *bada katha*, *dholo* (big drums), *changu* (drum), *bainsi* (flute) and the *madala* (large drum). The *badakatha* is a big wooden drum, one side of which is covered with goat's hide and the other side with cow's hide stretched and tied tightly to the body with leather strips. Two persons on their shoulders carry it while the third man plays it with sticks. It is now found specifically in the Gupta-ganga village of Juang pirh. The *dholo*, smaller in size is a hallow cylindrical wooden body, covered with goat's hide on both sides, which are held together with leather strips. Both these drums are used during the ritual dances. *Changu* is the most common, important and the oldest musical instrument of the Juangs. It has deep socio-religious meaning for them. An ability to play this flat tambourine-like drum is one of the essential pre-requisites for membership to the dormitory. For preparing this drum, the villagers collect the wood of tamarind (*tentuli*) or *karala* or *kendu* tree from the forest. Wooden planks are placed in a circular pit to achieve the barrel or round shape frame. After two days when the frame is dry, they call the blacksmith to join the two ends with the help of iron nails and to make holes around at an interval of five to six centimeters. On one side of that, the Juang fix the prepared goat skin tightly, keeping the hairy part on top with the help of wooden nails with the assistance of ten to twelve villagers. The remaining skins are cut from the periphery before the final touch of shaving the furs with knife is imparted. The boys play it with fingers.

Elwin mentions a legend regarding the power of this changu and the drummer: "By slapping the dead-goat you assemble the girls, mean the *chang* hide-gong." (Elwin, 1943b: 277 and 1948:91). The bamboo flute, though rare, plays an important role as a musical instrument among the Juangs. Sometimes various types of human, animal and bride figures or geometric and zigzag lines are found on it. Often sun and lotus figures are also portrayed.

## DANCE RELATED BELIEFS

The Juangs practice a number of rites and rituals for their drums. On *Amba-Nua* they worship their *changu* and *dholo* and offer shares of chicken and rice piles from the *Gram Shri* (the village God). They believe that both the divine couple, Kanchuni and Bhima Badma, reside in the drums and they have full control over the sounds of drums. Unless the essential rituals for pacifying these are made, the drums do not produce sufficient sound, even if beaten heavily. Even during marriages, offerings of chicken and rice grains are made to them, so that the villagers win the changu competition by defeating opponents in playing the drum. Elwin records a legend: "To see a *chang* broken during the dance means that some one will die" (Elwin: 1948:142).

Describing the dance briefly, the first ever recorded author on Juangs writes as follows:

"The Puttooa (refereed in this paper as Juang) Women are in the habit of dancing in a circle to the noise of a large drum (refered in this paper as changu) beat by the men. They move round and round in the same measured step, occasionally advancing towards the musicians and then retreating, the body bent forward i what the Melbourne Secretary would call, a recumbent posture, the left hand holding the end of the necklace and the right hand hanging down (Samuells: 298)." His paper was accompanied with Drawing of Changu dance by Major Strange.

Folk dance is deep rooted among the Juangs and carvings of dances are found on their flutes, doors, combs, local lighters, tobacco cases, wall paintings and on dormitory pillars. Though in recent times such activities are comparatively less in evidence, dancing and drumming are still a living art. A wind of change is slowly blowing in these remote areas due to the spread of education and other developmental activities, and the simple living youths are often influenced by civilization that is quite alien. The rigidity of their codes and taboos is gradually breaking up It is not surprising therefore, that they feel distant from their age-old tradition of dance.

Today they are a far cry from he kind of Juangs Bose speaks of: "I remember the moonlit night, when the sky was glorious. They went on dancing until day broke, and one by one they left the dancing ground near the youth dormitory for attending to their daily chores. In the morning I asked one of them how they could pass the whole night without sleep and spend it in dancing and singing. An elderly Juang replied, we have enough sorrows all the day, why should we waste the night also in brooding over these sorrows?" (Bose: 1971:74).

## ACKNOWLEDGMENTS

The author is grateful to the Horace C. Beck Fund, administered by Naomi Rubin of the Chicago Midwest Bead Society and Peter Francis, Jr., of the Center for Bead Research, U.S.A., for partial financial support, and to the Deccan College Postgraduate

Research Institute Library, Pune and Harijan and Tribal Welfare Department Library, Bhubaneswar, India for academic support. He thanks Drs. Vasant Shinde, Sachidananda Kanungo, and Selvakumar for their guidance and comments on the first draft of this paper. He is also thankful to Ms. A. Nair, S. Ansari, A. Upadhaya and Mr. S, Panda for their help and assistance in the preparation of this article.

## Notes

1. A dormitcry (*mandagarh*) is made up of carved beams and pillars stands in the center of all the Juang villages of Keonjhar. This is the school of folk culture and the storehouse-cum-temple for the musical instruments. It is a big, comfortable habitation open along one side and with a high verandah. On the occasion of every important event in their corporate life, the males assemble here, encircling a continuously burning fire in the middle of the dormitory. Each and every auspicious event begins here. Visitors are entertained in the dormitory, including wedding guests.

2. The Juang believe that Gonasika is their original homeland, where they had a mythical origin. With the passing of time, some Juangs moved away from Gonasika. At present, those who do not reside within the territory of Gonasika are considered Bhagdiys, while those who reside are "Thaniya.

## REFERENCE

Bose, N.K. 1971 Tribal Life in India, National Book Trust, New Delhi.

Elwin, V. 1943, Ten Juang Dance Songs, Man in India, Vol. XXVIII: 4-146, Nos. 1 &2.

Kanungo, A.K. 1999, Beads among the Juangs of India, Beads, Vol. VIII.

Samuells, E.A. 1856 Notes on a Forest Race Called Puttoas or Juanga; Inhabiting Certain Tributary Mehals of Cuttack, *The Journal of the Asiatic Society of the Asiatic Society of Bengal*, Vol- XXV.

Watts, N.A. 1970 The Half-Clad Tribals of Eastern India: 140-153, Orient Longmans, Calcutta.

❑❑❑

# 20

# Gujarat's Tribal Fairs

*Anuja Arun Mujjumdar*

14% of population in Gujarat is tribal from Banaskatha District and specifically from Dant Taluka within it and extending further to the borders of Sabankatha, Vadodara Panchmahal, Bharuch, Surat, Valsad, and Dang Districts—you can see population of tribals in major number. This whole region is full of mountains, rivers, valleys and sectored forests.

Though the tribals live in midst of forest their life is quite pale. Their culture is united in their customs which is passed from one generation to other through experience. During festive occasions you can listen to their different traditional instruments (musical). For Tribals such fairs are for social, economics and religious getherings. These occasions gives them an opportunity to meet their relatives from far off places. Sometimes such opportunities are utilized to select marriage partners for their children. The young boys and girls get opportunities to express their love. Some tribes have custom to proposed to would be wife in such fairs. Some times such fairs adds up to the enemity between two rivals.

The youngsters (perform) dances with by holding each others hands. The various Instruments used are: Trumpet 'pipudi' Drum 'Dhal' Shenai, Tadpu. Their environmental background reflects in their dresses. In a way to express their gratitude towards god. Holi is one of the major festivals when such fairs are organized It's the tribal spirit which you can see in their laughter and eyes when they enjoy forgetting all their worries.

In some of such fairs you can see that all the people both tribal and non tribals get together and have fun together.

Given below is a table which provides brief information about fairs of tribals in Gujarat state.

**REFERENCES**

Raval J.S, Pandya, G & Rathod J, 1982, Fairs & Festivals of Tribals in Gujarat, Tribal Research and Training Centre, Gujarat.

*Note : Please turn over for information on fairs of Tribals Gujarat given in tabular form.*

## Tribal Fairs of Gujarat

### Table 1

| No. 1 | Name of Fair 2 | Name of Place 3 | No. of People 4 | Activity 5 | Distance 6 | Tribe & castes 7 | Notes 8 |
|---|---|---|---|---|---|---|---|
| 1. | Junagadh Dist Naganeli or URS of Naganshah Pir | Madhupur Jeunbupur Ta. Mahal | 6000 | Kavvali, Genba Dance, games | — Vayaj, walk on fire | Sidi | Sidi's from all over state & B'bay go to Naganshah pir's tomb as pilgrim. |
| 2. | Banaskatha Dungarpuri Bava's Fair | Shree Amirgodh Ta. Palanpur | 8000 to | Bhagan, katha & Dance 10000 | — | Tribal Garasia | Held near Iolob tree Bhil etc. |
| 3. | Sitala Mata's Fair | Parpada | 5000 10000 | Fair only | 3 miles from Cadotar | Tribal | — |
| | | | This fair is organised by Tribals themselves. | | | | |
| 4. | Gar Fair | Virampur | 2000 | Tribal Dance, Discussion among sarpanch | 18 miles by Bus from Chimosani | Tribal Wanshiping | Femai's pay tribute by gor they dance, sing & Garba. |
| 5. | Kadannath's Fair | Balunda Ta. Palampur Dist. Banaskatha | 2000 | Garba, Bhajan, Tribal Dance | 2 miles from iqubal | Tribal gadh | Tribal from Guj & Rajasthan one seen. |
| 6. | Dhuni's fair | Virampur | 1500 | Tribal Dance songs, Garba | 16 miles from Chimsani | Tribals seem | Traditional healers are |
| 8. | Shifla Satam Fair | Pratap in Danta Ta Banaskatha | 2000 To 3000 | Thank's Bhajan Kirtan Monk's Madal | 20 miles from Tarangaj Hill | Brahmans Rajput, Jains tribals | It's near Sitla Mata's Temple |
| 9. | Thakanji's Fair | Rajenea Dhananja | 2000 to 3000 | R as, song Bhajan | 20 mile from Dias | Specially Bhil | Thakanji is Krishna |
| 10. | Janmasthami Fair | Satsan Ta Dhanara | 2000 Bus | Bhajan Bhil | by walk People come | Kunbi | only close by |

*(Tables Cont. ...)*

| | | | | | | | |
|---|---|---|---|---|---|---|---|
| 11. | Kartaki Poonam | Jaia Tal Dhanana | 1500 to 2000 | Gerba 8 mg. | 15 mile from Raniwadi | Kanbi Rabani Bhil | In traditional temple of Mahadav |
| 12. | Thokanki Fair | Sankada Tal Dhonara | 1500 to 2000 | Bhajan Song Garba | 20 mile from Disa | Kanbi Rabani | People from about 10 villages come |
| 13. | Sabarkatha Navratri or Chitvichi | Gun Bhakri Tal Khed Brhma | 25000 | Falk Dance Song, Bhagan | 37 mile from khedbrahma | Tribals from Sabulcotha Triveni sangam Banaskatha Rajasthan | Fair held on & if one takes Bath-illness gets cured |
| 14. | Anand Fair | Amba Mahuda Ta. khed | 15000 | Tribal Dance & song | 30 mile from | Tribals Khedbvahava | Due to clashes this fair was banned and again started by sabankath tribal & Ambamahuda Ashram. |
| 20. | Shamlaji (Gada ghar) Fair | Shamlaji Tal Bhilloda Sabankatha | 15000 | Mari garound Drama, Magic sell of clothes utencils Adivasi Market and Dance. | 30 mile from Himat-nagas | specially Tribals & others too | This fair is held approx. since last 1000 years. |
| 21. | Shamlaji | — | 8000 ved 8 | Bhagan | sons Ras. | — | |
| 22. | Bhavnathan or Bhuvneshwar's mela mela | Desan | 10000 12000 | Tribal Dance, song and other activities | 21 mile from Himatnagan like no. 2. | Tribals and others | Fair is at Bhuvneshwar Mahada |
| 24. | Bhavnath mela Shivratri | Desan | 7000 | Tribal group dance and song | | Tribals and others | All Shiv temples at Bhiloda, Meghraj Bhiloda, Meghraj and Vijaynagan are full. |

(Tables Cont. ...)

| | | | | | | | |
|---|---|---|---|---|---|---|---|
| 25. | Panchma Dist Janmasthami | Delol Ta. Kalal and Jambugoda Ta. Panchmal | 2000 -3000 | Bhajan 5000 | 2 mile from Donal 7 mile from Bodali tribals | Bhil Niak, Rathva, & other | Nv. Ramna Temple people allowes mahal gethes there. |
| 26. | Mathkotla | Kotal Santanam Ta | 25000 to 30000 | sale of house hold items and tribal weapons | 23 mile from lugvada | Bhil | At Mahadev temple near Mahavir |
| 27. | Chul Fair | Abhadlod | 1000 | Bhil dance | 7 mile with drum | Bhils from | They walk ones Patel fire, this day tribes is celebrated by all tribals over Gujarat |
| 28. | Holi | Randhirpur | 4000 to 5000 | sale of horse hold goods | 11 mile from piplod cane and clay utencils | Hindus tribals century | fair is held in a temple built in 13th century |
| 29. | Dawala's Fair or teth month | Oaj Kajan | 200000 | Ramkuku, plays sale of goods, circus, film | 211 miles from Naresh was | Bhil & others | The stones in Namada are at this time worshipped as Shiva |
| | Sindhvai Mata or | Kanvan Ta. Dabhoi | 10000 | Yagya, Horse Race | — | Vasava & others | on Deshera a procession up to Sindhvai mata temple |
| 30. | Navratri fair | | | | | | |
| 31. | Kali Chandas | Gadboriyad Ta. Naswadi | 5000 7000 | Utencils of 7000 | 7 mile from clay | Tribals & Narwadi | Fair started by Gadbariyad others Thakns 40 years ago. |
| 32. | Bhanuch Dist Fair of Pandra & Kalika | Deumagar Ta. Sagbara Mahal | 8000 to 10000 | Tribal Folk Dance | 30 mile from Netrang | Tribal | During this time tribals enjoy more as they have finished there work at farms. |

*(Tables Cont. ...)*

| | | | | | | | |
|---|---|---|---|---|---|---|---|
| 33. | Adapir's Fair | Rampura<br>Ta. Mantrol | 3000<br>to<br>4000 | Bhajan, Ras<br>and sale from<br>of handmade | 4 milk<br>Vasava<br>Jalvav<br>items | Bhil<br>Gamit<br>Chaudri | In this fair<br>both tomb<br>of Adapir and<br>Hanuman's temple<br>offerings are made |
| 34. | Khatla Shah Pir's<br>fair<br>or<br>God's Pilgrim | Vyara | 40000<br>to<br>60000 | Sale of all<br>items related<br>to tribal<br>life style<br>even cattles<br>& related things. | by Bus | Tribals<br>&<br>Muslims | to<br>pir to cure<br>from illness. |
| 35. | Kali Chandas<br>Fair | Dhaluan<br>Ta. Vyara | 8000<br>to<br>10000 | Cultural<br>programme<br>with tribal<br>Development<br>Department | 4 mile<br>from<br>Unai<br>gamit | Tribals<br>Katvalia<br>Bhil<br>Chandhi | Celebrated since<br>1935. In this<br>fair young<br>men and women<br>get opportunity<br>Niak to choose their<br>Dubla Spouses |
| 36. | Pir's Urs | Bilimara | 10000<br>resital | Kawali<br>&<br>Kuran | Bus | Dadhia | Pir's Danga |
| 37. | Nalyari Poonam | Bilimara | 10000 | — | Bus | Dodhia | Pray venue<br>& water God<br>on Bank of<br>Ambika river |
| 38. | Divsa's Fair | Bilimara | 10000 | — | Bus | Halpati | Dubla & Kali<br>women float<br>idals in Ambika river |
| 39. | Pilgram | Unai Maha's<br>Ta. vasad | 20000<br>to<br>25000 | Ramlila,<br>Bhavai<br>Play<br>Play | Railway<br>&<br>Bus<br>different | Tribals | Hotwater is<br>kept near<br>Unai Mata &<br>it is considered<br>that evens<br>skin diseases<br>Unai maha is<br>considered to<br>be creation of Sita |
| 40. | Gandhiji's<br>Fair | Salsumba | 20000 | Folk Dance<br>Sale of<br>tribal<br>Jewellery | — | Warli<br>Dubla<br>&<br>others | This fair is<br>considered<br>to be Ganga's<br>to be ganga's wish. |

# 21

# Toranmal Fair of the Tribals from Satpuda Mountain Ranges

*Dr. Robin D. Tribhuwan, & Kunj Bihari Nayak*

## A WORD ABOUT TORANMAL

The North-Western Satpuda mountain ranges has been a natural abode of the Bhil, Pawra, Gavits and Kotwalia tribes, since time immemorial. The Satpuda mountain ranges are geographically located on the border of Maharashtra, Madhya Pradesh and Gujarat, towards the north-West of Maharashtra, in Dhule and Nandurbar districts. Toranmal is however 600 kms from Pune. One has to go to Dhule or Nandurbar District first and then take a bus to Shahada and finally to Toranmal. Toranmal is one of the major pilgrim centers of Satpuda regions, as it is abode of one of the Shivlings. Both tribals and non tribals visit this place throughout the year. However, on the Maha Shivratri night, some where in the month of February, Toranmal is crowded, because tribals and non-tribals from Maharashtra, Gujrat and Madhya Pradesh come to participate in the fair.

The Toranmal Mela' is one of the most spectacular fair of the rural folks in the border region of Maharashtra and Madhya Pradesh. Originally, this mela was being observed by the Bhil tribes of this region. Today this fair is integrated in a Hindu festival popularly known as "Mahashivaratri" is celebrated as the second day of the festival, in the month of February every year. People from all walks of life irrespective of caste, class, age, sex and creed enjoy it with traditional geity and religious fervour.

## ORIGINAL BACKGROUND

According to Guru Pirbadrinath (the present chief), the origin of the Mela goes back to antiquity. There are two major traditions of thought. On the one side, it is ingrained in traditional myths and legends which races it's mythological evolution. The mythology of the Hindu Shaiva culture is integrated with the tribal festival of Toranmal. Today there is a common belief that Lord Shiv conceived as "Adi-Guru" preceding Guru Gorakhnath who used to travel and meditate on the top of the Satpuda Parbat (the mountain valley of present toranmal village). Therefore, Lord Shiv is worshipped together with the original tribal sage guru Gorakhnath Baba and the "Mahashivratri" is celebrated as the central day of the Toranmal Mela. Such process of synchronisation or acculturation seems to be undermining the original tribal culture since the mainstream Hindu culture specially the cultural symbols of Shaivism has been projected as a unit of dominant ideology over the Toranmal Mela. However, people of this region instead of having any critical understanding presume this Mela as sacred and worship the Guru Gorakhnath Baba as an incarnation succeeded by the Lord Shiv (Adiguru).

On the other side, the genesis of the Toranmal Mela is derived from the historic empire of a Hindu King Faja Vikramaditya, approximately from the period 2000 years back. Since then or some time ago, the warrier Bhil tribes used to rever an ancient sage Guru Gorakhnath Baba as their spiritual teacher and traditional leader. Some incidents of miracle are associated with the personality of their great guru. One incident was that once upon a time, the sage Gorakhnath Baba was meditating on a mountain near toranmal Lake. That day, the king Bhartthar (elder brother of the great emperor Raja Vikramaditya), had gone for hunting in the jungle of that valley. By the way he shot an innocent swan which being seriously hurt, fell down in front of the sage. The king asked the sage to handover it since he had hunted. The sage asked the king to give life to the innocent bird if the later had right to kill it. The king felt sad and expressed his inability to do so. Then the sage sprinkled a little sacred water collected from the Torannmal Lake. By the blessing of lord Shiv, the dead swan got back life. The king was astonished, and considered the sage as his guru and started worshipping him with all followers. Even after his departure, the Bhil tribe continued the tradition of revering the great sage from generation to generation. Till today, it is being observed by all the people in the Toranmal region.

Although after Guru Gorakhnath Baba there have been thirty two generations (pidhi) of successive spiritual teachers, for it's genesis, but mainly five of them have been very popular i maintaining this age-old tradition of Toranmal Mela. They are: Guru Bhartthari, Guru Badrinath, Guru Sunath, Guru Mangalnath and now-a-days Guru Yogipir Badrinath.

## THE PRESENT SCENARIO

The present scenario of the Toranmal Mela is described under the following headlines.

1. **Geographical Structure And Population:** The Toranmal Mela as a distinct tribal fair ad festival is observed today in a Bhil tribal village popularly known as Toranmal village. This village is situated near Toranmal lake and hill-station. Since the village stands on the top of the Satpuda Parbat (Seven layers of mountains) it is named as such. The surrounding area of the village has unique physical appearance and it is clothed with such a beautiful natural scenery that it enchants everyone whosoever visit. It has a sound and heathy moderate climate that attracts people from far off places. The village stands approximately 20 kms, away from Shahada of Dhule District in Maharashtra. It is a small village consisting of more than 1800 people belonging to different Hindu caste groups like Thakurs, Patils and others including the original Bhil habitants.

2. **A Brief Socio-economic Profile:** After independence and particularly since 1980s, the village has witnessed visible modern forces of change not only in terms of transport and communication, but also in respect of people's participation in culture and politics and their sharing in economic standard pf life. Even if people's quality of life has improved to a some extent. There is one small health centre, a Zilla Parishad School, one post-office, a phandi (police station) and a Government run guest-house in the village. Besides a number of Government houses are seen besides, road upto the Toranmal hill-station. The State Government seems to be active in welfaristic works ad schemes.

All these forces of change have brought about considerable improvement in peoples way of life or life-style. People belonging to different sources of income i.e. agriculture, business and service. This is not to say that the people of this region are very well-off and are largely modernized. Inspite of such modern forces of change, the living standards of a large section of the village belonging to poor, Dalit and Adivasi has not improved to a great extent. Only few sections like the migrant Thakurs and Patils seem to be comparatively progressive and dominant influencing every aspect of village community affairs.

However, the principle of unity in diversity is very much visible in various socio-cultural programmes observed in the village. Modern forces of chance like education, transport and communication, modern health care etc. have not taken people away from their closet attachment to their traditional culture and original nature which is evident from their observance of various cultural activities and ceremonies. One such instance is found in the Toranmal Mela organised by village panchayat.

3. **A Glimpse of Toranmal Mela:** The Toranmal Mela is one of the most famous and spectacular fair of the region. It is one of the most important cultural affair of the rural folks in the toranmal village. This Mela as mentioned above, is celebrated only for three days centring round the Mahashivratri in the month of February every year. Although the village panchyat systematically organises the Mela, still the rural folks coming from far-off places of this bordering region of Maharashtra and Madhya Pradesh enjoy it and voluntarily contribute for it's devotees.

People irrespective of caste, class, creed, age and sex celebrate the festival with full spiritual feeling and traditional geity. During this Mela, people are treated equal under the single umbrella of spiritual almighty. Everyone considers the lake water and the land of this village as pure and sacred. Therefore, when the Mela is on, no devotee hesitates to drink the dirty water of the nearby lake and to sleep overnight on the cleanless open ground of the village. Each and everybody feels purified and contented after having a holy bath in the lake. All believe that a bath in the lake will certainly washaway all the impurities in their body and mind which leads to the union of their body, mind and spirit. This signifies a core value in their strong faith and feeling towards the Mela. Besides a phenomenon is observed as strange in this bath that some devotees due to strong faith on the infinite power of the lake-deity, madly dance in the lake while chanting hymns or reciting various names of deities. Even if, they loose their sense and fall down. For this incident all other devotees blindly believe that there is a miracle behind it. The deities, for a while, enter into the mind and heart of those dancing devotees.

4. **The Mela As a System:** The devotees from far off place flock together in groups into the village, just one day before the great Hindu day well-known as "Mahashivaratri". From the very first day the village gets crowded with

thousands of devotees. Here too, the market does not keep itself away from the sacred religion. It becomes a good source of income for people. Some of them belong to the village while others come from distant places just to milk fast profit. Small temporary and shifting shops line up on both sides of the village road. Special transport facilities are arranged for the smooth to and fro travelling of the devotees. The village road, up to the Baba Gorakhnath and "Shiv temple, is decorated with mango and, banyan leaves, colourful flowers and electric bulbs. For three days, both days and nights the village road looks like a flowing river of human beings and the frequent announcement of spiritual songs, music and reciting in the micro-phone associated with noise of the crowd seem to be a unique melody of the village.

At first, each and every devotee visits the lake just to have a holy bath. Groups of devotees after having bath offer a ritual to the lake deity. In this ritual, each group erects a small stone conceiving it as the lake deity, pours a jug of water and handful rice on the stone, smears vermilion on it and them keeps on coconut on a tiny jug of water collected from the lake, chants various names of deities like Gorakhnath Baba, Lord Shiv, Goddess Durga, Mother Lake and so on. After offering dhup and deep the devotees break their respective coconuts, through away half into the lake and take the other half as Prasad. Finally, they bring that worshipped unbroken coconut, as kept on a tiny brass jug with the burning incense the devotees break their respective coconuts, throw away half into the lake ad take the other half as "Prasad".

Since hundreds of devotees come together to offer coconuts to Lord Shiva, they stand-up in a long queue for the smooth visit. Here too, they never feel impaitient and restles for standing in the queue. The temple is situated at 100 metres height by the side of the lake. The Shiva temple is named after Guru 'Gorakhnath baba. After visiting Lords Shivlinga and offering coconut, every devotee meets the present sage Guru Pir Badrinath Baba who sits in the nearby hermitage. Then, the devotees go to visit another nearby temple called as Toraneshwari temple which was established in 1998. After this, they again go back to the lakeside, where they take rest until a special temple prasad called is distributed among them which is served in the early morning, the day after Mahashivratri. Till then all the devotees in order to maintain their hungry fast, prepare a kind of cakes by the side of the lake. Such a cakes are made of wheat flour, water, sugar or masala and groundnut oil or ghee. After these are rolled on are burnt on open oven fueled by cow-dung. While the temple prasad is prepared only on Mahashivratri. Before distribution, it looks like a large cake made of wheat flour, coconut, cow or buffalo ghee, water, sugar and masala. After making a mixture of all these items in a large bowl, it is at first fried on a big oven and then it is tied by a long, clean cloth and burnt half on open fire fueled by cow-dung. One miracle is observed here that the long cloth tied on the cake does not get burnt but the cake gets fried without any harm. For this, people believe that it is due to the cursy of "Guru Gorakhnath Baba. Afterall, the cake is ritually offered to the Lord Shiva at 12'o clock at night and distributed among all devotees by the temple sage and his associates.

Until this Maha-prasad is served, all the devotees wait near the lake, sing devotional group songs, beat drums, blow horns, play other musical instruments and devotionally dance with the rhythm of music. This mela is held only once in a year. During mela, the Toranmal village echoes with various types of nama-japa, and bhajan-kirtan. Such mela, the Toranmal village echoes with various types of nama-japa, and bhajan-kirtan. Such mela has been holding on the age old tradition and culture of the village. The mela fulfills not only spiritual aims of the devotees, but also material needs of some people particularly local shop-keepers.

During mela a large number of small shops line-up on the village road. The shops consists of bettle-shops, grocery, stationary, vegetables, hotels, restaurants, ready-made and cloth shops, utensil, toy-shops, flowers and fruits, traditional Ayurvedic and tribal system of medicine and all that is available in a big town. The local people, particularly tribals still today have strong faith on traditional culture, their mind and body are systematically socialized and linked with the age-old customs, traditions, myths-legends and blind beliefs that the patients naturally get cured by using such medicinal herbs, roots etc, collected from the Nature. This is called as indigenous system of medicine. The tribal people, since time immemorial, have been utilizing various types of herbs, roots, leaves, branches of trees, fruits and flowers available in the nearby jungles and hills, to be recovered from different kinds of infectious diseases, from the malevolent forces or harmful influence of spirits and ghosts and from the epidemics. Infact, here the indigenous system of knowledge, wisdom skills and techniques transmitted from generation to generation through the medium of traditional culture works well. Although the modern system of education and medicine has been enforced in the village, but a large number of rural folks, particularly, the poor adivasi have not discarded their traditional system of knowledge, skills and training that still continues today. It is mainly because people are very much socialized and bound by the age-old tradition and culture.

However, this is not to substantiate that the forces of modernization or modernity has not changed the original courses of tradition. Infact, there has been some extent of transformation in the minds and attitude of people, in their life-style and behaviour as well as simultaneously in their social structure. For instance, earlier in this Toranmal fair the traditional barter system was the only medium of exchange of market commodities among rural folks and the shop-keepers, but today it is only by cash. Similarly, the poor tribals who were not accustomed to using modern dresses, now-a-days they have been purchasing modern commodities from the market of the fair.

This Tornalmal Mela has become very famous today. Behind it's development lies the visible or invisible hands of some personalities. At first, the credit goes to the present sage Guru Pir Badrinath Baba and his associates who by their love and affection, leadership and persuation, have been able in organizing the village panchayat, generous people and the devotees in constructing temples like the Gorakhnath temple and the toraneshwari temple and the Shiva temple and as a whole in bringing about tremendous transformations in the affairs of the Mela. Besides, the villagers are grateful to the State Govt. for providing transport and communication facilities. Above all, the timely contribution help and co-operation of the villagers, devotees and generous people like Shri siting Member of Paliament and others who are very much visible in the fair and in it's overall development.

## CONCLUSION

This paper attempts to unearth some of the most common and distinctive features of an Indian fair and festival. Interestingly it highlights how religious values and ideologies stand as a back-bone while projecting traditional culture as a strong and deep-rooted foundation of Toranmal Mela. On the other side, ironically it upholds blind beliefs, unscientific rituals and strengthens the domination of mainstream Hindu idology and culture over that of the tribals Bhils by way of acculturation. After all, the Mela survives today only because of it's positive contributions to the functional needs of the rural and tribal community.

❑❑❑

# 22

# Bhima Shanker Tribal Fair

*Dr. Robin D. Tribhuwan*

1. ***Geographical Profile:*** Bhima Shanker is a hill top village situated in the northern part about 135 kms from Pune city in Maharashtra State. These range of mountains are a part of the Sahyadri Mountain ranges. This beautiful place is also declared as a wild life sanctuary. Bhima Shanker is known for its medicinal herbs.

The name of this holy pilgrim centre comes from the river "Bhima"-which originates from here and "Shanker" because it is believed to have given birth from the sweat of shanker or Shiva. Hence, "Bhima Shanker" is the name of this pilgrim centre.

2. ***Hindu Myth About Bhima Shanker:*** In his booklet, captioned "Bhagwan Shankerache Bara Jyotiling", Shri R.M. Joshi (1998: 33) mentions that during the olden days Bhima Shanker was inhabited by demons and giants (Rakshas). One such giant by the name "Tripurasur" created havoc on earth, in heaven and in the entire universe as it were. Every one was terrified, even the Gods did. No one could fight this deadly giant. Finally Bhagwan Shanker himself came down on the earth. He took the form of Bhim. When "Tripurasur" saw Bhagwan Shanker he was scared.

Bhagwan Shanker fought with the giant for days and finally killed him. Shanker was very tired and found this mountain to rest. His body was sweating so much that it formed a stream of water which later gathered in a big ditch to form the present "Bhima River". Soon many human devotees rushed to the spot and requested Lord shanker to make "Bhima Shanker" as his permanent place of presence. Bhagwan Shanker considered their request and lived there in the form of one of his "Jyotiling".

Yet another myth about the origin of this ling suggests that once upon a time there was a wood cutter who was cutting a huge tree. While cutting it, he hit on the root and to his surprise he saw blood coming out from the roots. He was scared that he ran away from the sight. Soon, he summoned others to witness this miracle. One of them brought a cow and made it to stand on the blood stream. To their surprise, blood stopped oozing from the roots. However, milk started pouring down from the uders of the cow. While the milk was pouring on the ground the earth tore apart and Bhagwan Shankers Joytirling came up. This later became the pilgrim centre of tribals and non-tribals.

The reference of Bhima Shanker is found in scriptures such as "Shivlilmrut" "Guru Charitra", "Stotraratnakar" etc. Similarly saints like Ramdas, Pandit Gangadhar, Dyeshwar Maharaj, Shridhar Swami, Narahmali, etc.

Great kings of the Maratha Kingdom, namely Shivaji Maharaj, Rajaram Maharaj, Raghunath Dada Peshva visited this temple regularly. In the year 1737 Shri Chintamaniji Antaji Naik and Bhide Savkar built the temple court. That same year Nana Phadhis built the penacle with main temple. The temple is built with black basalt rock. There is a big bell made up of brass on which 1729 B.C. is engraved. From the above stories, it is evident that the "Jyotiling" or the "Stone Statue" is ancient, while the temple has been built during the 17th century.

When do Devotees Visit Bhima Shanker: Bhima Shanker is visited by devotees every day, but particularly on Mondays. On Mahashivratri this place is over crowded for three days with devotees from all over the state. Majority of them are from Western Maharashtra. The tribals of the Konkan region, specially come to worship all the deities on Mahashivratri.

**Other Deities of Bhima Shanker**—Other pilgrim centers and deities on Bhima shanker mountain are:

*(i)* Moksha Kund

*(ii)* Dynan Kund

*(iii)* Gupta Bhimeshwar

*(iv)* Sarva Thirtha

*(v)* Papanashini Akhyatirtha

*(vi)* Vyavrapad Thirtha

*(vii)* Sakhshki

*(viii)* Vinayak

*(ix)* Gorakhnathaddra Muth

*(x)* Daitya Saharini Kamalja Devi

*(xi)* Kamalaja Tale and

*(xii)* Hanuman Tale

The Hindus believe that Bhima Shanker is one the twelve "Jyotirlings" of lord Shiva. The other eleven are as follows.

*(i)* Shri Somnath

*(ii)* Shri Mallikarjun

*(iii)* Shri Maha Kaleshwar

*(iv)* Shri Omkaramalleshwar

*(v)* Shri Vaidyanath

*(vi)* Shri Rameshwar

*(vii)* Shri Nagnath

*(viii)* Shri Vishveshwar

*(ix)* Shri Trimbakeshwar

*(x)* Shri Kedarnath

*(xi)* Shri Ghruneshwar

## Concluding Remarks

The Mahadev Kolis say that the temple of Bhima Shanker was once upon a time taken care by them. The Brahmans and the Gurav caste groups later on took over its administration. Today the tribals including Thakars, Katkaris, and Mahadev Kolis are merely participanats in the general fair and have no say in the temple's administration. However a small temple on the hill namely "Kalamja devi" is managed by the 'Lokhre' clan of Mahadev Koli tribe.

❑❑❑

# 23

# The Mahalaxmi Fair of Tribals in South Gujarat and Western Maharashtra

*Dr. Robin D. Tribhuwan*

## I. WHERE ABOUTS OF MAHALAXMI?

Mahalaxmi temple is situated on a mountain called "Musalya Donger". This mountain is surrounded by three tribal villages namely Ranshet, Sarani and vival Vedha, in Dahanu block of Thane District in the State of Maharashtra, India. Dahanu town is on the border of western Maharashtra and south Gujarat.

## II. A WORD ABOUT HISTORY OF MAHALAXMI FAIR

Primary data collected from elderly tribes men in thane revealed that the temple is very old. Their memory of its history however dates back to 1306, it was during that time the tribal king of Jawahar block situated in Thane, by the name Jayaba Mukne built the temple of Mahalaxmi. The Mukne kings who belonged to the Mahadev Koli tribe, since 1306 have been inaugurating the fair by installing the flag of Jawhar. Since then the honour of worshipping the goddess has been retained by the Muknes.

The kings of Jawahar have been instrumental in preserving and promoting tribal traditions in six blocks of Thane, namely Jawahar, Mokhada, Vikramgad, Dahanu, Talasari and Shahapur. In their book captioned, tribal Masks and Myths (2002)

Tribhuwan Robin and Laurence Savelli have also made reference of the efforts of Mukne kings in preserving and promoting the Bohada Mask festival of tribals in Thane and in Nasik as well. Thanks to the Mùkne kings for their contribution until members of this royal family left Jawhar after independence, and settled in Pune. Despite of leaving Jawhar, the modern Mukne sons still preside over traditional rituals of Jawahar Kingdom, which includes the worship of Mahalaxmi as well.

## III. WHO PRESIDES OVER THE TEMPLE RITUALS?

Qualitative data gathered from tribals and the priest himself revealed following facts.

1. The duty or responsibility of managing the temple, its activities including presiding over its rituals was bestowed upon a clan called "Satav". This clan hailed from the "Malhar Koli" tribe.

2. The current high priest of the Mahalaxmi temple is Bahiramji Satav, from the 'Satav' clan of "Malhar Koli" tribe.

3. Mahalaxmi goddess-the goddess of the mountains is the clan goddess of the Satav clan.

4. Members of 'Satva' clan are hence looked upon with respect by other clans of Malhar koli tribe and even other tribal groups as well.

5. The high priest performs the first Puja (ritual) before the fair starts. The high priest and members of his family refrain from eating non-vegetarian food alcohol or any narcotic substances. They have to keep a fast. The high priest cannot even have any interaction with his wife, including sexual relation, one month before the first puja. He is not to interact with other women as well, these are rituals of purification and repentance, before he really offers Mahalaxmi her first puja.

6 Nagara—a traditional drum made up of clay is played before the aarti (puja of Mahalaxmi goddess. This drum is played for ten days.

7 Tribals believe that during the preparatory phase if a drunkard, or a non-vegetarian consumer happens to climb the mountain and go near the temple. He gets lost, never goes down the mountain, vultures eat him up. For he or she has become a victim of the wrath of Mahalaxmi. The fair usually takes place in the months of April-May.

8. Tribals have told me an incidence of a drunkard who went up and was bitten up by honey bees (bigger variety) to death.
9. People say, earlier tribals used to give food grains and vegetables to the high priest. Later on the Mukne kings took care of them. Now people both tribals and non-tribals take care of the high priest.
10. In the early 19th century Mr. Vesiya a business man from Surat, visited Mahalaxmi temple and prayed to her for a wish of his, which was fulfilled. He therefore build a cement concrete structured temple and was responsible to introduce electricity in the temple.

Since then non-tribals especially from business community of Gujarat started interfering in Mahalaxmi fair affairs. They formed a trust. This also invited members of the Brahmin group, to work as priest and offer prasad to devotes. There was conflict between the tribal priest clan and the trustees.

This dispute was however solved by shri clintaman Vanga- the local, Member of Parliament, a member of Warli tribe. He took up this matter legally in the court, won the case and today the result is that the high priest of Mahalaxmi is shri Bahiram satav, of the Malharkoli tribe. Mr. chintaman Vanga thus, contributed in getting back the cultural rights of Malhar koli tribals.

## IV. TRIBES THAT PARTICIPATE

It was observed that members of Warli, Mahadev Koli, Kokna, Dhorkoli, Malhar Koli, Thakar, Katkari, Dubla and Naikda tribal participate in the fair. Some of the major tribes from Gujarat that come to Mahalaxmi are Bhils, Kuknas, Kotwalia, Warlis, Kothodis etc.

People of all age groups, both young and old come to enjoy themselves in Mahalaxmi fair. They sing, dance, buy and sell and enjoy themselves for ten days. Given themselves for ten days. Given below are glimpses of tribal events, happening of interactions that take place among the tribals.

## V. INTER-TRIBAL DRAMA

Tribals who participate in the fair organize several activities such as:

1. Dance, Music and Dramas, some of the famous dances performed here are tarpa dance, Dhol dance and Gauri dance. Tribals also organize "Tamashas"-i.e. traditional dramas.

2. Besides this folk songs called "Pawadas" are also sung.

3. Musicians from different tribes play music and sell musical instruments.

4. Tribal artisans demonstrate and sell their artifacts.

5. Traditional show men belonging to the non-tribal communities such as snake charmers, people who own monkeys and bears demonstrate tricks of these animals for the tribals.

6. Tribal traders sell their goods.

7. Tribal farmers and daily wage labourers exchange goods for food grains or minor forest produce.

8. Young boys and girls have courtship and select their life partners or atleast reveal their desire to get married a girl of boy here. This is the time when they can see many boys and girls from far and near villages of their own tribe.

9. Many tribals offer coconut and flowers to Mahalaxmi and also request her to fulfil their wishes.

10. One interesting aspect observed among tribal girls and women, while they walk towards Mahalaxmi temple in groups, they sing songs.

Most tribals living around Mahalaxmi temple start early in the morning at 4-o-clock in groups. Thus, from different parts one can hear these wild birds singing in different dialects. It is so melodious to hear them sing. As an anthropologist I joined several groups to go to mahalaxmi on all the ten days. It was tiring, yet thrilling experience.

11. Tribal young boys and girls who are in love with each other. For them this time and place is good for promoting sexual relations.

12. For children it is enjoyment of playing in swings, and giant wheels. They make their parents to buy baloons, clothes, toys, icecandis, sweets, snacks etc.

13. For tribal house wives, Mahalaxmi fair is platform to purchase house hold utensils, baskets, clothes and other items.

14. For tribal men, they have barter system with tribal and non-tribal communities. They purchase hunting and agricultural implements.

15. Mahalaxmi fair promotes inter-tribal socio-economic and cultural interaction and in the process sustains tradition. It promotes inter-tribal harmony and solidarity.

## VI. CHANGES IN MAHALAXMI FAIR

The temple of Mahalaxmi is situated close to Bombay–Ahemedabad highway. Since it is close to Gujarat, non-tribal interference in the fair is possing several problems or tribal traditions. Politicians and political parties are making it a platform to gain political popularity. Some tribal boys have also said, that their women and girls are sexually exploited if found alone on the mountain or in bushes. Hindi & Marathi film music is becoming a substitute for traditional songs, dramas & dance forms of the tribals. Non-tribal traders are dictating terms to the tribal traders and harassing them as well. There is a tension between modernity and traditionalism. Government authorities concerned with cultural and tourism ministries, along with genuine NGO's and politicians can help to preserve and promote past traditions of the fair.

□□□

# 24

# Devmogra and Asthamba Fairs

***Dr. Robin. D. Tribhuwan***

## INTRODUCTION

Popular among the tribes of south Gujarat and north-west Maharashtra are the fairs Dev Mogra and Asthamba. Interestingly both the fairs are attended by tribals from Gujarat, Maharashtra and Madhya Pradesh as well. Let us briefly look into the cultural and social significance of both these fairs

## DEVMOGRA FAIR

Devmogra is a name of a tribal deity. The temple of the deity is situated on a mountain, of Dhediya block in Baruch district of Gujarat state, in India. For the tribals in Dhule and Nandurbar district it close. From Nandurbar it takes 3½ to 4 hrs by bus. Most tribals however walk to reach Devmogra village. Given below are salient features of Dev mogra fair.

- ***(a)*** ***Period:*** The fair is held in the months of February-March, during the Shivratri festival. It lasts for 15 days after Mahashivratri festival.
- ***(b)*** **People and fair Activities** Nearly 5 to 7 lakhs people attend the fair out of which 90% are tribals. The fair is spread over on a area of 30 to 40 area of land on and at the foot of the mountain. Participates in the fair consists of

Traditional Medical practitioners who come to sell plant and animal medicines.

- Ornament makers and sellers
- Shamans called budvas and budvis
- Traders who sell food, clothes, utensils, cereals, pulses, minor forest produce, agricultural implements, hunting gadgets, tobacco, alcohol etc.
- Artisans, Dancers, Musicians singers and Drama artists
- Street artists, snake charmers, acrobat artists etc.
- Entertainers take part in the fair.
- Photographers both mobile and stationary, participate.
- Flower, coconut, incense stick vendors, are seen.
- The fair is full of people of all ages.
- Tribals and traders make temporary tents and live in them for the period or as long as they want to hangs around there.

**(c)** ***High Priest*:** The high priest of Devmogra, by the name ukhdya Bhagat was kind enough to give information about the high priest tradition. Ukhdya Bhagat said, he belong to the seventh generation of the high priests who served Devmogra. Ukhdya is survived by three sons. The eldest one is Bhima, who would take over after his father's death. When I collected data from Ukhdya Bhagat, he was alive. I was shocked to hear about the death of Ukhdya recently. I am not aware whether, Bhima his eldest son, has taken over after Ukhdya.

**(d)** ***Myth about Devmogra:*** When I talked to Ukhdya Bhagat, the then high priest, he said the myth about installation of Devmogra goes back seven generations ago. He said, his great father, the first high priest of the temple, saw a vision. In the vision he saw a form of Devmogra. She asked him to install her statue and a temple. She instructed him to make the statue of gold. She said people should worship me. After he appeared to the high priest. Ukhdya's fore father did not take need of her instructions. He was busy in his work. When she reappeared in the vision, he told her it is difficult to make gold statue, because I cannot gather so much money. He however promised her that the statue will be made up of five metals (Pancha dhatu). He also took an oath to install the temple. He punished himself for not making Devmogra statue in gold, by cutting his little finger and by offering her his own blood, to her.

Ukhdya told me, since that time onwards in every generation atleast one member of the family has a crooked little finger. Ukhdya's son Bhima and his eldest daughter who is married off in another village, both have crooked little fingers.

*(e)* ***Survival of the high priest:*** The high priest of Devmogra who belong to the Bhil tribe is taken care by tribals of Devmogra. They give him cereals, pulses, vegetables, clothes and money too. These offering are kept in a winnowing pan, which is kept outside his house near the temple.

However, during the Mahashivratri season, that is the time when the actual fair is held. Ukhdya would receive food grains and pulses for the whole year, not only for himself but his family as well.

*(f)* ***Role of Sakhbara Kings:*** Sakhbara is a town, situated 35 kms away from Dev mogra. It is known for the seat of a royal family of the Vasava (bhil) kings. Since the establishment of Devmogra temple, the first puja on the Mahashivratri at the beginning of the fair is presided over by the king. Even today, members of the royal family of vasava clan perform this puja. He offers flowers and coconut to the deity.

*(g)* ***Types of offering:*** Devmogra is given two types of offerings namely:

*(i)* Coconut and flowers, and,

*(ii)* Sacrifices of goat and chicken

These are offered by the high priest and her devotees.

*(h)* ***Other Deities:*** Raja Pantha and Ganda Thakur are other deities worshipped by tribals during the fair. Their idols are at the foot of the mountain. Both Raja pantha and Ganda Thakur are mythological warrior deities of the Bhil, Gamit and Pawra Pantheon. At some point of history these king may have helped the tribals and hence found a place in the Bhil spiritual pantheon.

## II. ASTHAMBA FAIR

Yet another popular fair of the tribals from south Gujarat and north-west Maharashtra is the Asthamba fair. This fair is held during Diwali festival season for 10 to 15 days. Geographically Asthamba is situated in...block of Dhule district. Asthamba is a mythological character from Hindu epic called Mahabharat. Tribals say he is also known as Ashvasthama, a male character and son of Dronacharya.

According to Mahabharat Dronacharya was the teacher of "Eklavya"-a Bhil tribal boy. Although Dronacharya never taught "Eklavya". This tribal boy made his statue and learnt to shoot with arrows. Once while walking in the jungle with his Brahman students Dronacharya came across a dog having several arrows in his mouth. Dronacharya wanted to know who the hunter was. When he met Eklavya, he was surprised to see his own statue. After having talked to Eklavya, he found out that the Bhil boy was a excellent shooter. Eklavya wanted to give gift to the Guru. Dronacharya demanded his thumb, the Bhil boy immediately cut it and offered it to his teacher.

Well, that is how the mythological co-relation of Dronacharya and the Bhils is associated. As compared to other fairs, these two fairs are held in remote areas and the number of tribals here are more than than non-tribals.

❑❑❑